In *The Discerning Life* Steve Mac
ment smack in the middle of everyd.
Discernment must never be sequestered into issues of decision making
alone. No, it is discovered in a joy-filled, hair-raising, bewildering awareness of the living presence of God in the push and pull of daily life. I thank
God for *The Discerning Life*.

> **Richard J. Foster,** author of several books, including
> *Celebration of Discipline* and *Sanctuary of the Soul*

You're holding in your hands a new spiritual classic. Both brilliant and
beautiful, *The Discerning Life* may well be the book Steve Macchia was
born to write. Every chapter unlocks new insights and treasures of devo-
tion for any believer who aspires to live a life dedicated to "practicing a
preference for God."

> **Gary Thomas,** author of *Sacred Pathways*

For a world we know to be infused with the divine presence, it's dis-
turbingly easy to miss. Steve Macchia, through his long, steady life of
discipleship, has learned how to notice what many of us are overlooking,
and in this book he shows us how we also can discern the Presence, thereby
enjoying intimacy with the Triune God who is eager to fill us with abundant life.

> **Eric E. Peterson,** pastor of Colbert
> Presbyterian Church, Colbert, WA

Wise, winsome, and worship-evoking, *The Discerning Life* will awaken you
to the wonder of God's presence not only in your times of prayer but in
your everyday work, your family and friendships, and your rest and play.
This beautiful book will help you see God in your everything.

> **Ken Shigematsu,** pastor and author of *God in My Everything*

The approach Steve Macchia takes in *The Discerning Life* reminds me of Dallas Willard's primary focus in *Hearing God*. Both offer the wonderful reminder that listening for the voice of God does not begin with a "how-to" manual but with developing the habit of continuously seeking awareness of his presence that leads to the intimacy of divine friendship.

Gary W. Moon, PhD, author and founding executive director of the
Martin Institute and Dallas Willard Center, Westmont College

Practicing a preference for God. That is the piquant phrase Steve Macchia uses to describe the life of discernment. But his book itself is that—a radiant testament to a preference for God. And the man himself is that—a living embodiment of a preference for God. I am truly and deeply grateful to Steve that he, yet again, has made his wisdom available to me and to you, so that we, too, can practice a preference for God.

Mark Buchanan, author of *God Walk*

The Discerning Life is clearly a masterpiece of God's divine impartation to Steve Macchia. This kairos word is an inclusive invitation for followers of Christ to continually abide in his presence. Consequently, they will embrace the totality of the discipline of discernment. God's gift of discernment is not for the elect few but is for all disciples. Living a life of discernment cannot be boxed in traditionalism and elitism but is for kingdom-minded citizens who desire to know God more personally and intimately. Encountering his presence is not an overnight wonder but is imparted to those who are attentive to pursing the abundant life while traveling on their discerning spiritual journey.

Rev. Dr. Barbara L. Peacock, author of *Soul
Care in African American Practice*

Out of his many years of experience and learning—both as disciple and guide—Steve Macchia has given us a fresh take on spiritual discernment. He pictures discernment not as a tool or technique but as a lifestyle of sensing and being obedient to God. Discernment as he describes it is a way of life, not just a help in making decisions. He includes some unexpected topics, such as the importance of hospitality and empathy and self-awareness, as we open our lives to the gaze and guidance of God. Both those seeking help and those pointing others along the way will find his thoughts helpful and hopeful.

Leighton Ford, author and founding
president, Leighton Ford Ministries

Steve Macchia in *The Discerning Life* calls us to nothing less than a spiritual awakening at the deepest level. This book charts a path to greater attentiveness and daily awe of God's presence and work even in the quotidian tasks of life. Like a master Sherpa, Macchia leads us to discover new heights of wonderment and Presence amid a broken world.

Timothy C. Tennent, PhD, president, professor of
world Christianity, Asbury Theological Seminary

In *The Discerning Life*, Steve Macchia leads us into a powerful practice of discerning God in every aspect of our lives. With the wisdom and nuance of someone who practices deeply what he teaches, Macchia provides much-needed guidance for anyone seeking to increase their attentiveness to the movement of God's Spirit in their day-to-day lives. This is a book for every Christ-follower.

Dr. Alison Cook, counselor and author

To follow Jesus is to become fully alive to God every day. That means that a core part of our formation is learning how to recognize God's presence—his gifts, his confirmations and corrections, his invitations and more—in our daily lives. Steve Macchia has spent decades teaching people to do just that. In this book, he imparts his considerable wisdom to us, serving as a sage for our journey, teaching us how to notice not just the world but God at work in His world. We learn in these pages that discernment is about much more than decision-making; it's about the joyful discovery of grace and glory in ordinary life.

Rev. Dr. Glenn Packiam, pastor and author

How would you cultivate a discerning life? Frankly, most of us don't have the best eyes that see how God is working, ears to hear his voice, or a heart that longs for his presence. If you'd like to grow more in a lifestyle that continuously seeks God's presence, power, peace, and purposes, this engaging book is for you.

Michael Martin, author, and president and CEO of ECFA

Here's an idea—go deep on this book with colleagues and friends. The stories are page-turners (think *This Old House*—the perfect discernment metaphor). The "Practicing a Preference for God" summaries are so helpful. And the lists, oh my, the lists! Steve Macchia resists formulaic, pious claptrap and instead delivers deep and soul-challenging content: discernment definitions and postures, soul-neglect causes, stumbling blocks to listening, poignant discernment questions, Jesus' favorite topics—you'll love the lists! And this honest warning: "All of this will take a lifetime to rehearse." OK, no pressure—just jump in. I love this book.

John Pearson, author and management consultant

I love it when I come across a book so rich with grounded and thoughtful insights that it could only come from a lifetime of lived experience—this is such a book.

Nathan Foster, author, and director of community life at Renovaré

Discernment is key to living well in God's presence, but we often settle for just figuring out what to do next. Discernment is more communion-cultivating than mere decision-making, more a way of life than a technology for navigating a few crisis moments in our lives. Steve Macchia has written a wise book rooted in deep experience in discerning God's presence in his own life and work.

Alan Fadling, author

We have read many spiritual-formation books in our thirty years in ministry. We have never read one as unique, inspiring, and yet practical as *The Discerning Life*. If this book doesn't inspire you to strive for spiritual discernment, we don't know what will. We feel privileged to know Stephen and have been blessed to watch him live out the principles described in this book in his own life.

Kenneth and Jolene Hodder, commissioners
and national leaders of the Salvation Army

So much of our lives are spent attempting to discern the will of God for one wrong reason or another. We don't want to make a mistake or wander from the razor-width path of perfection or displease the unpleasable tyrant. Not so for Steve Macchia and this fresh approach on discernment. It is not a puzzle to be solved or the successful completion of a multiple-choice test but a lifelong process of listening, paying attention, and practicing a daily preference for God—not just in the times of big decisions. Written from deep experience and his own life of practice, this book is full of wisdom, insight, and, yes, discernment.

Fred Smith, founder of The Gathering

Steve Macchia has a profound biblical understanding of the full nature and vital importance of spiritual discernment. His ability to artfully convey that understanding and winsomely help his readers clear pathways for making spiritual discernment a way of life is a gift to us all. *The Discerning Life* is a book packed full of equal parts wisdom, joy, and practical insight. Highly recommended.

Jeff Crosby, editor and compiler of *Days of Grace through the Year*

Steve Machia once again has shared his keen insight and wisdom in his latest book, *The Discerning Life*. Filled with rich and warm personal stories, the reader will relish the rich biblical instruction that fills this book. If ever there was a day when a follower of Jesus needs discernment and clarity of soul, now is the time. This book will help the reader in their spiritual journey to go deeper, grow closer to God, and walk with greater integrity in the world. A must read.

Lt. Colonel Tim Foley, DMin, author and divisional
leader, northwest division, of The Salvation Army

From weary Moses at the end of his life to the fresh, hopeful prayers of people I sacramentally confirm, to my own recurrent longings, the heart-cry of God's people remains essentially unchanged: "Satisfy us with your love, let us see your work in our world, let your favor rest on us" (cf. Ps 90:12–17). We can endure most anything if we know God is with us. Steve Macchia invites us into a rich conversation about a life of spiritual discernment, a life centered in the active everyday awareness of God's presence, power, and peace. *The Discerning Life* is the fruit of Steve's own lifelong pursuit of God and his prayerful ministry to countless others. Full of transformational wisdom about a "with-God life," this book is worth savoring and embracing like you would a lifelong friend's most loving, heartfelt counsel.

Bishop Steven A Breedlove, diocese of Christ our
Hope, Anglican Church in North America

As followers of Jesus, we are all "under construction," undergoing heart renovations. *The Discerning Life* provides a skilled carpenter's perspective on how to perceive and enter into the deeper work the Lord is carrying out in this lifelong process.

David A. Currie, professor of pastoral theology, dean of the
doctor of ministry program, and vice-president of cohort-
based education at Gordon-Conwell Theological Seminary

The world seems lost these days. So many voices calling out to us: "Come this way!" "Come that way!" How can we ever find our way? *The Discerning Life* is more than a road map to help us find our way. It is a gentle and graceful sieve—removing what is unnecessary and unhelpful in making good and healthy decisions and seeking guidance. This book provides a process of making solid decisions. What is most important for you to know is that the author, Steve Macchia, has followed his own advice and counsel he's given us here. I've witnessed him discern a major opportunity offered him and decided it was not right for him. A leader who can say no is a trusted leader in a world when so many say yes just to please or not ruffle our spiritual feathers. These words, in this beautiful book, can be trusted, and this is a faithful guide to help us all find a path that is a good one, a trusted one, and in the end, a right one. It will be a keepsake that you will return to for many decisions facing you in these confusing times in which we are living.

Stephen W. Smith, author and president of Potter's Inn

In this wonderful book on the discerning life, Steve Machia unpacks the biblical and spiritual features of discernment in ways that individuals and groups can make use of to great benefit. Filled with practical wisdom, this book will enable the believer to discern and embrace what God wants in their lives and in the world—individually and corporately. This book is a must-read for all Christian leaders, and for any others who feel called to attend, discern, and mind the present leadings of the resurrected Lord.

Paul N. Anderson, professor of biblical and
Quaker Studies, George Fox University

Steve Macchia writes what he lives and lives what he writes. I've witnessed his life of discernment for nearly three decades. Leaders today need help in their deeper life, and Steve brings it. Books are aplenty on the techniques of leadership, but they are exceedingly rare on the soul of a leader. For those of us who desire a life of God-in-everything meaning that transcends the many burdens we bear, Steve has something to say.

Barry H. Corey, author and president of Biola
University in Southern California

The walk of the believer, as intended by God, is one that is neither aimless, confused, directionless, meaningless, or unclear. Rather it is intended to be one of direction, clarity, focus, meaning, and purpose. The pursuit of God's intention is not accidental or happenstance. It is intentional. Such an intentional pursuit is called spiritual discernment. In his book, *The Discerning Life*, Dr. Macchia provides a blueprint for the intentional pursuit of God and the meaning, direction, point, and purpose that is found in him. Anchored in Scripture and informed by his life as a scholar and fellow navigator, Stephen alerts us to vital characteristics such as attentiveness, listening, presence, hospitality, empathy, and focus. Throughout the book, I found myself challenged by the constant call to "practice a preference for God." In an age where we are so easily distracted by the noisy and the needless, *The Discerning Life* invites us to find the one thing that is necessary that will not be taken away.

Bishop Claude R. Alexander, senior pastor of The Park Church

THE
Discerning Life

OTHER BOOKS BY STEPHEN A. MACCHIA

Becoming a Healthy Church: Ten Traits of a Vital Ministry

Becoming a Healthy Church Workbook

Becoming a Healthy Disciple: Ten Traits of a Vital Christian

Becoming a Healthy Disciple Small Group Study and Worship Guide

Becoming a Healthy Team: Five Traits of Vital Leadership

Becoming a Healthy Team Workbook

Crafting a Rule of Life: An Invitation to the Well-Ordered Way

Broken and Whole: A Leader's Path to Spiritual Transformation

Legacy: 60 Life Reflections for the Next Generation

*Silencio: Reflective Practices for Nurturing
Your Soul (Contributing Editor)*

Wellspring: 31 Days to Wholehearted Living

Path of a Beloved Disciple: 31 Days in the Gospel of John

Come Home, My Soul: 31 Days of Praying the Living Word

The Promises of Christmas: 25 Advent and Christmas Reflections

Outstretched Arms of Grace: A 40-Day Lenten Devotional

THE
Discerning
Life

An Invitation to

NOTICE GOD IN EVERYTHING

STEPHEN A. MACCHIA

ZONDERVAN
REFLECTIVE

ZONDERVAN REFLECTIVE

The Discerning Life
Copyright © 2022 by Stephen A. Macchia

Requests for information should be addressed to:
Zondervan, *3900 Sparks Dr. SE, Grand Rapids, Michigan 49546*

Zondervan titles may be purchased in bulk for educational, business, fundraising, or sales promotional use. For information, please email SpecialMarkets@Zondervan.com.

ISBN 978-0-310-12792-5 (audio)

Library of Congress Cataloging-in-Publication Data

Names: Macchia, Stephen A., 1956- author.
Title: The discerning life : an invitation to notice God in everything / Stephen A. Macchia.
Description: Grand Rapids : Zondervan, 2022.
Identifiers: LCCN 2021042976 (print) | LCCN 2021042977 (ebook) | ISBN 9780310127901 (paperback) | ISBN 9780310127918 (ebook)
Subjects: LCSH: Discernment (Christian theology) | Desire for God. | Christian life.
Classification: LCC BV4509.5 .M25325 2022 (print) | LCC BV4509.5 (ebook) | DDC 235—dc23/eng/20211004
LC record available at https://lccn.loc.gov/2021042976
LC ebook record available at https://lccn.loc.gov/2021042977

The use of the content of Rueben P. Job's material from *A Guide to Spiritual Discernment*, compiled by Rueben P. Job, Upper Room Publications, 1996, is used by permission.

Unless otherwise noted, Scripture quotations are from The Holy Bible, New International Version®, NIV®. Copyright © 1973, 1978, 1984, 2011 by Biblica, Inc.® Used by permission of Zondervan. All rights reserved worldwide. www.Zondervan.com. The "NIV" and "New International Version" are trademarks registered in the United States Patent and Trademark Office by Biblica, Inc.®

Scripture quotations marked ESV are taken from the ESV® Bible (The Holy Bible, English Standard Version®). Copyright © 2001 by Crossway, a publishing ministry of Good News Publishers. Used by permission. All rights reserved.

Scripture quotations marked THE MESSAGE are taken from *THE MESSAGE*. Copyright © 1993, 2002, 2018 by Eugene H. Peterson. Used by permission of NavPress. All rights reserved. Represented by Tyndale House Publishers, Inc.

Scripture quotations marked RSV are taken from the Revised Standard Version of the Bible. Copyright © 1946, 1952, and 1971 National Council of the Churches of Christ in the United States of America. Used by permission. All rights reserved worldwide.

Any internet addresses (websites, blogs, etc.) and telephone numbers in this book are offered as a resource. They are not intended in any way to be or imply an endorsement by Zondervan, nor does Zondervan vouch for the content of these sites and numbers for the life of this book.

Cover design: Tammy Johnson Design
Cover photo: © Genz Twins / Shutterstock
Interior design: Sara Colley

Printed in the United States of America

22 23 24 25 26 27 28 29 30   /TRM/   12 11 10 9 8 7 6 5 4 3 2 1

To Ruth Lynn Macchia
beloved soul mate and devoted partner in the discerning life
together we are learning how to practice a preference for God

and to
Br. David Vryhof, SSJE

and
Methodist Bishop Rueben P. Job (1928–2015)
spiritual mentors and friends
guides to spiritual discernment

CONTENTS

Grace and truth

There's No Place Like Home

"The Word became flesh and made his dwelling among us. We have seen his glory, the glory of the one and only Son, who came from the Father, full of grace and truth."

John 1:14

Far too often, spiritual discernment has been pigeon-holed into the exclusive realm of decision-making, learning how to make good choices and know God's will methodically and predictably. We want a simple system to follow: set up the room, put people in place, consider the right options, add a prayer, and then press the button of discernment. For some people, spiritual discernment is reserved for major ministry or organizational decisions, like calling the right pastor or determining where to plant a church. For others, it's a tool used to spiritualize every single decision: *God, what fabric softener do you want me to buy at the store this week?*

But spiritual discernment is so much more. It's the choice of the bold and courageous to know God intimately. It's an invitation to all who desire a lifestyle that continuously seeks God's presence, power, peace, and purposes. It's a lifestyle for those who want to see God working throughout their personal lives—in good times, hard times, major inflection points, and everyday moments too.

Spiritual discernment is much more than a how-to manual for making good selections from a list of options. It certainly includes wise decision-making, but it begins with a relationship with God and the ability to notice God when he shows up, whether he reveals himself clearly or mysteriously. The discerning life grows from a heart that recognizes God's loving voice, responds to his gentle beckoning, and knows with certainty that our true home is found in God alone. We embrace the discerning life by learning to tune out the many distractions demanding our attention and daily practice a preference for God.

Imagine for a moment how different your life would be if, at the end of a long day, you were able to point to at least a handful of ways you clearly noticed God in your life. You could rest in that reality, giving thanks to the Father for his goodness, faithfulness, trustworthiness, and grace. Then, you could point out God to others, giving thanks together in response to what you experienced collectively. You wouldn't have to wait for someone else to remind you of God's great delight in making himself known. Instead, you would be the one who acknowledges God's presence and then faithfully looks for him more frequently throughout the day.

Friend, God wants you to notice him, and it is within your grasp to discern his presence. Your true home in God is available today. The adventure of walking with him daily awaits you.

Still, the discerning life needs to be cultivated. We don't consistently have eyes to see him, ears to hear his voice, or a heart that longs for his presence. We are born with a fresh innocence, pliable to the love that's poured out upon us as children, enjoying the fascinations that accompany each new experience. Over time our childlike wonder dissipates as our hearts harden to the presence of God. We begin to lean more toward our human capabilities and away from a healthy dependence on God. As this wide-eyed childlikeness and resplendent wonder gradually diminishes, we lose sight of our faithful companion, Jesus, the lover of our souls and the shepherd of our hearts.

Think back to the first time you noticed the sunshine and the shadows of others as you walked the beach. Can you recall the joy of standing at the edge of the ocean, your toes getting lost under the sand, your fingers grasping a seashell, and your body being held as the current came and went? Over time, such memories get complicated by the tumult of the tides, and our innocence washes away. Our eyes and ears lose the ability to see and hear God in our midst. So it is with our soul and the awakening we long for in Christ.

God knows all about this waning heart condition. He's been consistent in his desire to make himself known since the dawn of time. It's always been a challenge to get, foster, and maintain the attention of the people of God. But God doesn't quit. His patience is relentless. He wants his beloved to know that he resides in their midst. With every moment of our lives, God is giving us yet another chance to notice his love through the beauty in the world, the actions of others, the Scriptures, and yes, even in the breath you are breathing right now.

And he loves it when, with childlike innocence, we notice his abiding presence and receive his loving embrace. He welcomes us home from our wanderings along the edges of the sea of life, and we vanish restfully in his embrace to resume our companionship once more. All of this is available to you today.

The Glorious Incarnation

God waited patiently for generations to deliver the gift of the Incarnation. He revealed himself miraculously and mysteriously at the perfect time—God's chosen time. Those who were open to receive the gift of Jesus the Messiah were radically changed from the inside out.

From the moment of Jesus's miraculous and mysterious conception by the Holy Spirit, his earthly mission and ministry was to be embodied in an extraordinary with-ness, a presence unlike any other. For those who had eyes to see, ears to hear, and hearts to respond, it was unmistakable, quite remarkable, and completely transformational.

The incarnation of Jesus ushered in a new way of perceiving God's presence, power, and peace. Rueben P. Job, a mentor to many discerning pilgrims of the past century, including yours truly, called it a life marked by "practicing a preference for God," fully realized and graciously exemplified in Jesus. That same life was offered to all who encountered Jesus, the lover of their souls. The dawn of a new day of incarnational attentiveness had arrived. Those who met Jesus and received and embraced his divinity were surprisingly and delightfully changed, never to be the same again.

That same invitation to pursue intimacy with Jesus is ours today. It is an invitation to the discerning life—noticing everywhere, every day, and in everything, the loving presence, power, peace, and purposes of God.

God is with us. He desires to be noticed. He longs to be known. He seeks to be welcomed into the home of our hearts as we are consistently welcomed into his.

Throughout the Older Testament, the people of God awaited

the miracle of the Incarnation, the awe-inspiring arrival of Messiah Jesus, born humbly and faithfully as the prophets foretold. The early pages of the Gospel narratives give us a few important snapshots of those who witnessed his entry into earth, the residence we call home. Zechariah, Elizabeth, Joseph, and Mary experienced the discerning life firsthand. Theirs was an intimate encounter with angelic visitations and the empowering presence of the Spirit.

For them to miss seeing and hearing from God would have required a deliberate turning away with a stiff arm, a deaf ear, or a hard heart. Thankfully, they were each ripe for a fresh encounter with the Living God, and the Lord used them powerfully for a grand and eternal purpose: witnessing the humble arrival of the long-awaited Messiah, Jesus. Their hearts were warmed and prepared for all that was in store for them. God reached out to them with a mighty and merciful hand, seeking to take up full residence within, and they welcomed him into the home of their hearts with receptive joy.

Think for a moment about what was asked of and offered to Mary, a virgin betrothed to a man named Joseph, a descendent of David. The promise to David so long ago—that a Messiah would come from his house and lineage—was embodied in Jesus. And he came through the discerning life of Mary, who received in her womb the miraculous Son of God. The angel Gabriel comforted Mary, urged her not to be afraid, and promised the Holy Spirit's presence and power. He convinced Mary of the validity of God's protection.

In response, Mary sang. A virgin became a mother, and her womb became a home for Jesus, Emmanuel, God with us. And now *we* sing.

Just as Joseph and Mary, the shepherds and wise men, said yes to God's work in their hearts, so too are we to welcome Jesus into the center of our hearts. We too can experience Emmanuel, God with us, noticeably but mysteriously changing us day by day, one moment after another. He radically enters our lives and invites us to receive his miraculous love today and forever.

Presence, Grace, and Hospitality

The analogies for discernment are plentiful. One could liken discernment to traders on the floor of the New York Stock Exchange making rapid moves within a given time frame; physicians in the ER making swift and life-saving decisions; or police, firefighters, and other first responders coming swiftly to the aid of those in need. Discernment is required of any who are called upon to make quick and bold decisions in the moment.

Others might see discernment in politics, where finding compromise is paramount; in sports, where game plans matter; or in entertainment, when an emotional response is created from what appears on-screen. Some may equate discernment with preparing to teach in a classroom, choosing the content and presentation style most appropriate for one's students. Still others may see discernment as the ability to act promptly, calculate, ruminate, stimulate, regulate, and make decisions precipitously. In such nimble settings, the smarter and swifter you are, the better your results—hopefully.

But in the world of *spiritual* discernment, fast and first and most are not the way we are invited to live and learn as followers of Jesus. At times the discerning life will require agility and the God-given ability to pivot swiftly and gracefully. However, there is another pace, posture, and process for those in pursuit of spiritual discernment as a lifestyle. It's the pace of God, the One who lives with and among us in the daily rhythms of our hearts and households. It's a way of life that slows us down, fills us up, and opens us to a greater and deeper attentiveness and a richer, more fulfilling existence. As a result, more apt analogies for spiritual discernment are organic and related to everyday life.

We could, for example, consider the analogy of creation. Discerning God is indeed like observing the created order of how mountains and rivers, trees and plants, animals and wildlife, seasons and weather patterns all work in harmony with one another. Noticing the intricacies of creation keeps us appropriately focused on discerning God. We observe the created order and its need for water, nutrients, and sunlight. We watch how all of creation grows and matures as God ordains. We see how weather patterns express the power of God and the growth of all living things. Likewise, weather forecasting is akin to discernment, detecting the conditions of the environment and offering a prognosis for the days ahead.

For the purposes of this book, the metaphor we'll be using is centered on the homes we occupy and the hospitality and house care we engage in to maintain the quality of our daily lives. To do so, we must notice the condition of our homes, discern and attend to what's needed, and find joy in the results. These are things we can all relate to regardless of the size of our home.

Just as our physical home needs daily care, so too does our discerning heart. In our homes, we practice forms of hospitality for those who visit or reside there: family, friends, or even alone. In soul hospitality, God invites us to abide in him as he chooses to reside in us. Therefore, we are to make the house of our hearts hospitable to him, noticing his presence, inviting his residence, and preparing for his arrival continuously, prayerfully, and graciously. In so doing, we practice a preference for God.

Jesus came to us miraculously in the first Advent and lived among us as the Incarnate One. He suffered and died on our behalf so we can experience the fullness of eternal life, today and forever. I like to imagine him waiting patiently on the porch of heaven, his glance of love fixed upon us as his beloved. And all he's longing for is that we would notice him in return. As we notice him, we are invited to trust his presence, his power, his myriad gifts of grace, as he comes alongside us and delights to abide with us all the days of our lives.

Since we don't live our lives in isolation, we are also invited to encourage others to abide in Jesus and make their home in him too. God resides in and with the people of God as the new temple, without walls, awaiting eternity together. In Jesus, God dwells in our midst, making himself known and continuously beckoning us to come close and follow him. The discerning life is an intimately communal life for all who know and love and follow Jesus.

In this regard, Christ's home is my heart, and my home is Christ's heart, just like the words of Jesus: "Remain in me, as I also remain in you" (John 15:4). There's no place like home.

Our Discernment Home

Our earthly homes look completely different today from those in ancient times. We no longer live in modest first-century dwellings or in elaborate cedar palaces like those described in the Old Testament. Yet no matter your physical abode today, a home can be a vibrant metaphor for the state of your soul, the condition of your heart, and your longing (or not) for God. God delights to dwell with us in whatever home we live in and longs to be welcomed in with the kind of hospitality he graciously offers to all his beloved.

Imagine inviting Jesus into your physical home. No room off limits to the Savior's presence. He's not entertained just in the front room, the parlor, or at the dining room table. No, you invite him to make himself at home in any room available, regardless of the physical condition of each room. This metaphor speaks powerfully to those in pursuit of a discerning life—inviting, noticing, and receiving Jesus fully into the home of our heart, where nothing is off limits, and everything is made known to him. There, we are either receptive or resistant to the resonant work of God in the intimate crevices of our soul. The Messiah Jesus has been sent to be with you in the home of your heart, where he longs to become the primary dweller *and* the exclusive provider of the hospitality your soul desires.

This book is about spiritual discernment as a way of life. It's offered to you as an encouragement to open up the home of your heart to the deep work of God. Consider the parallel priorities of house care with soul care. Both keep us on our toes and on our knees. Both apply to our daily existence and our costly affection. Both are ever before us, beckoning us to notice, affirm, and give thanks for the life we are embracing today.

In each chapter, I will share with you some of the quirks of the home my wife, Ruth, and I have occupied for nearly four decades. This unique address has proven to be an ongoing teacher to our family concerning our life of discernment. We have had plenty of opportunities to turn to God for his wisdom and direction. God has continually taught us to trust him in all matters large and small. As you look around at your own home today, perhaps there are lessons to be learned in your living metaphor for spiritual discernment. Remain open and let's see what God will unveil.

In the pages ahead of us, we will first *define spiritual discernment*, noticing the transformational impact of a lifestyle marked by it. Then we will unpack our topic from the following vantage points:

We will begin with *biblical attentiveness*, delighting in how the Scriptures reveal the discerning life among the people of God throughout the generations.

We will then explore *prayerful listening* as the posture for discernment, caring for our soul as the primary seedbed for a discerning heart.

Our *relational presence* is best expressed in our compassion toward family, friends, and other discerning pilgrims sharing this extremely personal and transformational journey with us.

Within the gracious presence of *communal hospitality* in and among our spiritual community, we will consider ways to nurture our spiritual health and vitality together.

Then, we will look at ways to express *contextual empathy* toward our wider culture as well as our groups and personal contexts where good discernment can take root.

The *intentional focus* of Jesus will inform our pursuit of a with-God life defined by purposeful, unhurried presence among those we've been called to sacrificially serve.

A robust *practical process* will be defined by phases and questions and will include time-tested practices and rhythms to follow prayerfully in discernment, either alone or with others.

The *radical lifestyle* of embracing the distinct call of God that's upon us as Christ-followers will invite us to lean fully into building up the kingdom of God this side of heaven.

Then we will find a word on *restful trust*, the heart of the matter for all who desire the richness of the discerning life.

Finally, we will conclude with a suggested way of *Practicing a Preference for God*, a 40-day journey building on the good work of Rueben P. Job and utilizing portions of his *Guide to Spiritual Discernment*.[1]

By practicing a preference for God, the pathway that leads into a discerning life is open to us all. This starts in our hearts, and then moves into all aspects of our personal lives and ministries, our leadership and our service to others. With God taking up residence in our heart's home, we are positioned well for the discerning life at home, among others, and most importantly, with God.

Are you ready to begin?

CHAPTER 1

What Is Spiritual Discernment?

"So that you may live a life worthy of the Lord and please him in every way: bearing fruit in every good work, growing in the knowledge of God, being strengthened with all power according to his glorious might so that you may have great endurance and patience."

Colossians 1:10–11

Sometimes noticing God and practicing a life of discernment is as obvious as the nose on your face. Or, in my case, the rotten marinara sauce on the ceiling.

It had been a long week of minor renovations in our household, but they were finally complete. The kitchen walls had been repainted a soft gray, and the ceiling sparkled in bright white. The carpenters and painters were finally gone. We could check the project off our long list of home improvement needs. It was time to reclaim our

home, freed from the high cost of fixer-upper professionals hovering, making their mess, and leaving us to clean it up all over again. Perhaps you know the drill.

Thankfully, we liked the end result very much. Our eighty-year-old home was being transformed one project at a time. Our joy increased.

Our home is older than most in the US, and each time we have attempted to make a change, we have found sizeable surprises to repair before achieving the new look we desired. This particular kitchen reno was the fourth time we had worked on that room since purchasing our home in September of 1984.

The initial kitchen project was a simple cleanup from the prior owners. The open socket of dangling wires behind the refrigerator needed immediate repair. We replaced the green refrigerator—yes, they used to have green enamel painted refrigerators—with a new yellow model. We still keep that green one in our basement as a backup fridge. (As our repairperson said, "They don't make them like this anymore!") In addition, we restored a small wooden table and chair set for the only available corner as an eat-in option in the tiny kitchen. That was all we could afford.

Since then, we've made vast improvements to that kitchen. Renovation projects two, three, and four came over the next two decades. The original kitchen is long gone, and a completely refreshed space has replaced it under this roof of ours.

You'll learn more about this quirky home in future chapters, but for now, back to my story.

It was Friday afternoon. We were both exhausted from a full week of drilling, sanding, and painting by the crew. We had just finished cleaning up from the workers for the umpteenth time since the project began, and we were ready to simply be home that night and prepare a simple supper.

Ruth suggested we cook some pasta, pulled out the saucepan, and started boiling water. She asked me to go downstairs to the basement stash of grocery items to get some marinara sauce. When I returned and opened the jar, a mighty explosion of red sauce filled the air. Pasta sauce with mushrooms and onions erupted from the jar like lava from a volcano.

Red sauce sprayed across the cabinets within reach, poured along the countertops, attacked the newly painted walls and ceiling, and covered every other inch of the hard wood floors. Somehow it even landed on the area rugs in the adjacent hallway. It was on every one of the antique kitchen nick knacks we had collected over the years and displayed in the newly painted shelves. The coffee pot, the mixer, the wire vegetable baskets, the accumulated mail, the phone, the front of the microwave, the window of the wall oven, the cabinet handles, drawer pulls, the curtain over the sink, and yes, our faces, clothes, and eyeglasses were all drenched in sauce. It was everywhere.

We looked at each other in horror. What had just happened? How? Why? The tomato sauce must have been rotten! Had it been downstairs *that* long? Apparently, tomato sauce expires, and when it does, it can explode.

We sprinted into action. We wiped each other off as best as possible, cleaned our glasses so we could see clearly, and changed clothes. Then we got to work. We found the necessary buckets and towels. We rubbed and scrubbed. We washed and cleansed.

But the cabinets were still sticky and stinky. The countertops and floors were in good shape after our deep clean. We spotted the rug with carpet cleaner and scrubbed the antique kitchen items like never before. But the walls and ceilings, all newly painted, were stained with red splotches that wouldn't wash off.

Within a handful of days, the painters came to our rescue and restored the beauty of our beloved kitchen. We were back to normal within a week's time. All that was left was the memory of an amazing experience in the life of our household and marriage. It was something we would never forget. Even writing out the story makes me cringe a bit in the retelling.

Sometimes Discerning God Is Obvious; Other Times It Isn't

Discerning the presence and power of God can be as obvious as bright red tomato sauce splattered on the walls and ceilings of your kitchen, requiring immediate clean up. But only sometimes.

I am really good at discerning God when I'm watching a gorgeous sunset and offering praise to my Maker. Or when I'm in a worship service and a teenager offers a powerful testimony of his life with God. Or when I sit with a couple who entered my office broken and tattered and leave with renewed zeal for genuine reconciliation. In these instances, I get all choked up with delight. I see God at work, I'm ready to receive his presence, and I open myself wide to his work of redemption. His personal affection for all he created, including yours truly, is a delight to behold.

This can also be seen in the way we make decisions—the aspect of spiritual discernment most people want to jump ahead to. If the building you are in is burning, the smartest decision is also the most obvious: exit swiftly and safely. If one option in front of you is moral and the other is immoral, then the right decision is obvious: pick the moral decision. If the choice is between kindness and unkindness, always make kindness your priority. Yes, life is filled with obvious forms of discernment that emanate from a decisive and deliberate heart.

In the world of spiritual discernment, I call this "the obvious." This is when it's beyond the shadow of a doubt that God is in our midst, when one option is unequivocally the right one, or when acting compassionately in Christ is to your and others' full advantage. These situations are similar to the times when Jesus clearly instructed his disciples to teach, heal, and offer acts of compassion. It is also like when Saul, the hater of the church, was stricken on the road to Damascus with a blinding light, was thrust to the ground, heard the voice of Jesus, and was led to Damascus so he could see again and be filled with the Holy Spirit. This example of obvious discernment was made clear when the scales fell from Saul's eyes and his sight was restored. He couldn't help but notice Jesus, be moved to repentance, and commence a completely new trajectory for the rest of his life.

It's wonderful when basic levels of noticing God and living a discerning life are easy and clear. There are plenty of times every day when such discernment is obvious. Is it time for a meal? Eat. Is it time for a walk? Exercise. Is it time for a day's work? Accomplish it. Is it trash day? Take out the trash. Is it wiser to get up and walk outside to see a beautiful sunrise or sit on the couch and watch the TV? Get up and walk!

Even in the realm of the spiritual life, there are times of obvious discernment. Are you convicted of sin? Repent. Are you in need of guidance? Pray. Has a friend called for help? Serve. Have you been invited to donate? Give. Are you curious to learn? Read. Are you moved to tears? Cry. Is your heart moved to joy? Clap or dance or shout "Hallelujah!"

But the discerning life isn't always filled with the obvious or easy or readily accessible. God's presence isn't always evident. The right decision isn't always apparent. Following Christ isn't always easy or to a person's clear advantage (at least in the short term). Even though I'm convinced of God's empowering presence in each and every moment of every single day, I'm not always keen to notice. Perhaps you can relate.

Most of the time, we need to practice noticing God and responding in kind. This doesn't come naturally, but it can be attained rather simply, with intentionality. If you're patient, gracious, and willing to learn, you can begin to consistently practice a preference for God. The more you do so, the greater the wisdom you'll have when God's presence is not so obvious to discern.

The subject of spiritual discernment has captured my heart and mind for many years. It began for me when God woke me up with a dream that resulted in leaving one ministry leadership post to start something new: Leadership Transformations, Inc. (LTI).[1] That organization is the fruit of noticing. It took months for me to get clarity on the way forward, but thanks be to God, I had wise people surrounding me as we discerned God and leaned forward in his presence, power, and direction. I'm forever indebted to my discernment team of friends who helped me listen and respond. LTI's focus is on the spiritual formation, discernment, and renewal of leaders and teams. Discernment is at the epicenter of our shared calling. We deal with this topic daily and continue to learn together as we serve.

Early in LTI's history, I was invited to participate in a national discernment initiative with Paul Anderson and his team at George Fox University in Portland. This group of discernmentarians from across the United States were all in search of the same end: leading others in a lifestyle of discernment. Central to this yearlong endeavor were the following biblical, theological, and historical convictions:

- Christ is alive and wants to lead the church.
- His will is not divided, and it can be known if it will be sought.
- No one has sole access to God's truth and Christ's leadings, but neither is anyone deprived of such access.
- Authentic Christian discernment begins and ends with submitting oneself totally to the lordship of Christ, aspiring to conform faithfully to the clear teaching of Scripture, the wisdom of the church, and the witness of the Holy Spirit.
- Effective Christian leadership helps people understand the issues better . . . helps people distinguish between matters of reference and matters of conscience . . . helps people come to a unitive sense of God's leading.[2]

This initiative thrust LTI into an ongoing discovery process that remains at the forefront of our ministry priorities today. There is no more important topic for the church to wrestle with today than to know God, notice him at work in, through, and all around us, and to aid others in embracing and fulfilling the discerning life.

The topic is smack-dab in the center of every Christian's experience. I welcome you to explore discernment as a way of life, not just relevant in times of important and obvious decision-making, but in the everyday experiences of life in relationship with God, with the people of God, and in the world we are invited to love and serve in the name of God.

Unless we learn how to discern God's presence, his power, his protection, and his peace, we will not be able to discern the will of God. Discerning God precedes the discernment of his will. It's a must for the people of God today.

The Road to Emmaus

Scripture also gives us pictures of what it looks like when discernment isn't so obvious.

Along the road home to Emmaus, two disciples walk with their heads down and their hearts dejected (Luke 24:13–35). They are heading home from Jerusalem, and the seven-mile journey has been rather depressing. They had hoped Jesus was their long-awaited Messiah, but instead they witnessed his arrest and crucifixion. The darkness of the clouds in the sky feel to them like a metaphor for the state of their own hearts and souls. How could things have gone so poorly after so much grand anticipation?

As they walk, they discuss the events of the previous day. They don't notice when someone joins them. It is Jesus, but they are kept from recognizing him.

He inquires, "What are you discussing together as you walk along?" (v. 17).

Their faces remain downcast. Cleopas, the only named disciple of the pair, asks their fellow traveler, "Are you the only one visiting Jerusalem who does not know the things that have happened there in these days?" (v. 18). Here's my modern translation: "Are you, like, the only clueless one?"

Apparently. Because Jesus then asks them, "What things?" (v. 19).

Still unaware of the unfolding situation, the two inform their companion about the things that had transpired "about Jesus of Nazareth."

> He was a prophet, powerful in word and deed before God and all the people. The chief priests and our rulers handed him over to be sentenced to death, and they crucified him; but we had hoped that he was the one who was going to redeem Israel. And what is more, it is the third day since all this took place. In addition, some of our women amazed us. They went to the tomb early this morning but didn't find his body. They came and told us that they had seen a vision of angels, who said he was alive. Then some of our companions went to the tomb and found it just as the women had said, but they did not see Jesus. (vv. 19–24)

At this point, Jesus begins to increase their understanding, awareness, and discernment of his presence. As we read this passage, we're amazed at how clueless the two disciples were (much like we would be too). Jesus lovingly rebukes the closed eyes of their hearts: "How foolish you are, and how slow to believe all that the prophets have spoken! Did not the Messiah have to suffer these things and then enter his glory?" (vv. 25–26).

And then, "beginning with Moses and all the Prophets, he explained to them what was said in all the Scriptures concerning himself" (v. 27).

That much intrigued them, but not enough to reveal who was speaking to them. As they approach their home village, Jesus keeps walking as if he is heading to a further-than-Emmaus destination. The two have the sense to invite him in: "'Stay with us, for it is nearly evening; the day is almost over.' So he went in to stay with them" (vv. 28–29).

The household of the disciples becomes their Holy of Holies. We have no idea how large or small that household was. We don't know how many rooms. We don't know who else lived with them. We don't know if it's a public inn or a family dwelling. We aren't sure if they are related to one another, as many suppose. But we know that they invite him in, to eat, rest, and enjoy company.

When they sit at the table together to partake of a simple meal, their gracious hospitality to this stranger (Jesus) is reversed into the soul hospitality of their guest. At the table, Jesus is the one to take bread, give thanks, break it, and serve it to them (v. 30). And in that gentle moment, the resurrected Jesus is revealed to the disciples as the host, breaking the bread and offering the gift, all with a spirit of thankfulness.

Can you imagine what it was like to be present at that table on that night, only a day after the tomb was emptied miraculously and the risen Jesus was set free from the bondage of his earthly existence? The Scriptures tell us that "their eyes were opened and they recognized him, and he disappeared from their sight" (v. 31).

Astonishing. Bewildering. Delightful. Life changing. They saw Jesus. They recognize him. The eyes of their hearts are opened wide to receive, recognize, and rejoice.

Sometimes Jesus is obvious to discern. Many times he is not. But when we do see him, like the two disciples, we can't help but exclaim, "Were not our hearts burning within us while he talked with us on the road and opened the Scriptures to us?" (v. 32). Like the two disciples, when we discern the presence of Jesus, we run back into our worlds with shouts of acclamation: "It is true! The Lord has risen" (v. 34).

The Emmaus Road story is a prime example of spiritual discernment. In it, we see that a lifestyle of discernment includes the following:

- A road on which we travel through life.
- Companions who join us along the way.
- A home in which to reside and process.
- Eyes to see, ears to hear, and hearts to feel.
- Willingness to listen carefully and prayerfully.
- Responses of celebration, thankfulness, offering, and obedience.

Are you willing to walk this way?

Burning, Burned Out, or Heartburn

A lifestyle of discernment is best described by the burning of the heart that the two disciples shared in common: "Were not our hearts burning within us?" Yes, their hearts were burning with delight, with joy, in worship, and in relationship with the living Jesus, who was with them and in their midst. When their eyes were finally opened wide to see Jesus, their hearts fluttered and burst into flame from within. Their previous experience of despondency and downheartedness was replaced with exuberance and joy. They couldn't wait to tell their friends about Jesus. Their hearts were burning with joy.

A burning heart for Jesus is much different than a burned-out heart or heartburn. A burned-out heart believes in the work ethic of constant effort for swift results, accompanied by adrenaline rush and productivity. The goal is success at any cost. For example, imagine a pastor whose church and reputation are growing, who pushes and pushes until everyone is burning the candle at both ends. Eventually those excessive efforts snuff out their effectiveness. Burnout brings everything to a grinding halt. There's nothing left to offer in a burned-out person, and cynicism, skepticism, and negativity result.

Heartburn is what we experience when we're tense, stressed, irritable, flummoxed, and controlling. It comes with the territory of the nerved, the nervous, and the unnerving. It's what happens when our circumstances are out of our control and we're ready to explode. Imagine church leaders wound up so tightly that they lash out instead of ministering. This occurs when the people of God, who are supposed to excel in the way of love, are instead engaged in unending conflict, which often leads to division. When our lives and ministries are experiencing heartburn, leaders need to address these issues head on. Repeated cases of relational heartburn will never reap positive fruit for God's kingdom and glory.

Burned-out hearts and heartburn are unhealthy. But a burning heart for God, kept aflame by the presence of Jesus and the empowerment of the Spirit, is a picture of the abundant life Jesus wants for us. We're invited to receive that life from our loving heavenly Father. It's the goal of a discerning life, and a profound indicator for how well we're doing fulfilling our call to a discerning life. Is your heart aflame with the love of Jesus, or are you experiencing burnout due to overworking or heartburn brought on by relational instability?

John Wesley, the founder of Methodism, describes his conversion and renewal experience at Aldersgate (a street in London known as the place where he came to a living faith) as his "heart being strangely warmed"[3] by his profound experience with God. John Calvin's symbol of an open hand holding a flaming heart described how he wanted to present his heart aflame with the love of God. Both Arminians and Calvinists seem to be on board with the meaningful nature of a burning heart. Perhaps a fellowship of the burning heart will emerge among the convinced. Will that include you?

What Is Discernment?

In the simplest of terms, a complex word like *discernment* can be understood in the following ways:

- perceiving and noticing the present, attentive to the now, and in anticipation of the next—like holding hands and looking both ways before safely crossing the street
- separating mentally one aspect of life from another; the often quiet and patient sorting out and sifting through—like a well-tuned ear listening for the various instruments of an orchestra or a piano tuner attentive to his or her craft
- coming to greater clarity over time—perceiving life like the layers of an onion, peeling back one layer at a time until reaching the core
- distinguishing between good and evil, right from wrong, authentic from counterfeit—like a compass within that points to true north and keeps us from going astray
- recognizing that one's viewpoint can be crowded out instead of seen more fully from above—noticing the difference between the trees in front of you and the forest that surrounds you

Throughout the history of the church, people have defined discernment in a variety of ways. Evan B. Howard writes,

> The debates among the Socinians (reason), the Quakers (Spirit), the Catholics (tradition), the Reformers (Scripture), the Anglicans (Scripture, tradition, reason), the Anabaptists (Scripture, Spirit, local community), the Puritans (Scripture, Spirit), and the Methodists (Scripture, tradition, reason, experience) were not

ivory-tower feuds. They were also explorations of the sources of discernment. . . . Christian spirituality is about relationship with God. A life of discernment—appreciating God in the ordinary, watching the hand of God over time in our lives, and determining the guiding presence of God in key situations—is the means by which that relationship is navigated.[4]

One might say spiritual discernment is like learning to think God's thoughts after him, thoughtfully, prayerfully, and particularly. It includes judgment and discrimination so as to avoid landing in nonbiblical or un-Christlike sand traps. It's learning to think biblically about all aspects of a Christian's life. And it's clearly recognizing and distinguishing the difference between that which is from God and that which is from the enemy of our souls, the devil.

Often, when the term *spiritual discernment* is used, its apex (and often the only real focus) is decision-making. How does one discern the will of God, the ways of God, the wishes of God? And, in particular situations that are left with specific decisions to make, what does God want from us? While this is a worthwhile pursuit and one that we will explore together, we need to remember that *a lifestyle of spiritual discernment precedes a specific discernment question.*

Are we living out discernment as a daily and ongoing priority? That's our central question. The answer will come when we notice God, delight in God, converse with God, point God out to others, abide in God, and trust in God. In other words, it comes when we practice a preference for God, alone and with others in our family, friendship circle, community, work, and church.

Practicing a preference for God—noticing God in everything—is the essence of spiritual discernment and the pathway to a discerning life.

The first to love ## Tap, Tap, Tap

God is a loving initiator. It's what I most appreciate about God. He is the first to love. He is the first to give and forgive. He is first to call and empower. He is first to affirm us as his beloved and equip us as his broken and blessed children. He is the One who metaphorically stands on the porch of heaven and continuously sees us and waits for us to come to our senses and turn back home.

And when we finally do come to our senses, like in the parable of the prodigal son (Luke 15:11–32), it's God who is prodigal (wastefully extravagant) in his affection for us. His way of loving is gentle and generous, simple and beautiful: a robe for our back, a ring for our finger, a kiss for our cheek, new shoes for our tired feet, and a party for our wayward heart. His way of relating to us is always love. Always personal. Always gracious. Always. He's never there with a finger of shame or blame pointing in our direction. Rather, it's always an extended and outstretched hand to receive, greet, welcome us home, and restore us back into community.

It's so like God to be fully present when we're clueless and absent. His love for us is genuinely gracious and delightfully affectionate. He is so interested in us that his eyes are peeled on us 24/7, never stopping, never turning away, never distracted, never absent, never ending. His moment-by-moment focus is us, day and night, every minute of our lives, no matter where we live or what generation or ethnicity or social status we represent.

And he holds us close to himself, no matter where we are in life. He holds us tightly, and he initiates love, grace, mercy, and peace into our troubled hearts and personal lives—all the time. No exceptions. Always and forever.

But are we aware of his presence? He's tapping on the shoulder of our hearts all the time: tap, tap, tap . . . tap, tap, tap. As Christ-followers, it's incumbent on us to notice the tap and not brush it aside, shun God's presence, or be so numbed or hardened or oblivious as to miss it altogether.

The discerning life begins, ends, and is filled at every moment in between with practicing a preference for God. It makes so much sense: practice takes time, preference is overarching, and noticing God is our primary objective. Our awareness is in our noticing the tap, tap, tap of God's presence, power, and peace. Discernment is about love, and a discerning life is measured, protected, and empowered by love that emanates first and foremost from the hand and heart of Almighty God—Father, Son, and Spirit.

Psalm 139 is often referred to as the "Omni Psalm" because the psalmist is reminding us that God is *all-knowing* (omniscient—he knows you, vv. 1–6); *ever-present* (omnipresent—he is with you, vv. 7–12), and *all-powerful* (omnipotent—he created you and loves you, vv. 13–18). God is the giver of *shalom*, the peace that surpasses all knowledge and sustains us in our daily lives. And he invites us to trust deeply that he will care for us and protect us as we plead with him to "search me, O God, and know my heart; test me and know my anxious thoughts. See if there is any offensive way in me, and lead me in the way everlasting" (vv. 23–24) This is the kind of love that's discernable for all who know, love, and serve God.

Are you aware of the tap, tap, tap of God's presence, power, and peace? That's the benchmark from which we attain our understanding of spiritual discernment. It's not so much about what we know about God or what God's marching orders are for us. It's about what we notice and then receive personally and directly from God by continually attending to the relationally loving work of God in the Scriptures, in history, in the created world, and in our own lives. That's how we come to know God personally, relationally, and transformationally.

Our motivation? God. Our inspiration? God. Our destination? God.

Why *Spiritual* Discernment?

We call it "spiritual" discernment because of the movement of God's Spirit alive and at work in, through, with, and around us as God's beloved ones. The word *spiritual* belongs in the beginning of the phrase because as trinitarian Christians (those who acknowledge that God is known as the three-in-one triune God: Father, Son, and Holy Spirit) we acknowledge the powerful work of the Holy Spirit, the person of the Godhead given to us in order that we may live with and for God with fullness, wholeness, and abundance.

God loves us so much that when Jesus was preparing his disciples for his inevitable departure, he promised to send along a Comforter, the Spirit himself.

> If you love me, keep my commands. And I will ask the Father, and he will give you another advocate to help you and be with you forever—the Spirit of truth. . . . I will not leave you as orphans. . . . But the Advocate, the Holy Spirit, whom the Father will send in my name, will teach you all things and will remind you of everything I have said to you. Peace I leave with you; my peace I give you. (John 14:15–18, 26–27)

The Spirit himself dwells within us. And he longs for us to know him and perceive and discern his presence, his power, his peace, and his purpose. The Spirit we know as Holy is the One who empowers our discernment and our very lives. There is no other Spirit but God's, and when we use the term *spiritual discernment*, we are continually referencing the Holy Spirit.

An experiential knowledge of God is evidenced in the work of God's Spirit in, through, and all around us as believers. It's inherently a subjective experience because it's rooted in a relationship of love and affection. Who among us can quantify love? As a result, it can be misunderstood and misinterpreted. Since we tend to distrust our emotions or emotional experiences, the work of God's Spirit often gets discredited.

The remedy for this is actually to pay *more* attention to our heart's affections—our emotions—and not less. God is the author of our emotions, and when we express love and affection, it's fabulous to do so from the heart and not simply with our matter-of-fact minds. But we also tend to fear disappointment with God: *What if I don't hear from or notice God?* These fears are exactly what we need to bring to God, inviting him to work transformationally in us and through us, always for his glory.

The work of the Spirit is distinct and worth understanding more completely. In summary, the Spirit is the One who pours life into us and occupies every nook and cranny of our hearts.

- The Spirit brings us under conviction of our sinfulness and our need for holiness, turning our brokenness into joyfulness and faithfulness. He converts us from a life of oppression and self-absorption to a life of freedom and God-consciousness. "When [the Advocate] comes, he will prove the world to be in the wrong about sin and righteousness and judgment" (John 16:8).
- The Spirit assures us of our status as dearly loved children of

God, continually quickening our hearts to remain in alignment with his love. "The Spirit himself testifies with our spirit that we are God's children" (Rom. 8:16).

- The Spirit shines a bright light on the truth and trustworthiness of God and invites us to cooperate with the marching orders of our heavenly Father, birthing within us the hope and renewal only he can provide. "When he, the Spirit of truth, comes, he will guide you into all the truth. He will not speak on his own; he will speak only what he hears, and he will tell you what is yet to come" (John 16:13).

- The Spirit guides, enlightens, comforts, heals, and sustains us in times of deliberation and decision-making, counseling and consoling us, and ultimately is the One who completes the work of God in us. "Those who are led by the Spirit of God are the children of God" (Rom. 8:14).

When we trust God's Spirit dwelling within us, we can be assured of our discernment as we practice a preference for God.

A Way of Life

As believers in Jesus, we are invited to live the discerning life by choosing to prefer God's Word, his will, and his ways over our own or any preferences espoused by our unbelieving culture. Christ Jesus our Lord cares very much about our deformed and misinformed souls and delights to reform, conform, and transform them for his glory. Our priorities must emanate from the priorities of God.

The discerning life is for individuals, families, small groups, ministry teams, churches, and organizations. Discernment is for our daily life and is achieved by our deliberate and determined attentiveness, not just in special times of big decision-making, but as a moment-by-moment and day-by-day growing awareness of God's divine invitation to come close, draw near, and follow him into a deeper place of intimacy and companionship.

Such a lifestyle of practicing a preference for God begins first and foremost in the hearts and lives of individuals, then moves to communities and teams that are tired of the old way of manipulating agendas and desire instead to be molded and shaped by God. From that invitation to intimacy, God offers his divine intention to empower us to fulfill our rule of life as we fulfill his will for our lives on a daily basis and throughout our lifetime.

Ideally, it will become a conviction shared by all who embrace and embody the life-changing gospel of Jesus. When we practice a preference for God with those of like heart and mind, then our community life is transformed from the inside out. Leaders create the space for this to occur, as it doesn't naturally develop, nor is it passed to others by osmosis. The discerning life is for all, but not all will live it unless we start a revolution of sorts, a movement defined by spiritual discernment as a way of life.

If practicing a preference for God is our daily priority, then our posture matters. The discerning life is marked by the following postures:

- humility—content and open-handed; never arrogant; motivations in check
- listening—far more than talking; attentively and non-judgmentally present
- honesty—full disclosure and without pretense, posturing, or hiding what's true

- abandonment—willingly releasing our preconceived notions in order to remain open
- indifference—caring less about process or outcome; open to various possibilities; suspending one's desires, even for a time
- detachment—letting go of our attachments in order to properly attach to God
- openness—honoring another's opinion, option, and opportunity
- friendship—seeing the other as wiser, smarter, and choosing to prefer others for the sake of harmony, unity, and grace
- community—the our/we/us is always more important than I/me/mine
- consolation—peace, joy, delight, harmony, grace; held in times of desolation
- prayerfulness—prayerfully permeating and not merely punctuating the process; staying open, amiable, pliable, lucid, transparent, graced, forgiving
- decisions—not made prematurely or under compulsion, but freely, generously, hospitably, relationally, compassionately, organically, and systemically

Each of these postures will be touched on in the coming pages. None of them are easy to live, but with the guidance of the Spirit and the help of our spiritual communities, we can indeed choose to live this way with and for God.

Yes, sometimes discernment is as obvious as tomato sauce on our walls and ceiling. But Ruth and I learned our lesson that infamous Friday night: check the expiration date before opening a jar of tomato sauce. Take time to notice. Left too long, the steady build-up of food particles, bacteria, mold, and other living things contained therein will create gas, and the result won't be pretty. Don't make assumptions about what appears to the naked eye as obvious. Keep your guard up, even and especially when you're exhausted. And when opening a jar of tomato sauce, it's always best to wrap it with a towel just in case.

So it is with spiritual discernment. At times it's obvious what God is up to. Enjoy a lovely sunset. Engage in a community worship service. Rejoice and give thanks for a story of restored relationships. But when it gets harder to distinguish and discern, to see God and the things he wants for you, lean fully into your relationship with a loving Father and wait for his empowering presence to help you discern his presence and trust him unconditionally. The more familiar you are with him in the obvious times, the more you'll be able to notice him when things are less clear.

Spiritual discernment becomes a part of us as we embrace the lifestyle of practicing a preference for God, noticing God in everything, and receiving the hospitality of God in the very places where we are learning to be hospitable to others and even ourselves. Only then will we be able to faithfully walk our road to Damascus or Emmaus or Jerusalem or wherever it is that God will lead.

All of this will take a lifetime to rehearse.

PRACTICING A PREFERENCE FOR GOD

Don't turn to the next page too quickly. As you reflect on the content of this chapter, consider areas of your life where you recently noticed God in the obvious. Perhaps it was in the beauty of his creation; what did you see of God's handiwork? Or maybe it was in your prayer closet when your heart was strangely warmed by the Word of God. Or in a conversation with a friend when you felt known, seen, and loved. Or in a difficult circumstance when you felt alone in what you believed to be right and true, but were accompanied affectionately by Jesus.

How is God seeking to reveal himself to you today? Acknowledge his tap, tap, tap, and point him out to others. Give voice to what you notice. Spiritual discernment—noticing God's presence, power, and peace by practicing a preference for God in everything—can indeed evidence itself in obvious ways. Keep the eyes of your heart wide open to prefer God today. Practicing hospitality in your heart begins with a willingness to "let it be to me according to your word" (Luke 1:38 ESV).

Here are a few spiritual exercises to put into practice as you reflect on this chapter:

- **The Obvious:** Where does God show up the most obviously for you? Where is he easiest to notice? Go there often. It's good for your soul.
- **Burning Heart:** When was the last time you had a burning heart of awareness of God? Do you feel that way now? If so, soak in it. If not, spend some time recalling that burning-heart feeling. What might be keeping you from it—heartburn, burnout, or something else?
- **Tap, Tap, Tap:** Do you notice God's initiatives toward you, and feel his drawing you toward himself 24/7? Or do you more often feel like you're the one searching for God? Why do you think that is?

CHAPTER 2

Attentiveness

Spiritual Discernment Is Biblical

"The LORD your God is with you, the Mighty Warrior who saves. He will take great delight in you; in his love he will no longer rebuke you, but will rejoice over you with singing."

Zephaniah 3:17

The discerning life is available to all who are open to receive it. But for many, the choice has already been made: life is more predictable when it's fulfilled in our own power and strength. This can be true even of Christians who have professed Jesus as their Lord and Savior.

We in the body of Christ don't necessarily mean to close off God from our daily routines. It's just that we have been in the habit of self-empowerment for so long that we do so without consideration of another way to live: Spirit-empowered. Our routines have been so predictably patterned that we are unaware of the consequences of

From Self to Spirit

our choices or of the available option to live with so much more. The discerning life is the invitation to shift from self to Spirit, from just enough to an abundance.

Our family has lived in our quirky home for the entirety of our children's lives. Every decade, give or take a year, we've had to replace our hot water heater. When the leaks begin to produce droplets or puddles of water on the basement floor, it's time to call the plumber.

On a recent water-heater-replacement visit, our plumber noted that the water pressure was quite low in our house. It wasn't the first time he shared this insight, but this time it caught our attention because he said we could not sell the house with such low pressure. We asked what this would cost to fix and learned it would require a total replacement of the water line from the street to our home—not a simple or cheap project.

By that time, we had raised our family in a low-water-pressure house for well over thirty years. We knew not to run the dishwasher when we were doing laundry. If we were using water inside, we couldn't water the lawn outside. We learned not to flush a toilet when someone was taking a shower, or else we risked scorching or freezing the person in the shower. Without thinking about it, we had slowly adjusted our lifestyle to accommodate low water pressure.

Simply put, we didn't know any better. We thought everyone in our town had low water pressure. We sincerely thought it was our lot in life. And we got used to living this way.

But the plumber's warning shook us out of our self-deception. Ruth and I looked at the options, considered the cost, and thought about the timing. We decided to bite the bullet and get it done. It had to be replaced sooner or later. Why wait?

When the big, burly digger dudes showed up at our doorstep to excavate our front yard and replace our water main, they thought they could do it swiftly. (Clearly, they had never worked at the Macchia's home!) Their strategy was to dig close to the house to find the main, then dig about ten feet away, find the main, and pull the pipe. But at that point, the pipe broke. So they tried again about ten feet further from the house. They dug down to the main and pulled the pipe. It broke again. The main was so deteriorated by rust that it was a miracle it had held any water whatsoever.

Before long, our entire front yard had been excavated, and one hundred feet of rusted pipe had been removed. The simple water-main-replacement project had expanded far beyond everyone's expectations. The workers placed one hundred feet of newly coiled copper replacement piping in our basement, ready to be rolled out six feet underground to the street. When they reached the entry point into our house, the biggest of the big, burly digger dudes said to me, "It's amazing you've had any water in this house. There's just a nail-head's width of a hole here at the point of entry."

With that, he and his buddies began to replace the water main. By sunset, the front yard had been put back together again (well, sort of), and the new main was attached from the house to the street. We had water pressure once more.

And boy, did we have water pressure! After the workers left our house, Ruth and I became giddy about our strong water pressure. We playfully turned on the water in one sink and then flushed the toilet, noticing no difference in the pressure either place. After taking a shower, Ruth noted, "I had so much pressure it actually hurt to take a shower!" We were glad to have the work done and looked forward to the future—until we went downstairs and noticed water streaming from the boiler of our oil heater.

Apparently, the pressure was too much for that piece of machinery. We panicked. I called the plumber. He came as quickly as possible and stopped the floodwaters from consuming our basement.

I asked the plumber, "Are the pipes in our house going to explode behind every wall and under every floor with this new water pressure?" He assured me that would not happen, and thankfully it didn't. He looked over our situation and modified a few settings, and we were back to life as it could now be lived—with normal water pressure.

The shock of going from very low to normal water pressure overnight taught us one main lesson: we lived with a "nail-head's width" of water pressure for over thirty years when we could have had so much more. We and our children knew nothing other than low water pressure.

So it is with the Christian life. Far too many of us are satisfied with a "nail-head's width" of God—just enough to get by—when we could have so much more. Too many churches and organizations do the same, satisfied that we know the basics about God when what's available to us in Christ is so much more.

The Abundant Life

People earnestly pursuing a discerning life eventually realize that God offers much more than they are used to. We don't have to be burdened by a scarcity mindset or a just-enough-to-get-by approach. We don't have to live our spiritual lives with extremely low spiritual (water) pressure. The fullness of the life of the Spirit of God is always there, waiting for us. All we need to do is widen the nail-head's width of our soul and receive its abundance.

That's what practicing a life of spiritual discernment is all about: preferring the fullness of God. Not just a pennies-for-charity worth of God. Not just church on Sunday and an occasional act of service or writing a check to a worthy cause or showing up at our children's church programs. There is so much more of God to receive.

Living with a posture of receptivity opens us up to the abundant life. In this posture, we acknowledge our natural propensity to take matters into our own hands, and instead prefer God's loving hands of gracious kindness, undeserved mercy, and everlasting love. Instead of making all of our own choices, we defer to God and invite him to lead the way. Instead of finding satisfaction with a minimum of cross-bearing for others, we invite the full load of burden-bearing for the sake of the community. Our discerning life is for ourselves, yes, but more importantly, it's for God and his kingdom, his church, his community, and his world. It's for others.

This invitation to enjoy the abundant life is repeated in the biblical text over and over. Jesus made it crystal clear when he said, "I have come that they may have life, and have it to the full" (John 10:10). This is Jesus's mission statement, his clarion call, his unmistakable desire for all his followers. Then and now, freely and generously, he wants to offer everyone his life-changing presence, power, protection, and peace—all because of love.

Love—vast as an ocean, abundant, lavish, generous, over-the-top, and eternal. God's love is unconditional, grace-filled, and joy-drenched. It's magnificent, glorious, marvelous, wonderful, amazing, and inconceivable. Yet it's also affectionate, warm, intimate, and heartfelt. What words would you add to describe how you feel about God's love? Write them down and thank God for his immeasurable love.

The key to the discerning life is much more than acknowledging God's love. More importantly, we may receive it for ourselves, today and every hour of each new day, being transformed by God's love from the inside out as a result. Love is the air of the kingdom of God. To breathe it deeply is to be changed by it forever.

The apostle Paul prays for the Ephesians to know the love of Christ:

> And I pray that you, being rooted and established in love, may have power, together with all the Lord's holy people, to grasp how wide and long and high and deep is the love of Christ, and to know this love that surpasses knowledge—that you may be filled to the measure of all the fullness of God. (Eph. 3:17–19)

We read such a familiar passage and far too often have a ho-hum response. *God's love. Yup, I get it. And I believe in it. And I share it with others.* But has it truly penetrated the deepest recesses of your soul?

On a spiritual retreat a handful of years ago, I was sitting with a spiritual mentor, detoxing my hurting soul. I was sharing about feelings of abandonment from those I thought had my best interests in mind but had turned against me. I was not in a good place. After listening to my story, this godly man encouraged me to do one of the strangest things ever suggested to me: wink at myself in the mirror. At least once a day. For the foreseeable future.

That sounded so bizarre! But his point was to do this as a reminder of God's unconditional love for me each day. This spiritual leader shared that our lives will be filled with disappointment, heartache, suffering, and sorrow. That reality we cannot change. But the inner reservoir of our soul can indeed be opened to receive love once more, over and over and over again. That's the way of God, and if we're to live a discerning life, it's to become our way too.

My spiritual friend did not want the wink to be prideful or self-aggrandizing. He meant it to be a here-and-now reminder that when God looks at me, he does so with profound affection and a deep love that upends all that the world does to destroy my soul. (And there's plenty of that to go around today.) The way of love God offers is completely upside down in comparison to even the finest form of love the world has to offer.

He then suggested I sit prayerfully with the story of the prodigal son in Luke 15. I did this for the rest of my time on retreat. The prodigal son (also known as the prodigal father, or as Tim Keller has relabeled it, the prodigal God) is a parable that comes alive every time it's prayerfully considered. It's all about extravagance—offered by the Father, received by one son, and shunned by another.

Prodigals

A few months after the spiritual retreat, I had the honor of traveling to St. Petersburg, Russia, and visiting the Hermitage Museum. There, Rembrandt's masterpiece "The Return of the Prodigal Son" hangs among several of his other paintings. It was one of the final oil paintings completed by Rembrandt prior to his death in 1669, and it depicts the merciful, forgiving, and loving hospitality of the father toward his wayward son. Filled with bold contrast between light and dark, the painting captivated me artistically, emotionally, relationally, and spiritually.

Henri Nouwen had prompted me, in his book that shares the title of Rembrandt's painting, to take as much time as possible prayerfully noticing the contours of the painting. He encourages readers to ponder the meaning of the story and to grasp the depth of their own receptivity of God's mercy, grace, love, and forgiveness. We were at the museum on a busy day, and it was filled with tourists from around the world. The hustle and bustle made it difficult to prayerfully sit with the painting. But after nearly two hours in that space, the significance of the experience hit me hard. I am like the prodigal son. I am like the older brother. I am like the loving father. I was on that canvas.

From the vantage point of the youngest son in the story, I realized he's lost in the extravagant selfishness of his own domain. He asks for his share of the estate prematurely and self-righteously, and the father gladly divides his property between his youngest and oldest sons. The younger son sets off for a distant country and squanders his wealth in wild living. After spending everything, he endures a famine in his new homeland and ends up living among the pigs, feeding them but starving himself.

When he "comes to his senses" and realizes the error of his ways, he sets his mind toward home—his true home, where his father still resides (Luke 15:17). He determines what he will say to his father upon his return: "I have sinned against heaven and against you. I am no longer worthy to be called your son; make me like one of your hired servants" (vv. 18–19).

But on his return journey, while he's still a long way off, his father sees him coming. And what proceeds from here is a display of the unconditional and extravagant love of the father for his wayward son:

> His father . . . was filled with compassion for him; he ran to his son, threw his arms around him and kissed him. The son said to him, "Father, I have sinned against heaven and against you. I am no longer worthy to be called your son." But the father said to his servants, "Quick! Bring the best robe and put it on him. Put a ring on his finger and sandals on his feet. Bring the fattened calf and kill it. Let's have a feast and celebrate. For this son of mine was dead and is alive again; he was lost and is found." So they began to celebrate. (vv. 20–24)

The father winks love. The young son receives love in abundance. A discerning life is born, reformed, and transformed from the inside out.

But that's not true for everyone in the story. The older son is outraged by this display of affection. When he returns from his workday in the field, he hears music and dancing. What in the world is going on? One of the servants tells him that his younger brother returned and his father killed the fattened calf because his son was safe and sound. "The older brother became angry and refused to go in," regardless of his father's pleading to join the celebration (v. 28). He recounts the many ways he has been faithful, slaving for his father and never disobeying his orders. "But when this son of yours who has squandered your property with prostitutes comes home, you kill the fattened calf for him!" (vv. 29–30).

The father winks to the older son: "'My son,' the father said, 'you are always with me, and everything I have is yours. But we had to celebrate and be glad, because this brother of yours was dead and is alive again; he was lost and is found'" (vv. 31–32).

The older son (figuratively) spits in the father's eyes. He wants nothing to do with his father's wink of affection. To him, this is foolishness and unnecessary tolerance. No work should yield no celebration. In his eyes, the father's actions are disgraceful and ridiculous!

That's exactly the point. Abundant love, especially to the self-righteous and the sinner, makes no sense whatsoever. But to those who come to their senses and turn back home, extravagant love is their healing balm.

A wink from heaven daily received creates a discerning life, transformed from the inside out.

The Older Brother and the Loving Father

Practicing a preference for God begins with receiving the loving attentiveness of God: his eyes on us from afar, his running in our direction, his hug of affection, his kiss on the cheek, his robe of protection, his ring of honor, his sandals of grace, his celebration of joy—all that is life-giving, freely, generously, and extravagantly offered to us by God. Our sins are forgiven. Relationship is restored. Reconciliation is received. Transformation is experienced. Discernment has begun.

But in this glorious renewal process, we must acknowledge the older brother within us too. I can't help but read this passage in Luke 15 and find myself in all of the main characters—for sure in the careless, sinful, and repentant younger son, but also in the careful, obedient, and resourceful older son. The older son worked hard but grew bitter as he compared himself with his brother. He never fully received the love of the father, but instead kept turning away from the father's unconditional affection and strove instead to earn it. Does that sound familiar?

If we're honest with ourselves, the older brother resides in our hearts too. It's easy to get caught up in a good-works mentality. Do the right thing. Do it again tomorrow and the next day. Get rewarded for doing so. Demand more over time. Expect others to toe the line and do likewise. Keep working harder. Gain advantage and power over others. Look down on those who can't compete. Keep up the work ethic and make sure it translates to the next generation. Don't give up.

But that attitude does not produce the discerning life. It's a life of self-determination that grows bitter, not better, over time.

It's fascinating to read about the older brother and wonder about all the variations possible for this member of the family: the older brother who is a hard worker but unaware of grace, the older brother who honors rules and regulations and has little tolerance for those who don't follow them with perfection, the older brother who's neat and tidy and looks down on the creative or mysterious, and the older brother who thinks in terms of law, merit, and reward rather than love and grace.

The older brother is hard to live with and even harder to be. Yet we gravitate toward speaking and acting and even feeling like the older brother. He resides in us, and he needs to be released so our hearts don't harden into his likeness.

What attributes do you embody today that look like the older brother? Answering that question is a good starting point for genuine transformation. Notice the older brother within and ask God, the prodigal (extravagant) Lover of your soul, to do radical surgery deep within until you too can rejoice in the kindness of God toward the younger sons in and around you.

And then there's the father in this story. We know the father in this parable represents God the Father, the extravagant Father who loves to love and who does so with grace, tenderness, and unconditional generosity. We are called to do likewise, to represent the Father as we relate with one another as his beloved children. We are God's chosen ones, dearly loved by the Father and commissioned to be like him in this world.

The Father delights to offer forgiveness freely to his wayward children. It's the most transformational offering the Father has for his lost-now-found beloved child. Like being welcomed home and from the moment you arrive at the door the welcome mat is aglow, the scent inside is love, the greeting is warm, the conversation is deep, the meal is delicious, the ambiance is beautiful, the love is palpable. The Father's love and forgiveness are combined in the hospitality of grace.

The apostle Paul picks up where Jesus left off in this regard by pinpointing the need to cheer one another on to love and good deeds as representatives of the Father. This delight in God begins with our receptivity and grows outward with our generosity. All the "one another" passages in the New Testament give voice to the way of love more than fifty times. God invites us to live abundantly among one another, and in doing so to:

- love one another,
- be devoted to one another,
- live in harmony with one another,
- build up one another,
- accept one another,
- care for one another,
- serve one another,
- bear one another's burdens,
- forgive one another,
- be patient with one another,
- be kind and compassionate to one another,
- comfort one another,
- encourage one another,
- show hospitality to one another,
- pray for one another.

The abundant life we share with others is not receptivity for personal gain or advantage, but for the sake of Christ's kingdom being received and released in and through us, in spite of us, and for the sake of others. It's the both-and approach, similar to what Jesus refers to in the Great Commandment and the Second Great Commandment: to love God with heart, soul, mind, and strength *and* to love our neighbors as we love ourselves (Mark 12:29–31). The abundant life weaves together love for God, others, and self.

That's the way of love.

We're in Good Company

This has been the desire of God since the dawn of time. God taps on the shoulder of the hearts of his children, seeking to get their attention and draw them close to himself, longing to whisper in their ear, wink at them, wrap his loving and forgiving arms around them, and welcome them home to himself. That's the way of God. It always has been and always will be.

But are we attentive to his loving initiatives, or are we too focused elsewhere to notice?

The biblical text is replete with examples of how God seeks the attention of his children. The variety of ways he makes himself known is both diverse and delightful.

For Abraham, God chose *dreams*. In Genesis 15, God comes to Abram in a vision and promises him more descendants than the number of stars in the night sky.

For Moses, the Spirit rested on him through an encounter with a *burning bush*. In Exodus 3, "the angel of the LORD appeared to him in flames of fire from within a bush" (v. 2) and commissions him to go to Pharaoh and bring the Israelites out of Egypt.

For the children of Israel, a *cloud and fire* led them. Exodus 13:21 says, "By day the LORD went ahead of them in a pillar of cloud to guide them on their way and by night in a pillar of fire to give them light, so that they could travel by day or night."

In both Old and New Testaments, they *cast lots* to attend

to God's direction. In Jonah 1:7, sailors do this to learn on whose account their calamity had struck. In Joshua 18, Joshua casts lots before the Lord and then divides the land among the sons of Israel according to their divisions. In Acts 1:26, the disciples cast lots to determine a new twelfth disciple.

For Samuel, he needed the help of an *older teacher* to hear the voice of God. In 1 Samuel 3, Eli sends young Samuel to lie down and listen attentively to God. When God calls out Samuel's name, the young boy responds, "Speak, for your servant is listening," thus beginning a robust relationship with the Lord (v. 10).

For Solomon, his heart cry and *fervent prayer* was for a discerning heart. In 1 Kings 3, as a young man, Solomon asks God straight up for "a discerning heart to govern [God's] people and to distinguish between right and wrong" (v. 9). And it is granted to him.

Prophets like Jeremiah longed for *eyes to see* the handiwork of God. In Jeremiah 6, the Lord invites the prophet to "stand at the crossroads and look; ask for the ancient paths, ask where the good way is, and walk in it, and you will find rest for your souls" (v. 16).

For Balaam, God uses his *donkey* to get him to open his eyes to see and his ears to listen for God's clarion instructions (Num. 22). His stubbornness and closed-heartedness are changed to repentance and ultimately the fulfillment of God's will for his people.

In the New Testament, particularly from Jesus himself, we see myriad examples of people noticing God. *Angels* come to worship, warn, witness, welcome, and watch with key characters in the biblical text like Elizabeth, Mary, Zechariah, and the company of shepherds and wise men awaiting the miraculous Advent of Jesus.

Signs and wonders in the early church, all offered as a gift from God to the people of God, accompanied the fresh movement of God. Those who lacked wisdom could simply ask for it (James 1:5–8).

How were they to discern the will of God? *Seek it with all your heart* (Rom. 12:1–2; Eph. 5:8–10; Phil. 1:9–11; Col. 1:9–14).

Over and above all these other examples, Jesus lovingly points to himself as the way to know God intimately and discerningly. The simplicity of his teaching invites us to consider our approach to God on an ongoing basis. Jesus's "I am" statements in John's Gospel are reassurances of his infinite and matchless affection for his beloved children.

Take some time to stop and reflect on these statements. They will undoubtedly enrich your fellowship with him, and ultimately with the triune God.

- "I am the bread of life" (John 6:35, 41, 48, 51). He satisfies my deepest longings and hunger.
- "I am the light of the world" (John 8:12). He shines a light on the path of righteousness.
- "I am the gate for the sheep" (John 10:7, 9). He summons me into the family of God.
- "I am the good shepherd" (John 10:11). He surrounds me with love and protection.
- "I am the resurrection and the life" (John 11:25). He secures my hope for all eternity.
- "I am the way and the truth and the life" (John 14:6). He serves as the only path of truth and life this side of heaven.
- "I am the true vine" (John 15:1, 5). He stewards well our relationship as vine and branch, pruning me out of his loving fruitfulness.

Jesus not only fulfills the promises he makes, but he chooses over and over again to make himself known to those who have eyes to see him, ears to hear his voice, and hearts that are open to receive his gifts of life, love, and salvation. He does this not only while living among his followers, but even after his resurrection and prior to his ascension to heaven.

The Scriptures point us to more than a dozen places where *Jesus appears* to his beloved disciples after his death and resurrection:

- To Mary Magdalene crying by the tomb (John 20:11–18)
- To the other women returning from the tomb
  (Matt. 28:8–10)
- To Cleopas and the other disciple on the road to Emmaus
  (Luke 24:13–32)
- To Peter in Jerusalem (Luke 24:33–35)
- To the eleven disciples and others in Jerusalem
  (Luke 24:36–49)
- To ten disciples without Thomas (John 20:19–25)
- To the eleven disciples with Thomas (John 20:26–29)
- To seven disciples by the Lake of Galilee (John 21:1–25)
- To eleven disciples on a mountain (Matt. 28:16–20)
- To 500 people at once (1 Cor. 15:6)
- To James (1 Cor. 15:7)
- To the eleven disciples at Jesus's ascension (Acts 1:4–11)
- To Paul on the road to Damascus (Acts 9:1–19; 1 Cor. 15:8)
- To John at Patmos (Rev. 1:9–20)
- To the churches (Rev. 2:1–3:22)

Over and over again, we find ourselves in good company with the ancients who preceded us in a life of discernment. They, like we, were granted ample opportunity to notice the work of God in their midst and respond with wide-open faithfulness to the mysterious, miraculous, and even mundane experiences of life. God's presence and power, his promises and peace, were offered over and over again. Some responded openly, humbly, receptively, and gratefully. Others stiff-armed God and missed out on his gift of abundant life.

So What? Now What?

It's worth asking once more: Are we attentive to the many ways God is seeking to make himself known to us today, as he so frequently did in the past? Or are we looking for love in all the wrong places? Are our eyes searching elsewhere? Are our ears listening to alternate voices? Are our hearts inclined toward ourselves instead of leaning toward God and the empowering work of his Spirit?

The hindrances to the discerning life are many. They are embodied in the older son in the story of the prodigal. They include many attributes commonly understood by all of us, because they reside in each of our hearts. The older son was unable to be the brother he could have been because of his pridefulness, which led to harsh judgment of his brother and father.

His pride manifested in his strong work ethic that led him into bitterness and strife. He believed that action, strenuous effort, and diligence would lead to rewards of eternal consequence. But this ethic was void of the joy of service and the delight of harvest when viewed in contrast with the younger brother. The older brother's obedience to work outstripped any need to extend grace or compassion to his wayward brother. He believed he alone was deserving of the blessing; his brother was unworthy. I can relate. Can you?

The older brother's pride also appeared in his expectation of reward for his efforts and energies expended on the family farm.

His work was all about what he would receive in return. Little in his heart cared for serving at his father's good pleasure or delighting in his father's joy. Instead, the older brother was devoid of relationship and affection, and was focused solely on the transactional nature of the job to be done. How easy it is to lapse into the functionality of our efforts, even if for religious purposes, instead of doing all for love's sake. I can relate. Can you?

His pride ended in resentment and animosity. In his mind, the contrast and comparisons were stark and alarming, and he offered a flippant and rather detestable response to his father and brother. After long days of hard work, the last thing the older brother wanted to see was grace in action. Especially when gifts were offered and a party was thrown for the one who had lost everything in riotous living. He extended no mercy toward the sinner. No grace. No kindness. No empathy. No support. How dare his wayward brother come home and receive so much attention from the father. I can relate. Can you?

The pride of the older brother had enveloped his heart and encompassed his mind. He could not see beyond himself. He could not reconcile the actions of his brother or his father. His was a disorienting life in desperate need of the gospel of grace, mercy, forgiveness, and love.

The discerning life, in contrast, is a life of love. Jesus loves us, this we know, for the Bible tells us so. And the Spirit confirms this affection with his empowering presence as evidence of the Father's extravagant forgiveness and grace. What will it take for you to notice and receive this for yourself, and then to understand that in order to give it away, you must be filled up with the abundance of God regularly?

The prodigal son was radically transformed by the prodigal love of the Father. His life of self-absorption was upended by the surprising gifts of forgiveness and grace. He missed the Father's loving care and daily provisions. Because of the 100 percent offered to him by the Father, he gave his 100 percent in return.

Do you know such love today? If so, then dwell therein. If not, then strive no more. Simply open up your heart to God and let him into the crevices of your life that long for a fully-with-God life. There's so much more than a nail-head's width heading your direction today. Perhaps there are some rusted pipes in your soul that are hindering the flow of God's Spirit in and through you. Or maybe you're noticing that you've lived with a just-enough view of God but long for so much more. Be assured that if you desire more of God, he will generously give himself to you. All you need to do is come to your senses, look toward home, and watch him run to you with forgiving and transformational love.

PRACTICING A PREFERENCE FOR GOD

Attending to and receiving the love of God may seem rather kindergarten-level. In fact, it is. As Jesus said, "Unless you change and become like little children, you will never enter the kingdom of heaven" (Matt. 18:3). When we think we're acting like adults, we can get ourselves into trouble. We think we know better; we lean on our own wisdom and strength, we exert our power over others, we take matters into our own hands—the list goes on.

Identifying one's propensities toward self and recognizing the temptations to take a self-defined pathway may awaken you to the need to turn around and head home to the heart of God.

Don't be afraid of what you see when you look in the mirror and notice the true you. Wink at that image of yourself and let your heart melt and be reformed and renewed by the love of Jesus, your Creator, Redeemer, and Friend. Let the mysteriously transforming power of God begin to form you. And then watch and wait for what's next. Let love be your guide.

Here are a few spiritual exercises to put into practice as you reflect on this chapter:

- **Attentiveness:** Be still and know God. Close this book and notice God in your midst. Yes, right now!
- **Prodigal:** Take some time to identify yourself in the prodigal parable. Who are you most like in the story: the younger son, the older son, or the father?
- **"One Another":** Think about a challenging relationship in your life. Flip back a few pages and reread the list of "one another" passages. Think of a creative way to express love to that person anonymously today.

CHAPTER 3

Listening

Spiritual Discernment Is Prayerful

"Be careful not to practice your righteousness in front of others to be seen by them. . . . But when you pray, go into your room, close the door and pray to your Father, who is unseen. Then your Father, who sees what is done in secret, will reward you."

Matthew 6:1, 6

The discerning life is a prayerful life—no ifs, ands, or buts about it. A prayerful life is an enduring, persevering life, in which prayer becomes the preferred response to any and every event that affects our personal lives. Practicing a prayerful preference for God is best fulfilled in a posture of listening.

I'm not talking about a prayerful life as if all we mean is offering a prayer at meals, bedtime, or in a church service. There is so much more to prayer than a handful of memorized ditties. The older I get, the harder it is to pray. And the longer my life continues, the more I realize I'm just a beginner. I'm a novice at prayer, continually learning what it means to pray and remain prayerful all my days.

A life of prayerful noticing is like a long winter with snow in the forecast every week. Just when you think you've safely cleared off the streets, sidewalks, and driveways, the white stuff appears once again, and all your hard work is quickly buried. So it is with prayer. Just when you think you're cruising forward and feeling good about the life of prayer you've created, another storm arrives, and you're back to square one.

Maybe you will be in your prayer closet, and you will sense the grace and peace of God as you pour out your heart in the pages of your journal. Or you will be in a delightful small group, feeling the love and saying "amen" with others like honey over a warm cinnamon bun. Or you will reach the end of a moving retreat experience, where the hugs are plentiful and genuine. Or you will be worshiping with others in your community, and hallelujahs fly freely as the tears flow.

And then you will leave the prayer closet, small group, retreat, or worship experience, and a wall of discouragement or disillusionment will hit you. The feel-good prayer experience will become a distant memory. You end up in a traffic jam and surprise yourself with the expletive that races off your lips. Or some negative self-talk starts racing in your mind. You enter the house, and your child has just thrown up or disobeyed and your home is a wreck. You will quickly long to return to that place of comfort and not have to deal with what's ahead or around or even within you. Another snowstorm (or hail, wind, fire, hurricane, tornado, flood) is forthcoming in your soul. I'm sure you can relate. Few among us prefer storms over sunshine, regardless of our geography, but that's what we must expect when we devote ourselves to a lifestyle of prayerful discernment.

In the northeast US, we've had our share of long-lasting winter storms. They feel like forever winters. A few years ago, one such season was labeled "snowmageddon" or "snowpocalypse" by those who weren't fond of the continuous accumulation of snow and ice, including yours truly. A major snowstorm was in the forecast nearly every week. We received a record-breaking 108.6 inches of snow and ice, and most of that fell within one month. Some people found the snow pretty. I was not among them.

Our quirky home didn't fare too well either. Ice dams formed along the north side of the house, which received zero sun and zero snow melt. Ice dams appear when a warm house streams heat out via gaps in the roof due to poorly placed insulation or no insulation whatsoever. This meets up with the cold snow that's accumulated on top of the roof, which melts but has nowhere to go since the gutters and downspouts are frozen. Then the melted snow freezes into large ice blocks and icicles overnight and with dipping temperatures. Without sun or higher than freezing temps, the ice dams grow and expand.

The problem with ice dams isn't so much what happens outside the house, but what happens inside. Water that has melted along the roofline eventually finds its way dripping inside the home, where it can trickle and flow. The condensation needs to go somewhere. In our situation, water from the ice dams entered our house via the walls and wallpaper, ceilings and light fixtures, flooring and window wells, door casings, and attic crawl spaces. It wreaked havoc in five rooms of our home during the snowmaggedon. I didn't see anything pretty about the snow by the time the water had weaved its way into every possible crevice on the north side of our house. My soul didn't appreciate the damage either.

Days of saturation turned into weeks. Our cries grew to weeping and wailing. Our biggest investment—our house—felt like it was being destroyed one drip at a time. It was death by moisture.[1]

Weeks into this mess, I finally found someone who could help me shovel the snow from the north side of our roof. We trudged to the side of the house in over four feet of snow, put a ladder up against the house, and climbed to the roof. Then the shoveling began, one square foot at a time. We carefully and prayerfully attended to the deep snow, thrusting it to the ground below, one heavy shovelful at a time. We even used a small snow blower and a pick axe to chip away the ice that had formed.

Snowstorms can be a huge nuisance. They are wonderful for the skiers and snowboarders, and the mountains look beautiful when they are white-capped. But not when they accumulate to the point of creating an avalanche, dangerous roads, collapsed roofs, or ice dams. Eventually too much accumulation wreaks havoc. So it is with our lives. Too much activity, too many responsibilities and relationships, too many long days, too many wants, too many hours at work, too many toys to maintain, too many pursuits that keep us from a faithful journey of walking with God.

In the prayer closet, we should be learning how to let go and to embrace a simpler life. If all we're doing is asking God for more things to attach to or preserve, our distracted heart will pursue all the wrong things. Meanwhile, like the ice dams, the leaking will enter the walls and ceilings, or like a collapsed roof, these things will destroy the very structure of our lives. Too much emphasis on accumulation ultimately hurts the soul—unless the thing we're pursuing more of is God.

The Deeper Life

During our recent "snowmageddon," depth was measured by way of accumulation above the ground, contrary to the way we usually talk about depth. Isn't depth something that typically measures below the surface?

Depth is subtractive. It is not additive. We don't dig a hole high; we dig it deep.

Similarly, in the spiritual life, depth relates to what's going on underneath the surface. A deeper life isn't measured by accumulation, unless what's gained is more of God. Depth is hidden and mysterious. Depth is experienced most abundantly in relation to what we lose or sacrifice or release. Even depth of knowledge, depth of compassion, depth of character, depth of insight, and depth of contentment require some form of letting go in order to fully receive. Preconceived notions need to be released in order for greater knowledge to be received. Creature comforts need to be released in order for compassion to be offered. Humility creates character. Wisdom forms insight. Contentment comes from letting go of that which previously defined you. In spiritual depth, we find life at its fullest by letting go. In so many profound ways, the spiritual life is *all* about letting go—not always complete detachment (as in the love of our spouse or child), but by holding people and things with a much looser grip, in order to mature as God desires.

The deeper life is singularly marked by humility—the dirt and humus and brokenness of life—not by what we stockpile in this life. Yet our definitions of success, accomplishment, and godliness defy such an attitude. We look at each other through the lens of accumulation: education, wealth, power, achievement, status, class. And we recognize one another's accumulation with accolades, awards, acknowledgements, and advancements. We say of such things, "Look at the depth of that life or experience," when we're actually pointing to the accumulation of things and experiences. As a result, we lose sight of God's invitation to the deeper life of humility and hiddenness, contentment and grace.

Perhaps we don't overtly say accumulation leads to depth, but inwardly we believe that one more _____ will lead to a life of depth and fulfillment. Yet accumulating things and notoriety doesn't necessarily translate to depth of spirituality, character, and more. Often, it's quite the contrary. When people return from short-term missions, they often say things like, "I was so moved by how content the people we served were even though they had nothing! I have so much; why am I not happier?" In other words, a sparse lifestyle gave the people they served a significant depth of contentment, so shouldn't a lavish lifestyle bring even deeper contentment? But that's missing the point. They're stuck in a mindset of depth through addition.

Jesus modeled a lifestyle of depth through subtraction. His life and ministry provoked varied responses from his followers.

The crowds were intrigued by his message and showed up *en masse* to have their ears tickled by his teaching. They weren't necessarily showing their depth by simply showing up.

The religious leaders were intimidated by his presence and sought to provoke and discredit him. They were definitely not deep, but instead rather shallow and competitive.

The ones he touched with compassionate healing were influenced by his miraculous powers. For most, their ultimate depth post-healing will remain unknown until heaven.

The disciples were invited to follow Jesus, and most of them did so to the very end. Most revealed depth, but not all—certainly not Judas, who sold his soul to accumulate thirty shekels of silver (which he later discarded in humiliating and devastating angst).

Jesus's mother Mary, the beloved disciple John, and several other humble ones (like the woman who washed his feet with her tears and hair) were intimate with Jesus and plunged into the depths of the Christlike life. Those who chose the deeper life of humility and who consistently said an enthusiastic yes to Jesus's invitations for intimacy were the ones most significantly transformed. Depth was not their stated goal, but it became their greatest gift and their eternal reward.

These humble ones walked close enough to Jesus to truly listen to him. They were courageous enough to follow him all the way to the cross. They were convinced that the pattern of their lives was to be modeled after the loving, self-effacing, sacrificial ways of Jesus. Ultimately, they lived discerning lives, loving as Jesus loved. It had nothing to do with accumulation, except perhaps of suffering. But it had everything to do with a life of prayerful, humble attentiveness. That was the depth that led to their transformation.

Lord, Teach Us to Pray

To love as Jesus loved meant that his followers had to learn how to practice a preference for the Father and the Spirit, just as Jesus modeled. Abiding as one with the Father and the Spirit was invitational and formational for Jesus's followers. To do so required a life of prayerfulness—even Jesus set apart time and space to focus on his heart priorities and his profound affection for the Father. And the disciples' simple request was for Jesus to teach them how to pray (Luke 11).

A discerning life comes out of one's prayerfulness. We will only go as deep with God as our prayer life allows. And we have a choice: to go along in a mile-wide and inch-deep life in pursuit of accumulation, or to plumb the depths of Christ and leave to God any expansion he chooses to accomplish through you.

Yes, Jesus, please teach us how to pray.

In the Sermon on the Mount, Jesus offers life-changing instructions about prayer. In Matthew 6, Jesus begins his reflections on piety by urging his listeners to "be careful not to practice [their] righteousness in front of others to be seen by them" (v. 1). Instead, when they give to the needy, they were to do so in secret. God the Father loves anonymous giving, not service announced with trumpet fanfare and public recognition.

And the same goes for prayer:

> And when you pray, do not be like the hypocrites, for they love to pray standing in the synagogues and on the street corners to be seen by others. Truly I tell you, they have received their reward in full. But when you pray, go into your room, close the door and pray to your Father, who is unseen. Then your Father, who sees what is done in secret, will reward you. And when you pray, do not keep on babbling like pagans, for they think they will be heard because of their many words. Do not be like them, for your Father knows what you need before you ask him. (vv. 5–8)

His point? Pray in the secret place, where intimacy is developed, not on the street corners in order to be seen by others. It's hard to be hypocritical when it's just you and the Father who knows you intimately and completely.

When you pray, this is how you should do so, says Jesus (vv. 9–15). Let's break it down word by word and phrase by phrase:

Our. Jesus begins by emphasizing the communal nature of the Lord's Prayer. We are to pray this way with all who know the Father from every corner of the planet and with those from every generation, including our own. We are to recall this communal reality as we pray this with others and in the solitude of our prayer closet.

We belong to the universal church, the people of God, the beloved congregation of the Father; he is ours, and we are his. The heart of God is best reflected in the unity of the body and the oneness of the church as the beloved children of God.

Father. Jesus offers us the Name to whom all our prayers belong. As children of God, we are privileged to call him our Father. His fatherhood is good, pure, gentle, truthful, gracious, kind, peaceful, restful, trustworthy, patient, faithful, compassionate, merciful, joyful, expectant, and loving. As we call on our Father, we come with confidence in the truest nature of his personhood, trusting him to father us over, above, and beyond the incomplete ways our earthly fathers seek to provide for us. God's father-love is perfect in every way.

In heaven. Jesus reminds us that the Father is eternal and everlasting. His presence is both in heaven and on earth, but his kingly reign is in heaven. We honor his kingship and his power by remembering always that his heavenly home is where we are invited to live with him for all eternity. It's hard to grasp the concept of heaven while we're fussing about here on earth, but Jesus teaches us to pray with heaven on our hearts and minds and a growing anticipation of eternal life in our spirits.

Hallowed be your name. Jesus reveres the name of God the Father. Sacred and holy is the name we use for God. We are not to treat it lightly or with anything less than reverence. With his name comes a bow of adoration and worship. As we pray, we are standing or sitting or lying prostrate before the Lord, knowing that we are in a holy place. Simply stating the name of God, our attitude should be honoring and respectful. From the dawn of time, God has been jealous for the sole affection of his bride, the church, the beloved.

Your kingdom come. Jesus invites the kingdom of God to be experienced fully by all who call upon the name of the Lord. The kingdom is where peace will reign supreme, where there is no more division among people. The kingdom was previously defined by Jesus in the Beatitudes as a reign in which the blessed are singled out as being poor in spirit, comforted, meek, merciful, and pure in heart. They are those who hunger and thirst for righteousness, are peacemakers, and are children of God. These are attributes of the kingdom that are birthed in the heart of God.

Your will be done. Jesus knows that unless we seek the will of God, we will pursue our own endeavors. When we are focused on ourselves, we seek control of our own will and impose it on others. When we pray for God's will to be done, we are in essence repeating another prayer from Jesus: "Not as I will, but as you will" (Matt. 26:39). That desire comes straight from the heart of God. As we pray and submit to the Father's will, we are being conformed by the Spirit to embody the way of Jesus. Inviting the will of God to be fulfilled is an attitude of faith and an act of faithfulness that delights the Lord.

On earth as it is in heaven. Jesus bridges the gap between heaven and earth by asking his disciples to model their lives on heavenly priorities. His kingdom and will are not simply for eternity, but for the here and now. And the present is to be a snapshot of eternal living. God's desire is for us to walk by faith and live faithfully today, a reflection of heaven on earth. There is to be no dichotomy between the two; but for that to be our reality, we need to pray. We are incapable of living heavenly on earth without the empowerment of God.

Give us today our daily bread. Jesus realizes we require basic necessities like bread in order to survive and thrive here on earth. As he teaches us to pray, he gives us permission to appeal to the Father for daily provision. In this appeal is an intrinsic warning not to get too far ahead of ourselves and begin hoarding for selfish gain or to become so focused on our own bread that we neglect sharing with others in need. Jesus's use of "us" and "our" reminds us that this portion of the prayer is for simple and daily sustenance for all.

And forgive us our debts (or trespasses). Jesus highlights the priority of forgiveness as the basis of all healthy relationships, beginning with the Father. God's full awareness of our many debts (or sins, transgressions, trespasses), accompanied by the Father's delight in canceling them, brings out the brightest of all promises from God. We are forgiven people who walk in newness of life, and in the Spirit we are completely free from the debts of our sinfulness. We cry out to God for his forgiveness, including his grace, mercy, and compassionate lovingkindness.

As we also have forgiven our debtors (or those who trespass against us). Jesus recognizes the importance of his disciples offering forgiveness to one another, particularly those who trespass against us. With our lives dominated by less than idyllic relationships this side of heaven, it's incumbent on us to practice forgiveness. Knowing with certainty that we live as forgiven ones, we thereby offer forgiveness and blessing to others, honoring those around us above ourselves. However, we cannot muster up the strength to forgive on our own. We appeal to the Father to grace us with the mind, heart, and will to forgive in Jesus's name.

And lead us not into temptation. Jesus urges us to depend on the Father in resisting every trial and temptation this life has to offer. This world lures us with plentiful opportunities to turn away from God and instead to consider the idols of money, sex, and power. Our affections are swiftly drawn away from God each time we succumb to the temptations before us. Only as we recognize our propensities to sin will we turn instead to prayer. The Lord invites us to be led back home to the embrace of the Father rather than remain in the grips of temptation.

But deliver us from the evil one. Jesus acknowledges the wiles of the enemy of our soul preying on us and summons us instead to greater attention as we pray. Unless we are delivered from the evil one, we will be ensnared by him. Therefore, apart from the work of God's Spirit, we are easily lulled by the offerings of the enemy. How remarkable that our Lord's Prayer would give credence to his archenemy. God knows we live in warfare all the time. Our prayers offer the helmet, shield, and sword of protection needed daily by all.

For yours is the kingdom, the power, and the glory forever. Amen. Jesus continually points us to the kingdom as our focus for life, service, and prayer. Although not included in the biblical teachings of Jesus, this conclusion to the Lord's Prayer was added later to focus our prayerful attention on the kingdom as children of the King. The kingdom of God is Jesus's favorite topic to teach about, and it should be on our lips as well. As a result, the power and glory of our prayers and the entirety of our discerning life belongs to the eternal King, who reigns forever and ever. And, as an appropriate ending to our prayers, we say "amen," a resounding declaration of the truth about God spoken of so clearly in our prayers. Everything about God and his kingdom and his sovereign will is "immovably true"—amen. The only conceivable response to every element of the Lord's Prayer, our prayer for a discerning life, is a resounding "amen!"

And then Jesus adds a P.S. to his instructions on prayer, in the context of one's personal piety, and it's about a central theme of prayerful noticing: forgiveness.

For if you forgive other people when they sin against you, your heavenly Father will also forgive you. But if you do not forgive others their sins, your Father will not forgive your sins. For Jesus, a life of prayerfulness reflects a life of forgiveness. Our prayers are to bring us into a graced place before the Father's throne of love and mercy. We have no life in Christ without being forgiven of our sins of omission (things we forget to say or do that honor God) and commission (things we choose to say or do that dishonor God). Forgiveness is central to our life with God, and in Jesus we see how forgiveness is the apex of all that he came to love and serve. His invitation is for us to live as a forgiven and forgiving people.

The Lord's Prayer is our discernment prayer, our model of excellence. It's filled with everything we'll ever need to unpack a prayerful life of discernment. Here in the Lord's Prayer we learn how to prayerfully practice a preference for God.

Our Prayer Closet

In every season of the soul, we need a space and time to practice a prayerful preference for God. Whether you call it a prayer closet, a prayer chair, or a prayer corner, this is where the rubber meets the road of discernment. Here, we forge a deeper life with God. Here, we encounter the crucible of transformation: silence and solitude. Here, in our willingness and priority of time alone with the Father, we notice his presence, power, and peace in the midst of our busy, active, noisy, colorful, and complex lives. Here, we learn to listen to the Father's voice amidst the cacophony of other voices in our world. Without a prayer closet, we are destined to live an inch deep and a mile wide.

For any number of reasons, we are highly allergic to spiritual depth. We're guilty of a self-ordained, self-empowered, self-absorbed life. And although we value the priority of prayer and believe in the importance of a prayer closet, we are far too busy for such a notion to be fully realized in our lives.

It reeks of weakness. It smacks of ritual. It sounds boring. I used to need it, but it's no longer necessary. Been there, done that, moving on.

For whatever reason, most of us simply don't have such a space and time to practice the discerning life in the secret place, where our soul is uncovered, revealed, and opened wide for God to enter and reign supreme. When we step away from the fray to be with Jesus, we notice he's been there the whole time, waiting for us to come to our senses and return home once more. We are simply too busy to pray. We need to slow down and keep turning toward and heading back home—over and over and over again.

I've said it before, and I'll say it again: a discerning life is a prayerful life. It's not simply a life punctuated by occasional prayers, but a life permeated by continual prayer. Is that your desire? Is this priority encouraged in your faith community and among the teams in which you participate?

A consistent visit to your prayer closet fulfills your soul's deepest longings. A prayer closet can be as simple as a dedicated time and space where you go with Bible, journal, and pen in hand to meet with God, as unhurried, unhindered, and uncluttered as possible. That's all that's needed—nothing more; nothing less.

Why are our prayer closets so frequently ignored? Like our own unkempt closets, why do they get overrun with clutter, unmanageable and neglected? The reasons for our soul-neglect are numerous:

- The *enemy of our souls* loves it when we ignore our prayer closets, and he will do everything possible to keep us distracted and distrustful of such a space and time.
- The *pride of the sovereign self* reinforces our independence and dismisses the need to be alone and quiet before the Lord as an act of weakness and unhealthy dependence.

- The *abundant access to technology* distracts our hearts, and
  we become more addicted to the constant influx of email,
  all forms of media, and a growing variety of modes of
  communication and entertainment.
- The *busyness of our schedules* leads to a hurried heart, looking
  for the adrenaline rush we desire through constant work,
  exhausting play, and a full but unfulfilled social life.
- The *idols of our hearts* lure us toward self-aggrandizement,
  self-advancement, and self-pleasure in the broad categories of
  idolatry via money, sex, and power.
- The *lack of Sabbath* in our busy, active, noisy lives leaves
  us inattentive to the need for life-giving rest, spiritual
  refreshment, and transformational renewal.
- The *unattended heartache* follows us around like an
  unwanted cyst, needing our attention to be healed, but
  instead left to fester in ignored infection.
- The *unconfessed sin* keeps us in relational bondage, and we
  forget that grace, mercy, and forgiveness are only a repentant
  prayer away.
- The *disordered priorities* of our lives keep us focused on all
  the wrong things and in all the wrong places, while we miss
  the simple joys of a with-God life.
- The *overall inattentiveness* of our daily lives leads to the
  demands of others and ourselves drowning out the voice of
  God and the invitation to a deeper life.

When we finally get beyond the distractions and neglect, and
into that dedicated space and time, we enter with heartfelt desire for
the deeper life—a life of humility, sacrifice, and the acknowledge-
ment of our personal, familial, communal, and cultural suffering.

No life is exempt from heartache and pain. God knows that full well, and he waits for us to acknowledge that before him and to hand it all over to him. Amazingly, he's there to receive and carry all of our pain. Our need to release that distress into his faithful and loving hands is a huge reason why we desperately need our prayer closet. There, we learn to let go of self and receive the loving embrace of God with complete abandon and simple trust.

Our relationship with God is enhanced the more we become aware of his abiding presence and peace. By praying the Lord's Prayer over and over again and letting it sink deeply into our souls, we become what we pray. We grow in our attentiveness to the Father's affections, for ourselves and for our wider world. We heighten our attentiveness to the kingdom we are a part of on earth as in heaven. We are unafraid to ask God for daily bread, daily forgiveness, daily deliverance, and daily power.

The prayer that Jesus taught his disciples belongs to us. It reminds us that our motivation in life is God. Our inspiration for life is God. Our destination after life is God.

And like the layers of an onion, our hearts are peeled back one layer at a time, one affectionate tear at a time. The more we are in God's presence, the deeper our soul is penetrated by the unconditional love of our gracious Father, redeeming Savior, and empowering Spirit.

As you ponder the state of your soul and the condition of your prayer closet, consider the following five key elements of a prayer-closet experience, the home for our listening life.

1. Solitude, Silence, Slowness, and Stillness

How comfortable are you with embracing the invitation to come away by yourself to be alone with Jesus?

Ask God to give you a desire for times of solitude and to see silence as a friend, not a foe. Alone we came into this world, and alone we will exit this life. To be comfortable alone with God is basic to our life with God. He's already 100-percent familiar with our lives, and we can enter that alone space without reticence or reservation and with anticipation and delight. Silence helps us concentrate on noticing and preferring God instead of missing him amid the cacophony of noise and distraction in our busy lives. In a life of prayer, we must embrace slowness as the pace of love. It's the only entrée to the stillness we long to embrace.

Some of the richest food for my soul is found when I notice the beauty of God's creation. A radiant sunrise, a thundering ocean, a golden orchard, a stunning mountain, a placid river, a gorgeous flower, an intricate seashell—all speak of the Lord's affection for what he so masterfully created. We are to enjoy the beauty and grandeur of his creation, and often the richest feast of creation can be found when we're alone and quiet (or with others but hushed by the stillness and wonder), slowing down long enough to notice and receive the fullness of such gifts.

Silence is good for the soul and is necessary for the deeper life of holy attentiveness. It's often considered the crucible of transformation, where the deep work of God occurs. Until we're able to silence the many other voices that seek our heart's attention in order to enter a place of holy stillness and reverence, we will miss the tender voice of God. His Father-heart toward us is filled to overflowing with affection and delight. In our quiet space of prayerful noticing, we posture ourselves to receive his voice of love. And that's something we would never want to miss. Solitude, silence, slowness, and stillness . . . the recipe for a prayerful life.

2. Scripture

How desirous are you of the Word of God, to receive it as a gift to be savored and embraced so that it comes alive from deep within your soul?

Invite God to illuminate your mind and heart as you ponder his Word. Consider *lectio divina* (sacred reading) as a way to prayerfully listen and attend to the Scriptures in the intimacy of your prayer closet. *Lectio* is a lovely way to pray the Word. Very simply, it is the repetitive reading of the same bite-size morsel of Scripture. For over 1,500 years, the church has found *lectio divina* a helpful, insightful, and transformational way to be present with God and his Word. Here are the six historical movements of *lectio* to try in your prayer closet:

> *Silencio.* Begin with silence, quieting your anxious heart and stilling your racing mind, letting go of your own agenda and submitting instead to God.
>
> *Lectio.* Read the passage a few times to acquaint yourself with the words and to enjoy the reading as if it's the first time you've ever heard this Word, sitting on the edge of your seat in anticipation and receptivity. If you are alone, read the passage aloud so that you are involving your senses of hearing and seeing.
>
> *Meditatio.* Read the passage again, noticing a word or phrase that jumps off the page and leaps into your heart; see if that particular word or phrase continues to call for your attention as you remain in the Word. Hold the Word close to your heart as you receive it as a gift from the Lord.
>
> *Oratio.* Read the passage again, asking God to clarify why the word or phrase is sticking to the roof of your hungry soul; listen for something your soul should especially notice, and

pray into the central message you are receiving. Remain in prayerful consideration of the words or phrase God has brought to your attention.

Contemplatio. Read the same Scripture again, slowly, reflectively, prayerfully, noticing the richness of the Word from as many angles as possible. Imagine the Word as a prism, from which you are seeing it through various lenses. Let the Word dwell deeply in your heart and soul and savor every morsel.

Incarnatio. Before you leave the Word, ask God to bring to light that which you are to carry with you into the day ahead in order to incarnate the Word into your life. Delight in the privilege of recalling, rehearsing, and revisiting the Word and watch how God lives it out through you in the hours and days ahead.

3. Prayer

How hopeful are you not only to learn how to pray with words but to listen attentively to the affectionate voice of God?

Listen attentively for the voice of the Father, the Son, and the Spirit. Like Samuel, listen with your ears: "Speak, LORD, for your servant is listening" (1 Sam. 3:7–11). Like Bartimaeus, listen with your eyes: "What do you want?" "I want to see" (Mark 10:46–52). Like Cleopas on the road to Emmaus, listen with your heart: "Were not our hearts burning within us?" (Luke 24:32).

So often we measure the quality of our prayer life by how much we have to say to God. We want to praise him in worshipful prayer. We want to confess to him in repentant prayer. We want to thank him in grateful prayer. We want to appeal to him in supplication prayer. We write out our prayers. We read written prayers. All of this is good prayerfulness.

Listening prayer, however, reminds us that we have two ears and one mouth. Let's double up the listening and remain all the more attentive to God's voice of affection as we lean into a deeper life of prayerful noticing. Listening in prayer opens for us a creative way to practice a preference for God in our body, mind, and spirit. In stillness, ask the Spirit to help you by his grace to focus on listening attentively. Rest in the quiet of your heart and mind. Be aware of your physical body, noticing any stiffness or anxiety, and ask God to comfort you. When you sense it's time, simply ask God for whatever you need or desire. Sit quietly and wait upon the Lord. Notice if he provides a word of comfort, a prick of conscience, an image, or simply an awareness of his presence. Hold that noticing, offer it back to God, and if necessary, seek discernment from a spiritual friend who can advise, affirm, and/or redirect you back to prayer.

We notice God in our body's posture—kneeling, closing or opening our eyes, folding or lifting our hands, lying prostrate on the ground, standing up with outstretched hands. We affirm the presence of God with an alert and attentive mind. We notice God's power and peace in the deepest recesses of our spirit. Prayerful noticing occurs in innumerable ways, thanks be to God. We have a lifetime to practice. Best to begin today. Lord, teach me to pray.

4. Reflection

How attentive are you becoming to the many ways God makes himself known to you throughout your day(s)?

In reflection, we notice the gifts and blessings God has entrusted to us and offer our thanks for each and every one. We remember and give thanks, similar to the many ways God's people practiced reflection in the biblical text, from placing rocks at the edge of the sea as tangible markers of the miraculous provision of God (Josh. 4:4–9), to remembering Jesus's sacrifice on the cross at the Lord's Supper (1 Cor. 11:24). Practicing some form of reflective discipline is always good for the soul.

Reflection can be as simple as giving voice to the gifts of the day, writing out words of gratitude in our journals, taking photographs as symbols of remembrance, or through the spiritual practice of *Examen*. Journaling is a way to recall what you're learning about God, his Word, his creation, and his people, the community of faith. Variations of journaling are plentiful; it's not about the way you journal but about the experience of closeness with God you experience as a result.

Noticing beauty and fostering wonder are life-giving forms of reflection. Taking time to reflect on the intricacies of creation brings us in touch with the complex majesty of life itself and the God who formed it all for his glory. Enjoying the vastness of God's handiwork in creation brings delight to our souls. Creating something of beauty or enjoying what others have created will enhance our reflective experience. Remain open to various forms of reflection.

Examen is the spiritual practice of noticing the life-giving movements of God throughout a particular period of time (day, week, month, season, year). There are various forms of the discipline of *Examen*, but all are designed to help us recall, reflect, and renew. Here's one simple way to practice *Examen:*

a. Become aware of God's presence by quieting your heart for meaningful reflection.
b. Review a particular period of time (day, week, month, year) and give thanks to God for the gifts you received from him and others.
c. Pay attention to your emotions (sad, angry, joyful, tearful) and the contexts for each noticing.

    d. Prayerfully respond to one main feature of the time frame and confess your need for God's grace. Seek or offer forgiveness if necessary.

    e. As you look ahead, consider how best to attend to specific matters brought to your heart and mind, asking for God's help in the day(s) ahead, looking forward to tomorrow with ever-increasing joy.

5. Sabbath Rest

How faithful are you to the weekly rhythm of Sabbath rest, as well as intentionally entering into Sabbath moments throughout your day(s)?

Sabbath is the key to the deeper life. It's the discipline you choose that reminds you there is only one God, and it's not you. Sabbath is a weekly and ongoing reminder of the need to rest and trust in God. We often forget that Sabbath is one of the Ten Commandments—it's that important. God himself instituted and followed it. After he created the heavens and the earth, he rested and enjoyed what he had established. So too are his children to both work hard and rest with intentionality. Doing so requires discipline and grace.

Sabbath rest is a choice of the will to stop what's normally done in our days in order to notice, celebrate, and consecrate the work of our hands into the heart, mind, and hands of Almighty God. The four steps we take into Sabbath are simple:

    a. Stop what you do as work.

    b. Rest from the labor of your hands.

    c. Enjoy the people around you and the God who gave them to you.

d. Renew your commitment to remain faithful to your calling, vocation, commitments, and relationships in the coming week.

In Sabbath rest we notice the wonder and majesty of God in worship with the family of God. We learn to trust God together, reminding each other of the faithfulness of God. We pay greater attention to the splendor of God's glorious creation as congregations, families, and individuals. In Sabbath rest we learn to notice the myriad ways God has gifted us with all that creation has to offer. We slow down and notice more deeply the awesomeness of God, from the smallest forms to the largest expressions of life. From a place of Sabbath rest, we can reengage with work and life from a renewed reservoir deep within us, living fully and restoratively.

The lens for our life of discernment is not a rearview mirror focusing on the past, nor is it a telescope looking toward the future. Instead, it's the mirror that forces us to look at the here and now. It's too easy to forget the now and instead be resentful or nostalgic about the past or anxious about the future. But when we claim the present in God, we affirm his lovingkindness and his myriad gifts of grace for today. In that place and posture of presence, we begin to notice God more prayerfully, and the state of our soul is enriched a hundredfold.

For that reason alone, the discerning life is encapsulated in our prayerful noticing now. When we are practicing that kind of active presence and inviting others around us to do likewise, we will enjoy the discerning life with others. Pointing out the fresh movements of God in worship, in creation, in relationships, in the Word, and in our prayerful practices will keep us intentionally focused in the right—and prayerfully present—direction.

In our prayerfulness, we wait on God—slow down and love him with all our heart, soul, mind, and strength. We rest in God—in a Sabbath lifestyle. We trust in God—who in turn helps us trust one another. We hope in God—by his grace and for his glory. We unite in God—in love and mission. We pray with God—asking, seeking, knocking, knowing, listening, and obeying.

There's so much to discover about prayerful noticing in this life. How kind of God to be patient, kind, and compassionate toward us as his beloved children.

PRACTICING A PREFERENCE FOR GOD

The deeper life of discernment is not about what we accumulate. Instead, it's what we let go of, knowing that in releasing things to God there is a receptivity from God that's far better. Like a seed that drops to the ground and dies before it sparks life, so it is with our discerning life.

Are you enamored today by what others have accumulated that you also desire? Can you trust God to rearrange your disordered affections? Will you say yes to Jesus's invitations and instructions for prayer, and will you establish once more a prayer closet that will keep welcoming you home to the Father's loving embrace?

Imagine what your life, your family's life, your friendships, your church, and your community would look and feel like if each member would begin practicing a preference for God. Lead the way today.

Here are a few spiritual exercises to put into practice as you reflect on this chapter:

- **The Lord's Prayer:** What phrase of Jesus's prayer means the most to you in this season? Why?
- **Prayer Closet:** Read back through the ways noted above to be prayerfully present to God. Pick one or two new ways to incorporate today.
- **Stillness:** Identify the barriers to your experience of peaceful stillness with God. Do any of the ones noted in this chapter sound familiar? Are there any other barriers not listed that might be hampering you?

.

CHAPTER 4

Presence

Spiritual Discernment Is Relational

"Love must be sincere. Hate what is evil; cling to what is good. Be devoted to one another in love. Honor one another above yourselves. Never be lacking in zeal, but keep your spiritual fervor, serving the Lord. Be joyful in hope, patient in affliction, faithful in prayer. Share with the Lord's people who are in need. Practice hospitality."

Romans 12:9–13

Spiritual discernment is intentionally, incarnationally, and intimately relational. The discerning life begins, continues, and ends in relationship—first with God, then with others, and including oneself. This is true for generation after generation, forever and ever. Our God is relational, and he invites us to focus on relational presence.

When Ruth and I first moved into our home, she was pregnant

with our first child. That step of faith felt ginormous in every regard. We had saved up a handful of shekels for a down payment, but without the generous no-interest loan from my supportive parents, we could not have moved from rented quarters. This was relational presence via parental support at its finest. We are forever grateful.

The home we purchased needed a lot of work. We identified the priority items on the punch list. Immediately rip up the purple shag carpet in the downstairs bedroom. Change out some loose wires in the kitchen. Buff the hardwood floors. Restore, caulk, and paint window sashes. Clean out the basement and garage. Paint several rooms. Change outdated light fixtures.

One of our top priorities was to strip the four layers of wallpaper in the living room and then repaint. For our cape-style home, that room was the first point of entry. We wanted it to feel open and inviting. So we began to tackle this project together one late afternoon in the fall of 1984.

I stood on a stepladder on the long interior wall, working above the mantel. It was early evening, just prior to sunset. Ruth was sitting on an upside-down five-gallon barrel, holding a work lamp so I could see what I was doing. It was the only form of light in the room. The scene was almost romantic. It's a memory permanently etched in my consciousness, like it was yesterday.

We were chatting about all the work we still had to accomplish before we could move in. Since Ruth was with child, we were leaning on friends and family members to help us as much as possible. But we didn't want to overdo things or set our expectations too high, so we worked as hard as possible on our own, late evenings, long weekends, and at every spare moment.

This project required extra energy for me. Scraping multiple layers of painted-over wallpaper wasn't my favorite home restoration project, and helpful products like wallpaper stripping agents weren't cheap, so I worked with warm water and lots of sweat to accomplish the goal. I moved four inches at a time (the width of my blade), working from right to left, layer by layer.

I had made it across the large main wall opposite the front door, and now I began working above the fireplace. Starting at the top of the wall, while I chatted away with Ruth, I kept scraping. When I got down about twelve inches from the ceiling, I noticed a dark pencil mark on the original plastered wall. I scraped and scraped until the letter A appeared.

Reveling in our discovery, I was intrigued by the fact that the letter was still intact. Obviously, the penciled letter was marked on the wall prior to the first layer of wallpaper.

I kept scraping. I had to whittle through four layers of wallpaper, two of which were painted over. Having done our share of wallpapering since, I understand why this happens. Old-fashioned wallpaper glue worked great. It held the wallpaper in place for decades, but it was a royal pain in the neck to scrape off. It was far easier to just add paint and train your eye to ignore the vertical lines created by the wallpaper edges every eighteen inches.

This isn't necessary with the latest strippable versions of wallpaper today: no glue, no mess, no hassle to install or remove. But in the early 1980s, wallpaper got stripped by steam, hot cloths, or stripping chemicals. And lots of personal energy. I kept scraping. The room was less than one-quarter finished.

As the wallpaper continued falling, more letters appeared on the plastered wall above the mantel. To our utter amazement, the revealed letters spelled ACCHIA. What were the chances our house's first owners shared our last name? Would we find an M preceding them? Not as we had hoped. When all the letters were revealed, the name CHIACCHIA was spelled over the mantel. The Chiacchia's had built our home in the early 1940s, and now we were the third family to own it.

On that October evening, Ruth and I felt at home. Our name was (almost) literally handwritten on the wall. We felt loved and assured that this was our place to reside. It couldn't have been much clearer on that night. We had worked so hard to get into this home, and the sweat equity we were giving to enhance this space was well worth it. Over the years, we would embrace similar challenges in keeping our home a place of love and service to each other and all who would cross that threshold into our humble abode.

We talked at length that night about the layers of wallpaper and the seasons of life experienced in that home for so many years, the conversations that must have ensued in front of the fireplace that sat gracefully under the mantel over which the handwritten letters were once penciled on the wall. What was life like for the Chiacchias in the early 1940s when their home—now ours—was built? How hard they must have worked to create this pleasant atmosphere.

Similarly, the layers of our relational lives are roughly hewn into the fibers of our being, beginning with what's written on the walls of our hearts. The stories being written about us today reflect where we came from. We are relational beings, meant to be in family and community, and the stories we create together add up to the distinct layers of our lives. Each layer is another new part of our story.

We look back with fondness and glee to that unique moment in our family history. We kept the letters visible for the remainder of the scraping process, sharing the story with all who would listen. Then, a few days later, we covered the letters with a prayer of thanksgiving and a fresh layer of paint. I think of that day often. How kind of God to love on us in such a creative way.

Relational Presence

If you were to scrape back all the accumulated layers on the walls of your soul—the many memories and conversations and experiences with others—you would find God's handwriting there. (Just like the many stories written in the wallpaper of the Chiacchia's house, with their name underneath.) God created, redeemed, and sustains us. He knows us by name. He formed and fashioned us in his likeness as a beautiful creation, a masterpiece. And he has destined us for intimate relationships, which include our life of worship, fellowship, and service to others.

Spiritual discernment is all about intentionally noticing our intimately loving God, and, in that noticing, showing gratitude for his abiding and unconditional presence. *Presence* is the defining word of that sentence. What does it mean to be present, first with God, and then with others, including ourselves? Learning how to be present begins with understanding how fully present God is with us.

The presence of Jesus was life-changing, from his earliest days on earth. His presence at the nativity was dramatic for all, beginning with Mary and Joseph, and advancing beyond that immediate-family circle to all who would come to know and adoringly worship him as the Christ child. From that point on, his fully present way was never interrupted, even to the very end.

Presence was always a relational priority for Jesus. It was a mainstay of his ministry with others. He was fully present at all times, and his invitation to his followers was to remain steadfastly present too. His gift to us as his beloved disciples is the constant and consistent presence of unconditional love.

When he eventually gets on his knees and begins to wash the feet of his disciples, Jesus is expressing the fullest extent of his love for them, as he "loved them to the end" (John 13:1). In the upper room, on the heels of his final meal with his band of brothers, he surprises them with the foot washing. "He got up from the meal, took off his outer clothing, and wrapped a towel around his waist. After that, he poured water into a basin and began to wash his disciples' feet, drying them with the towel that was wrapped around him" (vv. 4–5). Later, "when he had finished washing their feet, he put on his clothes and returned to his place" (v. 12). He then instructs them to do to others as he had done to them: "Now that I, your Lord and Teacher, have washed your feet, you also should wash one another's feet. . . . Now that you know these things, you will be blessed if you do them" (vv. 14, 17).

Peter resists it all at first, until he realizes the significance of this occasion and asks for not only his feet to be washed but his hands and head too (v. 9). In the moments to follow, Jesus predicts Peter's denial and Judas's betrayal. How heart-wrenching this all must have been.

Jesus's presence was received in the washing of their feet. Only hours later, his presence was rejected in betrayal and denial. How difficult it is to practice a preference for God, even for two of his own disciples.

Previously in Jesus's ministry, someone else had washed his feet. That time, his feet were washed by tears, kisses, and expensive perfume. They were washed by a woman—a sinful woman—who had crashed a dinner party held in the home of Simon the Pharisee. The contrast of response to the presence of Jesus between the learned host and the humble guest is startling to consider.

In Luke 7, we see this drama unfold. Jesus, invited by the Pharisee to have dinner with him, shows up and reclines at his table. The woman from the same town "who lived a sinful life [most likely a prostitute] learned that Jesus was eating at the Pharisee's house, so she came there with an alabaster jar of perfume" (v. 37). Perhaps this was the very perfume one of her clients had provided for a service she had previously rendered.

"As she stood behind him at his feet weeping," her tears fall gracefully on his feet. She wipes his feet with her hair, her tears, and her perfume (v. 38). All Simon can think to himself is, "If this man were a prophet, he would know who is touching him and what kind of woman she is—that she is a sinner" (v. 39). Does Simon really believe this information will make Jesus feel disgusted?

Jesus proceeds to dialogue with Simon the Pharisee, all the while leaving the woman at his feet to her repentance, her worship, her great affection for Jesus. Everything she offers to Jesus is for one reason alone: the intimate presence of love.

Simon is concerned about other things: his reputation, his pedigree, his power, his self-righteousness. His interactions with Jesus are noteworthy. Follow along.

> Jesus answered him, "Simon, I have something to tell you."
> "Tell me, teacher," he said. (v. 40)

And then Jesus tells Simon a story:

> "Two people owed money to a certain moneylender. One owed him five hundred denarii, and the other fifty. Neither of them had the money to pay him back, so he forgave the debts of both. Now which of them will love him more?"
> Simon replied, "I suppose the one who had the bigger debt forgiven."
> "You have judged correctly," Jesus said (vv. 41–43).

Then, to drive home the point, Jesus turns to the woman and tells the Pharisee,

> Do you see this woman? I came into your house. You did not give me any water for my feet, but she wet my feet with her tears and wiped them with her hair. You did not give me a kiss, but this woman, from the time I entered, has not stopped kissing my feet. You did not put oil on my head, but she has poured perfume on my feet. Therefore, I tell you, her many sins have been forgiven—as her great love has shown. But whoever has been forgiven little loves little. (vv. 44–47)

With sweeping forgiveness and grace, Jesus proclaims that her sins are forgiven. Her faith has saved her. His final words to her are, "Go in peace" (v. 50).

The Great Moneylender, the One who generously forgives debts, grants a full pardon to anyone who loves him. Those who love little—little people who think they are big in stature, prominence, and righteousness—are forgiven accordingly. Simon fell short in every regard. His littleness was evident to those who had eyes to see and ears to hear. Jesus made it crystal clear.

This smallness of heart was demonstrated by Simon's inability to truly see the woman. She was in his home, but his hard heart focused instead on the label he had affixed to her. "Sinner" was his judgment and condemnation of her. To him, she had no name, no reputation worth considering. This was in sharp contrast to Jesus, who saw her and praised her love, her hospitality, her courage, and her faith. Jesus's response was diametrically opposed to Simon's.

Let's not forget that Simon wasn't coldhearted only to the woman. His reception of Jesus into his home was similarly chilly.

Simon didn't perform even the most fundamental gestures of hospitality. He didn't give Jesus water for his dusty feet. He didn't offer him a welcoming kiss on the cheek. He didn't provide oil for his head. These were things Simon most likely provided for each of his other guests. But he didn't offer them to Jesus and certainly not to the sinful woman.

Simon's rejection of Jesus's presence was damning. He was blind to the presence of the woman. He was blind to the presence of the Savior. What about you? Do you have eyes to truly see Jesus and the people around you?

A Graced Presence

Jesus's presence transformed lives. In the upper room, this is what he offered his disciples at the table of grace during the Last Supper. He showed all of them the fullest extent of love, including his betrayer and the one who would deny him.

And, similarly, he offered his presence at another table of grace with the sinful woman in this life-changing pericope. Jesus saw the woman. He knew her. He accepted her. He recognized her debt. He offered complete forgiveness. He loved her in spite of herself. He was fully engaged in every moment of the interaction and was not thrown off by her affectionate response of kisses, tears, and expensive perfume.

The sinful woman in Luke 7 is our role model for the discerning life. Practicing a preference for God looks just like her. We should be aware of our sinfulness, desperate for forgiveness, and longing to be seen and known and loved in spite of our sin patterns, idiosyncrasies, and quirkiness. We are welcomed home to

God with the open arms of grace, and we are invited to offer the same to one another.

When we finally awaken to the reality of God's ever-present gift of his presence—his love and grace, hope and peace—we are ushered into a life of transformation. Discerning God's relational presence amidst our brokenness is the pathway to this kind of abundant living.

I trust this is what you're looking for.

At the table of grace, we receive an abundance of generous love and forgiveness. At the table of grace, we respond with our best offerings of gratitude. At the table of grace, we are powerfully altered by the One who knows and notices, who listens and attends with eyes and ears and a heart of affection.

Grace is contagious to those with open and receptive hearts. And it's offered back to God and then to others, including ourselves, with gratitude and generosity. Grace is the gift that keeps on giving, the presence of which alters the trajectory of your life today and forever. We have a fundamental choice to make: Will we prefer grace or judgment? Will we remain pliable in the hands of God, or will we consistently resist his tender grip and take matters into our own hands? Will we seek the heart of God on all matters large and small, or will we distance ourselves from God and prefer our own way instead? Will we love unconditionally, or will we remain manipulative in our response to others?

To live in graced presence with God and others is something we need to learn by practice. We are not naturally inclined to offer such grace, mercy, kindness, compassion, forgiveness, and love. But it's certainly possible for all who practice a preference for God. It's found at the table of grace, at the feet of Jesus, where he's washing our feet with affection, and where we are willing to do likewise with all who are in our orbit of relational presence.

A Listening Presence

My wife, a preschool teacher, would often say to her students, "I need to see your eyes when we're talking to each other." She would say the same to our children and to me. Our ears are not enough to fully listen and attend to others. Our eyes help us focus on being fully present. This starts with the eyes of our hearts as we listen to the voice of God. Our prayer closet, as we discussed in the previous chapter, is where we focus on developing a listening presence with God.

A listening presence is the priority practice for experiencing a discerning life with our family, friends, colleagues, and members of our faith communities. Learning how to purely listen to another person is a skill. It's an attribute of the heart that we need to develop by practice. It certainly doesn't come naturally to any of us.

Consider the many hindrances to a listening presence among your family, friends, and faith community. What keeps us from face-to-face, eye-to-eye, side-by-side time and all that is necessary for healthy relational presence? Here are some of the main stumbling blocks:

- *Distractions.* A plethora of items keep us unfocused and incapable of being fully present, such as our work, our technology, our to-do lists, and the needs of others.
- *Busyness.* We believe that a full schedule equals a fulfilling life and think it's really important to monitor our calendars, continually reordering our priorities and affections.
- *Narcissism.* This is our tendency toward self-absorption and self-protection that keeps us from noticing and attending to the needs of others by dying to self and living for God.
- *Unforgiveness.* Often, we are unwilling to offer grace, mercy,

81

and honest forgiveness to those who hurt or harm us; with or without complete reconciliation, our charge is to forgive.

- *Stubbornness.* This is the harsh, hard-hearted manner in which we connect with others, where we need to be right at all times and become incapable of backing down.
- *Hopelessness.* We feel that everything happening in and around us is fruitless, futile, or negative, which contributes to an attitude that can become debilitating for all.
- *Immaturity.* We are unable to rise to the occasion and express relational strength and focus, either by choosing to reject another or by responses that are laced with crude, naive, or irresponsible words, attitudes, and behaviors unbecoming a child of God.
- *Anger, sadness, or depression.* These are the immobilizing net effects of emotional instabilities brought about by circumstance, poor relationships, abuse, neglect, trauma, prejudice, and, in the case of depression, biological and physiological factors.
- *Lack of role models.* Many people don't have healthy role models who exemplify relationships that, although imperfect, are continually being refined, restored, and renewed.
- *Physical, mental, or intellectual limitations.* There are incapacitations brought on by restrictions outside the control of individuals, impacted by birth, heritage, or life-altering experiences.

Some of these restrictions to establishing a listening presence can be worked on and brought to betterment over time. Others are ongoing and need a compassionate response from the body of Christ. Regardless of the roadblocks to presence, it's incumbent on us to seek it as much as possible. It's worth the prayerful, intentional effort to create such an environment where listening presence can flourish.

A spiritually discerning community makes Jesus smile, as friends learn to love one another in the manner that Jesus exemplified. When relational presence is the stated priority for our own family and friends, as well as within the church, then all that we do together should follow suit.

Listening to one another is the heartbeat of a healthy, spiritually discerning community. The fruit of listening is a culture of grace, where kindness, patience, and forgiveness reign supreme. How we interact with one another is far more important than what we do together. However, when relationships are vibrant, the work and witness bears fruit that lasts. Jesus made that promise (John 15:16), and its within our grasp to fulfill.

But we need to learn how to listen first—as friends of Jesus and as friends with one another.

When our community life is laced with grace, the evidence of God's Spirit comes alive. The fruit of such is seen in love, joy, peace, patience, kindness, goodness, faithfulness, gentleness, and self-control. These are nine lovely attributes of the Spirit of God, demonstrated in the people of God.

Grace is both the means and the end result of pure listening. Impure listening barely offers an ear, never mind the necessary accompanying eyes. Impure listening is impatient and rather impervious to what's being said. It is more ready to reply and respond than to receive and ponder. It doesn't really care about what's being said, especially if it requires compassion, ownership, confession, or forgiveness. Impure listening is much more about the self than the other. It runs rampant in the world today, even in the body of Christ.

Pure listening is as open as possible. It sets aside personal agenda to embrace the words, attitudes, and affections of others. Pure listening is agenda-free. It's willing to slow down and pay attention to the tone of voice, the body language, and the words of others, which all combine to form the message. Pure listening comes from the heart more than the head. To purely listen to another is to seek compassion, empathy, and perseverance. When we offer ourselves to another through pure listening, we have all the time necessary to complete the cycle of speaking and listening, noticing and abandoning, receiving words and sentiments, and releasing the need to fix, control, or correct.

With pure listening as the goal, we recognize how far we have to go to achieve that objective. It's impossible to be totally pure in our listening, but by the grace of God, we can learn how to improve and begin to offer one another a more purified form of genuine listening.

Where should you start on this journey? Just listen! Don't feel the need to fix, correct, control, or suggest. Pure listening allows God the privilege of enlightening, awakening, and directing each and every one of us.

Pure listening is focused on others—either on God or another person. We need to learn how to be fully present in an uncluttered, unhindered, unhurried fashion. This begins in our prayer closet, listening intently to God. Then, it can expand into our daily lives, among those God has called us to serve within our families, friendships, workplaces, and wider communities.

Pure listening requires double the eyes and ears and half the tongue—especially in relationship with God. If we believe God has more important things to say to us than we to him, then it's best for us to focus more on listening than talking. It's the same with our human relationships, for we learn more about one another by being fully present with another through our attentive listening.

Pure listening is laced with grace—withholding judgment,

opinion, or suggestion. When we are fully and as-purely-as-possible present with another person, we are there to understand, empathize, and express compassionate interest in the details of the story being shared. We need to suspend our own experience or expertise and remain as fully present as possible. This is not an easy undertaking, and it takes practice to embody.

Pure listening responds—but only when invited to do so. Most family members and friends don't want to be fixed or corrected, but every single one of them wants to be listened to and loved just the way they are. Maintaining healthy boundaries in our listening presence allows us to share in the same space together without compulsion to lean in too close and offer too many words without first being asked.

You and I know when we are being listened to well. At different times, I've both excelled and failed at listening. I know what it's like to feel deeply loved simply by being listened to. And I know what it's like to be disregarded and ignored. In our LTI ministry, we teach others how to listen. We've been told by many, "I've never been listened to this well—ever."

I've led literally hundreds of spiritual formation groups with young leaders in seminary and groups of leaders on retreats. Each time I share my story, I can glance around the circle and know who's listening well—the ones who can repeat verbatim what I've said, without interpretation, comparison, or correction. And I know I'm listening well when I can do the same. But when I'm distracted, I easily forget the words spoken and fudge the details when given opportunity to recite back what I've heard. Listening well takes intentionality, focus, and lots of practice. Otherwise, we quickly shift back to the norm of poor attentiveness to the words, tones of voice, and body language of the one who's sharing.

When is the last time you were fully heard? Recall what happened to make it such a wonderful experience. Perhaps you were purely listened to, received at a table of grace, and allowed to inquire of God as to his interpretation, and ultimately, to his invitation.

A Discerning Presence

The discerning life is riddled with questions. Some of them are huge: "What is my calling?" or "Whom shall I marry?" or "What vocation should I pursue?" or "Where shall we live?"

But most of the time, our questions are more ordinary and rather simple. It's in the commonplace where God instructs us one step, one hour, one decision at a time. The result is a discerning life in which one practices a preference for God day by day.

In our relational presence, asking good questions results in ever-deepening affection for God and others. And then, we simply listen to the response. If you do so, you'll be amazed by what you'll learn about God, those around you, and the person you are becoming.

Here are a few ways to consider some of the most rudimentary relational inquiries in the discerning life.

1. Check In: "How Is It with Your Soul?"

This is a tremendous question, far better than the more typical "How are you?" It was originally coined by John Wesley as the way he would often query his followers. It's a wide-open question, designed to allow any answer to be acceptable. Frequently, we consider the state of our soul to represent our relationship with God (feeling close or distant, hungering or delighting). But it also can include how well we're doing in the following:

- Our physical bodies: "My soul is exhausted, hurting."
- Our relationships: "My soul is sad or feeling alienated."
- Our emotional state: "My soul is confused, frustrated."
- Our missional service: "My soul feels empty of purpose."
- Our geography: "My soul feels homeless or restless."
- Our economic status: "My soul is broke, lost, or in debt; or rich, heavily invested, or abundantly blessed."

Adding an object to your words can aid in communicating about the state of your soul. For example, share a toy race car to exemplify your fast-paced life, or a wilting plant to express how you are feeling about your neglected soul, or a candle to describe your flickering light and the darkness around you. You can focus your response to this question around a season: winter, spring, summer, or fall. Or choose an animal to describe the state of your soul. Ostrich

There are many ways to express the state of your soul. What's important is to give voice to your walk with God, knowing it's far better to learn this about another than to remain frivolous and superficial in our relational presence. Choose the deeper life among your friends and in your spiritual community.

2. Check Up: "How Are You Really Doing?"

Like a physical check up at the doctor's office, this question evokes a deeper look at our current reality. Friend to friend, we are invited to be honest with one another at a depth consistent with our relationship. We all need at least one relationship where we can be totally and completely honest. Without such a relationship, we limp along on our own strength even when we are crying out for companionship in the here and now.

The freedom to ask and be asked this question brings about the depth necessary to live a discerning life. When vocalized, the truth about you sets you free, and in freedom we are carried by God and upheld by the friends he gives us along the way. Looking squarely at our current reality helps us remain open and transparent, which ultimately leads to healing, restoration, and transformation.

3. Check Out: "What Discernment Questions Are You Pondering Today?"

By shifting outward in our growth as relational beings in pursuit of a discerning life, we are continuously in a state of discernment. The questions we are asking of God, others, and ourselves are plentiful. Each day brings to mind new questions that need answering: "What to wear?" "What to eat?" "Where to go?" "When to sleep?" "How to invest?" "Whom to see?"

Proactively ask others about the discernment questions they are considering. Bring these issues to light. Often, we answer them without much consideration or inadvertently avoid them because they aren't being acknowledged, brought out into the open for prayerful deliberation. In every serious aspect of discernment, we start by identifying the right question.

What's now is the entry point to what's next. As we lean into being fully present with God, ourselves, and others, we begin to notice some of the most fundamental questions about our daily lives. As we note the *now*, we can look forward to what's *next* with informed hearts and minds. Here are a handful of helpful questions to include as you pursue a discerning life:

- *What are you asking?* This is the most fundamental discernment question.

- *What do you need?* It's important to listen with compassion and grace.
- *What do you want?* These are the longings and desires of your heart.
- *What do you miss?* These are memories and histories we hold dearly.
- *What do you regret?* We all have missed opportunities and made poor decisions in the past.
- *What do you notice?* What do you see, hear, touch, smell, taste?
- *What do you sense?* These are feelings and empathies of the moment.
- *What do you know?* What are the facts and truths about your situation?
- *What seems right or wrong? Dark or light?* These are consolations and desolations. (We'll talk more about these in chapter 7.)
- *What do you need to release, forfeit, hold loosely, or disregard?* These are attachments that need to be detached in order to reattach to God and to more appropriate affections.
- *What is God inviting?* Where do we feel the welcoming presence and hospitality of God? Safety true relationship

Regardless of how large or small the question(s) may be, pressing the pause button on your busy life allows one the joy of reflection. Holding the question(s) prayerfully before the Lord, inviting others to join you in your inquiry, and writing out what you're noticing are ways that these questions can come alive in your soul.

We can trust God regardless of the size of the questions we ask. His enveloping presence surrounds us with grace to ask whatever we desire and to know with certainty that he's a God of clarity, not confusion. He will indeed make his way clear to all who follow him with listening love and prayerful obedience.

We can help each other in this regard. We need to learn how best to listen deeply in our relational presence. Knowing how to ask good questions and then to listen with purified grace will enable the discernment we long for in our faith community and in our individual lives.

Living a discerning life and practicing a preference for God will enlighten the path before us. Look today for the handwriting on the wall, for your name has been written there with love.

PRACTICING A PREFERENCE FOR GOD

Imagine what your family, friendships, and faith community would look like if they were earnestly practicing a preference for God. Imagine what your relational presence would become if you helped each other come to a table of grace each time you were together, where the generosity of God was evidenced and where gratitude abounds. As we look as close as possible at the disciples in the upper room and the woman at Jesus's feet, we can't help but notice a way of being together that was marked by unconditional relational presence.

Jesus has enlightened our pathway for the quality of our relationships here on earth—ones that are to be marked by unfathomable grace, unforgettable kindness, and unrelenting forgiveness. What would your relationships look like if these were your shared objectives? Perhaps an earnest pursuit of love, listening, and laughter will enhance and enliven your relational presence for all.

Here are a few spiritual exercises to put into practice as you reflect on this chapter:

- **Presence:** Sit with a friend to talk but leave your cell phone in the car or in another room. Notice the gift of presence. Was anything about this conversation different from usual?
- **Listening:** On a scale of 1 (low) to 10 (high), how do you rank as a pure listener? What is one thing you can start doing when you listen to jump up your score a point or two? Now do it!
- **Grace:** Imagine what your relationships would look like if grace were the centerpiece. How would this change your relationship with family members? What about a close friend? Someone else?

CHAPTER 5

Hospitality

Spiritual Discernment Is Communal

> *"Since we are surrounded by such a great cloud of witnesses, let us throw off everything that hinders and the sin that so easily entangles. And let us run with perseverance the race marked out for us, fixing our eyes on Jesus, the pioneer and perfecter of faith. . . . Consider him . . . so that you will not grow weary and lose heart."*
>
> Hebrews 12:1–3

Spiritual discernment isn't just for the individual; it's for the community. It's much more about us and we than I and me.

Let us run with perseverance the race marked out for us. Every marathoner needs running companions to keep in stride, friends on the sidelines offering cups of cold water, and cheering crowds offering words of encouragement all the way to the finish line.

We need our community in order to endure without growing

weary or losing heart, helping us keep our eye on the prize—the finished work of Christ in us. A discerning life requires a community of like-hearted and like-minded brothers and sisters who share this same desire for our entire lives. In this world of hindrance and entanglement, fixing our eyes on Jesus—in, among, and with our faith community—will keep us from growing weary and losing heart. The practice of Christian hospitality is the means by which true community is created, though it is costly for all involved.

So it is in the constant care of our homes. We need one another. Like the ongoing work of gracious hospitality, there's always something to fix, replace, rearrange, construct, reconstruct, restore, move, or clean. Our physical dwelling places need our continual attention. Sometimes the projects are rewarding and life-giving, while others can be exasperating. All of them are accomplished best with helpful guides and supporters by our side.

In my quirky home, most of the projects have leaned more toward exasperation than jubilation. Every project takes longer than anticipated, costs more than expected, and often requires double or triple the effort than first imagined. The joy of accomplishment eventually arrives, but it's usually through the eye of the needle of strenuous effort, likened to the work it takes to strengthen our community.

Oh, and it's worth noting for those who can empathize: most house projects are taxing on relationships, especially when the team or the helper is ill-informed, unprepared, unwilling, or simply not blessed with the gift of working with one's hands. As my dad once said, "In this life, there are tinkerers and there are thinkerers, and generally one person isn't both." I'm a thinkerer in desperate need of tinkerers to surround me.

I'm reminded of the time it was our turn to host Christmas for our extended family. We also wanted to have some friends over during the holiday week prior to New Year's. It was early on in our marriage, so we needed to make the best of what we had. At the very least, we knew we wanted a fresh Christmas tree to adorn our small living room.

We set out to buy the perfect tree. Our son Nate was a toddler at the time, and we had heard about a local tree farm that would make for a fun family experience. We packed up our car and brought along a saw to cut down our choice tree. When we got to the farm, we bundled up and headed into the forest of trees to make our selection. After a much longer than expected decision-making process, we chose *the* tree. I asked Nate to help me saw it down, knowing his efforts were more for the photo op.

We cut our tree down and proceeded to drag it to the front where we could pay for it, have it wrapped up for transport, and get it home. The tree farmer warned us that we had a big tree—perhaps we'd need to cut it back further once we got it home. Undeterred, we did our best to heave the tree onto our old van. This proved impossible for just Ruth and me, but with the assistance of two others, we successfully tied it onto the luggage rack. Driving home we kept a slow pace, fearful the tree would slide off the roof. Thankfully, we made it home without incident. When the twine was cut, it dropped off the car with a thud. Realizing my wife and son would not be able to help me get this up the front stairs and into the living room, I huffed my way forward, yanking the tree with me one laborious step at a time.

When the tree eventually landed in the living room, I immediately knew it was way too big. Picture an elephant in a VW beetle. I hacked off branches and cut off the base until the tree only consumed about one fourth of the room. Then I kept cutting and trimming until we were satisfied with the new size and shape of this "special" tree.

By the time we had cut the tree up to reasonable proportions, we realized the stand was too tiny for this monstrosity. I set off to the hardware store to get a new one and returned home only to discover that the tree's weight kept tipping it off kilter. Out came the wire to tie it to the mantle and keep it erect. I added several rocks to the stand, hoping it would help. It finally stood straight, but only by the grace of God.

With fear and trepidation, we decorated the tree, hoping each new ornament wouldn't send it crashing down. (Thankfully none of them did.) But our family and friends appreciated hearing our tree story; most had their own to tell too. That tree became the talk of the season—and the very last live tree we would ever purchase. Not only were we exhausted by the experience, but we discovered that year that I am actually allergic to pine trees. How ironic.

We learned some important lessons from that tree. Most significantly, there's a price to pay when we offer hospitality to others. Hospitality is much more complex than meets the eye. We rarely consider the work behind welcoming others into our circle, hosting a lovely party, or preparing a graced table for others to enjoy. Yet we need one another to do life well, so hospitality is not an option for those in pursuit of a discerning life.

We are meant for community, not isolation. Even monks who pray all day long live in community with other monks. When we are in community, we work hard to maintain a hospitable presence one with another. It takes a lot of work to consider the needs of others more important than your own, especially when you are sacrificing for the sake of those you're called to love and serve in the family, church, marketplace, neighborhood, and wider world in which we live.

That Christmas tree was a huge bundle of frustration, but it became a lasting memory. We went through it all for the sake of opening our home and sharing our lives with those we loved the most. We simply wanted to create a hospitable presence for others to enjoy.

Jesus Is Patient and Persistent

One of our dearest friends, upon entering our home and noticing all that was done prior to his arrival, once remarked to Ruth, "Preparation is the greatest sign of love." By this he meant: *When we enter your home and see all that you've done to prepare the meal, set the table, arrange the decor, and welcome us with open arms, we know we are loved in your presence. We feel safe and important. We know you care.* We have thought of that often over the years. In our hospitality, we attend to the details so everyone who arrives at our home knows that they matter.

I love how particular Jesus gets about the details of a faithful life, the importance of practicing hospitality, and sniffing out where it's not being appropriately provided. His continual focus with the disciples was to teach them to obey everything he had taught them. He leaves room for interpretation, according to the situations they found themselves in throughout the journey. But he certainly comforts his disciples with specificity.

When he sends out the Twelve in Matthew 10, his calling is secure: he gives them authority to drive out evil spirits and to heal every disease and sickness. He begins his litany of specificity with their names: "Simon (who is called Peter) and his brother Andrew; James son of Zebedee, and his brother John; Philip and Bartholomew; Thomas and Matthew the tax collector; James son of Alphaeus, and Thaddaeus; Simon the Zealot and Judas Iscariot, who betrayed him" (vv. 1–4).

His mission for them is to go to the lost sheep of Israel (v. 6). For Jesus, it is the lost who need to be found and welcomed into the kingdom of heaven. Consistently, Jesus cares for the lost, the least, the hurting, the needy, the sick, the disenfranchised, and any who are left behind. They are the ones with whom Jesus was most hospitable. His disciples are to carry on this legacy.

His message for them to preach is very simple: "The kingdom of heaven has come near" (v. 7). As we've already determined, Jesus is all about the kingdom of God. His life and teaching fulfill the kingdom that had been promised from the beginning of time. The prophets had foretold his coming as Messiah, the One to proclaim the kingdom at hand, as it was, is, and shall be evermore. The message of the disciples is the message of the King: embrace, enter, and find abundant and eternal life in the kingdom found only in Jesus.

His ministry for them is to be generously offered to all who are in need: "Heal the sick, raise the dead, cleanse those who have leprosy, drive out demons" (v. 8). The ministry of Jesus is focused on the hurting, those who suffer from disease, who without him are destined to die from despair, despondency, darkness, and even demonization. As freely as this redemptive work was received by the disciples themselves, so too are they set apart to offer it freely and hospitably to others.

Then, for the rest of Matthew 10, Jesus offers specific instructions for the disciples to follow, all to be fulfilled in community. They include:

- "Do not get any gold or silver or copper to take with you in your belts" (v. 9).

- Do not take a "bag for the journey or extra shirt or sandals or a staff, for the worker is worth his keep" (v. 10).
- "Whatever town or village you enter, search there for some worthy person and stay at their house until you leave" (v. 11).
- "As you enter the home, give it your greeting. If the home is deserving, let your peace rest on it; if it is not, let your peace return to you" (vv. 12–13).
- "If anyone will not welcome you or listen to your words, leave that home or town and shake the dust off your feet. Truly I tell you, it will be more bearable for Sodom and Gomorrah on the day of judgment than for that town" (vv. 14–15).
- "I am sending you out like sheep among wolves. Therefore be as shrewd as snakes and as innocent as doves. Be on your guard; you will be handed over to the local councils and be flogged in the synagogues. On my account you will be brought before governors and kings as witnesses to them and to the Gentiles" (vv. 16–18).

For the remainder of the chapter, Matthew brings to light the instructions of Jesus for his fledgling group of disciples, sent out on mission on his behalf. Jesus knows there is a marathon ahead of them, and he offers specific instructions for the way forward.

Jesus warns that "brother will betray brother to death, and a father his child; children will rebel against their parents and have them put to death" (v. 21). These are all signs of the judgment that would come upon all people. Jesus wants his disciples forewarned. But he also doesn't want them afraid. "There is nothing concealed that will not be disclosed, or hidden that will not be made known.... And even the very hairs on your head are all numbered" (vv. 26, 30).

His greatest longing is for his disciples to remain steadfast and faithful and to persevere together in community. He knows that for others to come to a living faith in God, his disciples need to be fully aware of the choices, consequences, and drama that will unfold. Following Jesus is serious business because it's kingdom work, and we are called to join his ministry of soul hospitality, offered freely and generously to all who would receive it.

For Jesus's disciples, their invitation to follow God began with taking up their crosses. This meant losing their lives for Jesus's sake and then finding them all over again as fully restored. And this led to the crescendo of his specific instructions: become receivable to others, welcoming others' hospitably in Jesus's name, in order that others may receive Christ for themselves.

Communal hospitality is articulated by Jesus in this way:

> Anyone who welcomes you welcomes me, and anyone who welcomes me welcomes the one who sent me. Whoever welcomes a prophet as a prophet will receive a prophet's reward, and whoever welcomes a righteous person as a righteous person will receive a righteous person's reward. And if anyone gives a cup of cold water to one of these little ones who is my disciple, truly I tell you, that person will certainly not lose their reward. (vv. 40–42)

Thus ends this chapter of specific instructions. The crux of the matter for Jesus was then and is today a spirit of welcoming hospitality, where the Spirit of Christ enters into the open arms of the one who longs to receive all that he has to offer.

And this welcoming spirit of graced hospitality is to be shared and received continuously by his disciples, one at a time and in community. This is communal hospitality focused on Jesus. Such hospitality is revered in the biblical text, specifically in the life of Jesus and among his community of disciples.

Jesus Is the One Thing

Everywhere Jesus traveled, we see evidence of either gracious hospitality or guarded hostility. With his friends Mary, Martha, and Lazarus, we note a wonderful example of loving hospitality. The story of their remarkable friendship is told in Luke 10:38–42 and John 11:1–12:8. Both passages are well worth prayerful review and reflection, as they depict welcoming hospitality at its finest.

Luke provides a refreshing pericope of comparison between Martha and Mary. Between the parable of the good Samaritan and Jesus's teaching on prayer, Luke inserts Jesus's admonition to his distracted friend Martha, who was worried and upset about many things. In contrast, he points out the endearing focus of Mary's singlehearted attention to the one thing that mattered most: sitting at the Lord's feet, listening to what he has to say.

Martha is often thrown under the bus for her improper expression of hospitality, when in fact she is the one who opens her home to Jesus (Luke 10:38). She is also the one who prepares for Jesus's presence. She obviously believes that preparation is her greatest sign of love. But because of her question, "Lord, don't you care that my sister has left me to do the work by myself?" (v. 40), her exasperation provides a teachable moment for Jesus. He lovingly and specifically urges her not to worry or fret about the many aspects of physical preparation, but to instead choose with Mary to perform one act of hospitality: unhurried, unhindered, uncluttered, undistracted relational presence and prayerful attentiveness.

The fully absorbed presence of Mary at Jesus's feet, listening to his teaching and receiving his love, is the one thing that he wants Martha to enjoy as well. Martha has indeed opened her home to Jesus, but Jesus wants her to open her heart as well. That is the one thing that matters most.

In John's Gospel, we see a much fuller exposition of their friendship. This time the focus is on Martha and Mary's brother, Lazarus, who was sick and has died. The sisters call for Jesus to come, heal his sickness, and raise him from the dead. Jesus sets out to their home, comforts the grieving sisters, and raises Lazarus from his deadly sleep. Lazarus is miraculously healed and set free from the pangs of death, fulfilling Jesus's proclamation: "I am the resurrection and the life. The one who believes in me will live, even though they die; and whoever lives by believing in me will never die" (John 11:25–26).

This infuriates the religious leaders, the chief priests and the Pharisees, who call a meeting of the Sanhedrin and plot to kill Jesus (vv. 45–57). The drama leading to Jesus's death is heating up among those who violently oppose his presence.

With this as a backdrop, John inserts another story of Mary's great affection for Jesus. Once again, Jesus is in the home of the three siblings, Martha, Mary, and Lazarus. Here, Martha is serving dinner, while Lazarus is reclining at the table with Jesus. Mary takes a pint of pure nard, an expensive perfume, and pours it on Jesus's feet, wiping his feet with her hair. The perfume fills the air with a lovely fragrance. One can only imagine the hospitality that was flourishing among them.

But in opposition to such waste, Judas Iscariot, who later betrays Jesus, objects to this display of fragrant affection. Judas cries out in exasperation, "Why wasn't this perfume sold and the money given to the poor? It was worth a year's wages" (John 12:5). John explains,

"He did not say this because he cared about the poor but because he was a thief; as keeper of the money bag, he used to help himself to what was put into it" (v. 6). This is yet another dramatic contrast between a faithful disciple and a hostile adversary of Jesus.

The stories of Martha, Mary, and Lazarus are depictions of the nature of hospitality Jesus clearly articulates in the series of instructions in Matthew 10. Where you are welcomed in Jesus's name, enter into fellowship among a community where all are received for Jesus's sake. But when confronted by self-righteous religious leaders or those who directly contradict Jesus, be wise and gentle, always choosing that which matters most in expressing one's affection for Jesus.

Always Choose the One Thing

In the early church, at the time of Pentecost, God's grace was powerfully at work in them all because of the presence and power of the Spirit. Jesus had promised to send them a Helper, the Spirit, and that was being fulfilled in their midst. Why? Because they

> devoted themselves to the apostles' teaching and to fellowship, to the breaking of bread and to prayer. Everyone was filled with awe at the many wonders and signs performed by the apostles. All the believers were together and had everything in common. They sold property and possessions to give to anyone who had need. Every day they continued to meet together in the temple courts. They broke bread in their homes and ate together with glad and sincere hearts, praising God and enjoying the favor of all the people. And the Lord added to their number daily those who were being saved. (Acts 2:42–47)

The early church chose to focus on the One Thing: God. They inclined their hearts fully in the direction of the Father, Son, and Holy Spirit. They were united in their fellowship in God's Spirit. They worshiped and prayed and loved and served together. Their communal hospitality was drenched with the Spirit we call Holy. Their communal love was fixed on Jesus, the pioneer and perfecter of their faith. Their communal effectiveness was blessed by the Father and multiplied in the hearts and lives of all who surrounded them. And God added to their number because of their faithfulness, perseverance, and profound trust in the Living God.

The season of Pentecost is remarkable and worth pondering. The One Thing that brought it about was the Spirit of God. The One Thing that mattered most was God. This is evidenced in living for Jesus, proclaiming his gospel, and receiving from him over and over again the fullness of his powerful presence.

When we imagine the church today in light of Pentecost, the One Thing we need to most highly regard is God—Father, Son, and Holy Spirit. For when we prefer God together as a community and entrust our existence into the hand of God as the people of God, we experience life with God like never before. And there's no turning back or away from God when we know with certainty that our lives are empty without God.

With (slight) apologies for so much God-talk, we simply cannot understand spiritual discernment without knowing what it means to depend on God. It's in our utter dependency on God that we discover afresh the fullness of the Spirit of God. When this is done in community, then our friendships, fellowship, and fruitfulness are multiplied beyond comprehension.

In our desire to control or manage the outcomes of our shared life in Christ, we get into trouble. When we stop looking to or for

God, we limit our effectiveness by trusting in our own strength, wisdom, competencies, plans, and ideas. Here, we look at each other as if we are in competition for control of our shared objectives. We get stirred up in consideration of how we can become bigger, better, bolder, and pursue now the new and the next. We get all fired up by the energy to complete as much as possible so that we feel good about our efforts.

It's way too easy to fall into this trap. Every ministry leader wants their ministry to be recognized, appreciated, and multiplied. We see this in the wider culture, and we want it for ourselves. We get pushed and shoved by the strongest voices in the crowd, and we often succumb. When highly successful people suggest something, we follow their advice. It's hard to say no. And the vicious circle goes round and round again.

But eventually we see the emptiness of such pursuit. We push and shove and manipulate and strategize and use every possible human endeavor to get what we set out to acquire. And it just about wipes us out. Our relationships begin to sour. The energy necessary to keep the ship afloat drains. We hit an iceberg we never saw coming. We suffer from the choices of our own making. We are devoid of meaning and purpose. The downward spiral of human effort eventually comes to an end.

What a contrast to Pentecost!

This is our fate unless we turn from such ways and pursue together a life of spiritual hospitality that begins with a repentant return to the Holy Spirit. We must choose to follow Jesus and his instruction manual for becoming hospitable to God and one another. In other words, we must come to our senses and return home to the Father's loving embrace. And invite our friends to do the same. We need to begin with the question, "God, what do you desire?" rather than "Let's brainstorm together and then pray for God's blessing on our decisions."

Imagine your community of family, friends, church, small group, and/or ministry team stepping to the plate and choosing to live in harmonious hospitality with God and one another. What would that look like today?

With scars to show the price I've paid, I have put a stake in the ground for the way forward, especially among the teams I serve. There is no turning back to the old way of human endeavor that reeks of self-righteous service and leads to human adulation. Instead, the pursuit moving forward is fully engulfed in creating, inviting, and engaging in Christ-centered and community-based team life that reflects Pentecost more than Wall Street; more than politics; more than success; more than the divisions that separate, alienate, and frustrate.

Easier Said Than Done

Spiritual discernment flourishes in communal contexts where we continuously point God out to one another and inquire of God together. It happens when we notice God in our worship, our relationships, and in our service to others in Jesus's name. When we care more about each other's soul-state and walk with God than posturing ourselves as wealthier, wittier, wiser, brighter, bigger, or better than each other.

When we can get past the false images we seek to project and pursue a more genuine presence with one another, then we are heading in the right direction. Are you relaxed, at home, and living with sincerity in your various relational contexts? If not, why not?

For leadership teams in particular, we need to begin to look around the table and notice who's there. Are the right people in the right seats? Do they fit their roles and fulfill their responsibilities? Do you share a common commitment to the organization, its vision and mission, that you are serving together? Do you embrace a distinct approach to leading via spiritual discernment principles and practices? Hospitality is the lens to look through, without which our teams will struggle and frustrate and potentially fail.

Effective leadership teams share many characteristics in common. Formative leadership teams stand alone in one priority: spiritual discernment. Their shared commitment is to practice a preference for God.

This kind of team shares a commitment to life together laced with prayer, grace, trust, kindness, patience, communication, forgiveness, and love. They value creativity, fruitfulness, discernment-based decision-making, conflict resolution, follow-through, fast failures, and a willingness to design and redesign as God so leads.

The hallmarks of a spiritually discerning leadership team (a ministry board, church elders, trustees, and even a small group sharing life together) are fourfold:

1. *Godly.* They share a common commitment to living a life of prayerfulness and dependence on God and lovingly hold each other to that daily priority.
2. *Gifted.* They willingly share their God-given gifts, passions, and personality with one another in life-giving ways and strive to serve cooperatively together.
3. *Gracious.* They create together a culture of grace, mercy, kindness, and forgiveness; and they steer clear of blame, shame, competition, ridicule, and any abuse of power.

4. *Generous.* They recognize that everything given to them comes from the hand of God and all that they steward together is to be offered back to God and given to others with generosity.

When these attributes are in place, the shared experience is delightful for all.

But when the gifted choose to become powerful and the godly become pious, when the gracious become judgmental and the generous become manipulative, then what was once delightful becomes intolerable. Unfortunately, it happens, overnight or over a longer period of time, and it needs to be guarded against at all costs. Otherwise, it will become costly, guaranteed. There are far too many examples of the souring effects of pridefulness on teams of all shapes and sizes, forms, and purposes.

Far too often, we select as leader the person who exhibits the most success in the marketplace rather than the one known more for their godliness. I've seen firsthand how destructive this can be for a team. Ego can dominate the room. Teams need to be led by those who value equipping, encouraging, and empowering others to thrive. It's not about them; it's always about others.

All persons around the table of discernment matter, and they bring with them who they are—the good, the bad, and the ugly. No one is perfect. To project unattainable expectations on others is to open the floodgates for disappointment, pain, and heartache among the team of leaders gathered for loftier purposes under God.

This is a human endeavor, not scientific, and it won't be perfected this side of heaven. But its pursuit will bring radical transformation to all who earnestly enter this journey. The pathway to a discerning life is to be creatively pursued, knowing that our shared life with God is like a prism of complexities, with no "right" way to handle one's community. We will experience trial and error, stops and starts, failures and successes, but when we persevere as saints (rather than as persnickety sinners), our growing God-awareness will lead us into a fruitful life of discernment.

Accepting our own humanness and the frailties of others on the team will lead us toward a communal hospitality that recognizes the strong and the weak among us as equals in the body we are becoming in Christ.

> God has placed the parts in the body, every one of them, just as he wanted them to be. If they were all one part, where would the body be? As it is, there are many parts, but one body. . . . Those parts of the body that seem to be weaker are indispensable. . . . Now you are the body of Christ, and each one of you is a part of it. (1 Cor. 12:18–27)

Who is sitting at the table will either make or break the experience of collective discernment. Not everyone is ready to join such a table because of what's required: humility of heart and hospitality of spirit.

Here are some of the possible personalities who will show up at your table:

- **The Wall Hugger:** the mostly silent onlooker, an observer who rarely speaks
- **The Bulldozer:** the powerful personality who seeks to control as much as possible
- **The Control Freak:** the driven and impatient one who simply must get his or her way

- **The Consensus Builder:** the collegial elongator of every conversation
- **The Golden Retriever:** the most pleasant of all, smiling and supportive to a fault
- **The Passive Aggressor:** the hard-to-read person—until he or she becomes agitated and lashes out
- **The Peacemaker:** the one who values peace at any price but becomes anxious under pressure or conflict
- **The Strategic Thinker:** the one who inserts his or her business acumen into most topics
- **The Depressing Downer:** the critical, skeptical person, always looking at the dark side
- **The Peppermint Patti:** the super positive, upbeat, syrupy-to-the-max individual
- **The Holier Than Thou:** the charismatic personality replete with spiritual lingo
- **The Class Clown:** the one who makes light of even the most challenging situations
- **The Bottom Liner:** the person who counts the cost and always says it as it is
- **The Doubter:** the member who always needs physical proof and shuns faith
- **The Impatient:** the competitive, impetuous, short-fused finger-tapper

All voices are to be welcomed and appreciated at the discernment table. But frankly, not every voice is helpful and constructive. Since we all have a propensity to bring our less-redeemed selves to the table or circle of discernment, we build trust through our sincerity of heart and our willingness to own our own brokenness. When these things are brought to the team circle of communal hospitality, then the experience is rich and abundant. When they're absent, you may feel as if you are in a dark hole of despondency and dread.

As leaders of teams or groups, we need to remember that every door has a hinge and a lock. Knowing when the door is to be open and when it should be closed will make for a spiritually hospitable community. Discerning both is what makes leadership so challenging yet critically important. Only saying no and keeping the door shut will lead to frustration and stagnation. But if we only say yes and keep the door open, then no boundaries will be kept in place. Learning when and why to say no and to close the door to intruders, falsehood, or relational destruction brought to the table by the ill-informed or wolves in sheep's clothing are the hardest decisions of all. To never say no in our discernment is to invite chaos and confusion to the group.

A team leader protects the spirit of hospitality among the team. This person knows the value of hospitable presence, which molds and shapes groups into outstanding places to serve. When every member of the team knows they are valued and are treated with kindness and grace, they will exceed expectations together. It's far better to err on the side of generous hospitality than to be considered tight fisted or withholding of the blessing of God.

What Matters Most

Mary, Martha, and Lazarus inform us of the way forward. As does the early church in their season of Pentecost. Choosing the One Thing created their life-altering experiences with God. So it is for us today. Communal hospitality will only happen when we say yes to Jesus and sit at his feet in adoring worship and when we invite the Spirit to do his unique and unifying work in our midst. Without God we are left to our own human abilities. And we will continue to pursue strength, willpower, and dominance over others when our calling is to welcome weakness redeemed by Jesus, power hunger overturned by the Father's grace, and dominance upended by dependence on the Holy Spirit.

Some believe that strong leaders make swift decisions and act unilaterally. If not, you are considered ineffective and weak, slow, and set up to fail. You must act decisively! But when we follow Jesus and lean on the Spirit to act in his time and his way, then we learn otherwise. Living out a spiritually discerning life is opposite to what the world teaches us.

What, then, makes for a discerning and hospitable community, whether in a church, a team, a family, or a group?

Attention. Attentively notice God in the daily, the ordinary, and the particular. The spiritual discipline of noticing God is the focal point of our formation into Christlikeness. It's choosing the One Thing—God—by sitting at Jesus's feet on a consistent basis in our personal prayer closets. And it's encouraging our friends and partners in life and ministry to do likewise, recounting together our God-noticings as ongoing encouragements to remain steadfast and faithful.

Incarnation. Interact with one another where our life-on-life breathes life-with-hope. Our shared spiritual identity as Christ-followers leads us into incarnational service. Here, we point out to one another the life changes experienced by those who are walking in submission to the lordship of Jesus. There is no greater joy than to see, affirm, celebrate, and encourage such faithfulness. It's our primary calling as lovers of God and servants to others.

Confirmation. Ask the right questions and keep each other focused on what matters. Living in community and pursuing the discerning life together naturally fosters ongoing conversation about the spiritual life. Here, we inquire of God on matters great and small. As we pursue the will of God, we lean on the Word of God and prayerfully invite the way of God to be mapped out with great and growing clarity. We say yes to his initiatives.

Affirmation. Remain guided by principles that sustain our communion as God's children. In a spiritually discerning community, we affirm first and foremost the principle of gracious hospitality. As God has come to us and continues to make himself known to us in Jesus, so we are invited to put our trust in Jesus together. Remaining in a hospitable posture prayerfully and relationally, we contribute to the ongoing affirmations of transformation.

Recognition. Realize that God will lead us forward no matter the obstacles or distractions. The leading and guiding, sustaining and multiplying work of God will move on day by day, season by season, year to year, generation to generation. Nothing is impossible when God is in the center of our lives, and no objective is too lofty to embrace and complete when God's will is at stake.

Resurrection. Know with certainty that God is in the business of making all things new. There is nothing static about the with-God life. Every moment of each new day is replete with a freshness and delight that only comes from the Spirit. Learning how to attend to the eternal work of God in and among us is the joy of our worshiping community. It's where our faith comes alive and our testimony is secure. We belong to God and his eternal kingdom.

Making the choice to contribute positively to the communal hospitality of friends and family, church and team will advance the kingdom of God. Decorating the tree together is far more enjoyable than struggling with a task far greater than one can adequately handle. It's refreshingly life-giving when we choose to help each other create something special together, for this is the way of love, which always makes Jesus smile.

PRACTICING A PREFERENCE FOR GOD

The discerning life cannot be lived in isolation. We are created for community—as human, hurtful, and humiliating as it may be. Choosing to participate in our various communal experiences with a hospitable presence will make all the difference in the world. Consider your own circle of relationships: family, friends, church, team, small group. Where are you most fully present, engaged in transformational ways? How can you contribute most positively to help any of these groups become more hospitable with one another? In what ways is God inviting you to practice an even greater preference for him in the community where you reside, relate, worship, and serve? Jot down a few ideas in your prayer journal and invite God to do a new, renewing, and restorative work in you today.

Here are a few spiritual exercises to put into practice as you reflect on this chapter:

- **Hospitality:** How do you show hospitality to people who visit your home? What about showing hospitality to a stranger or a person in need? What are the motivations behind each of these acts of hospitality? What does a hospitable heart look like to you? How grateful are you when others offer gracious hospitality?

- **One Thing:** What would it take for God to truly be first place in your heart? Reflecting on the ways you show hospitality to others in your physical home, how might you show God hospitality in your own heart? How has God shown you hospitality recently?
- **Team Life:** Think of a team or group you're a part of today. How can you positively contribute to the vitality of your team or group? Does your definition of hospitality have anything to contribute to that team dynamic?

CHAPTER 6

Empathy

Spiritual Discernment is Contextual

"And this is my prayer: that your love may abound more and more in knowledge and depth of insight, so that you may be able to discern what is best and may be pure and blameless for the day of Christ, filled with the fruit of righteousness that comes through Jesus Christ—to the glory and praise of God."

Philippians 1:9–11

Although the principles of discernment are constant, the context for discernment is unique to each person or setting. How discernment manifests itself in a rural context differs significantly from that in an urban setting. Our culture, ethnicity, politics, geography, theology, denomination, family, neighborhood, municipality, education, access to resources, and more all play into the context of our wisdom and discernment. This is true for all individuals and groups living a discerning life. We need to learn how to enhance our empathy for the differences that surround us in our daily contexts.

The apostle Paul's prayer for the church in Philippi (above) was that their knowledge and depth of insight would lead to discernment and righteousness in their immediate context and forever in the lives and communities to follow, all for the glory and praise of God. He is praying for them to be compassionate and empathetic toward one another as together the church is in pursuit of God, who knows and loves them perfectly.

Today, we need the same wisdom from God that leads to righteousness in Christ, continuously contextualized in our time and setting. We yearn for clear understanding of our context so the biblical, relational, and practical principles of discernment can be appropriately and empathically applied. We always practice a preference for God in a wider context that must routinely be considered. Some aspects of our context remain static while others are bound to change. Robust discernment maintains a posture of awareness of and empathy for our various contexts.

Ruth and I live in a historic town: Lexington, Massachusetts, where the minutemen met the British militia at the start of the Revolutionary War. It's the location where the initial skirmish occurred that ushered in the war between the British and the colonists, which ultimately led to our country's independence.

Anything that's old and still standing and functioning is a marvel to consider. Our hometown values the sights that remain on the national historical register, including Buckman Tavern and the Hancock-Clarke House, which are curated by the Historical Society. We have a historic district commission, designed to preserve and develop the historical and archeological assets of the town and oversee the renovations—down to details such as paint color—of these homes and buildings.

Another big priority in our town is the Conservation Commission, serving to protect and preserve our natural resources and to acquire land for conservation and recreation purposes. This commission has done extraordinary work in creating a patchwork of forests, fields, and wetlands that provide protection for wildlife and habitation for plants. Land trails, walking paths, community gardens, open space, recreation facilities, and land management have added significantly to the quality of life for the residents.

When we were newcomers to our town, all of this commission and committee work seemed excessive. Town meeting is our governing structure, with a town manager overseeing the various entities of community life. The infrastructure is a web of complementary and often competing priorities. The context of town life in our hamlet west of Boston is complex; there's always more at stake than meets the eye.

We experienced some of this complexity when we endeavored to build a garage addition onto our quirky home. It was a huge discernment question for us. Because we live across the street from wetlands, we would need to get permission from more than the typical approval entities. A few more town committees and commissions had to be involved. The building and planning boards needed to approve revised plot and construction plans. But the Conservation Commission held the key to receiving final permission to build.

They levied the most extreme measures in order for us to remain in compliance with the Rivers Protection Act, overseen by our town and reinforced by our state. This required additional effort to avoid water runoff into any river near one's property. Specifically, water from rain that would land on the roof of our new garage was not allowed to flow down our driveway, across the street, and into the brook ("river") fifty feet further away.

To remain in compliance with the regulations of the Conservation Commission, we were to construct an elaborate rain runoff system that would lead the rainwater down from our new garage roof, into the gutters and downspouts, and underground through pipes that would end in a collection basin (a massive heavy duty plastic container) underneath our front yard. The rest of our home's roof was exempt—grandfathered in, if you will—from these requirements that were specific only to our new garage roof.

We had talked about adding a garage for the first few decades of living in our home. Given the expected engineering difficulties, complex construction, and burdensome financial realities associated with this project, we avoided it for years. But the better side of wisdom and our most recent discernment process of whether to stay in our home or move out of town led us to believe that it was worth the effort and expense. There was hope for recouping our investment when we eventually sell this home and relocate.

We knew remaining in our home for the foreseeable future meant it was time for a garage, which meant we needed to agree to all the town's expectations. We certainly weren't alone in navigating such guidelines and regulations. It's all a part of living in our complex community context. We were challenged by the need to empathically understand and accept our context.

We had to learn everything that would be expected of us in order to discern what was best at that time and for the future. We don't regret our decision one iota. For the first time in sixty years of my life, I am living in a home with a garage. The improvements we made outstrip the complexity and the expense of compliance. Remember the "snowmageddon" story from chapter 3? That was pre-garage, and it was the primary homeownership experience that tipped the discernment scale in favor of the garage project. Simply put, shoveling 108 inches of the white stuff off and around our cars, in addition to our drive and walkway, did me in. I felt my age.

As crazy as it may sound to those with limited information about our setting, it took us nearly a decade of discernment to come to our decision and complete the construction. Our four decades in this home, our personal financial situation, our prayerful consideration of what was at stake, and our local community context all impacted the outcome. Our community set the expectations, and our construction team completed the task. But we were the ones in the center of discernment every step of the way.

Context Matters

When we are in the midst of a discerning life, we continuously ask the Lord one fundamental question: How is God inviting me (us) to live for him today *in my (our) context* as I (we) practice a preference for God and notice God in everything? Our discernment is the ongoing clarification of that invitation, and our response is the result of how well we attend, notice, pray, consider, decide, and act. Hopefully the response will be faithful to God's invitation.

For that essential question to take root in our hearts, the soil of our soul needs to be prepared to receive whatever seeds God scatters into it. God is the initiator, and we are the active recipient. The soil is the context of our discerning life. What is the condition of the soil of your soul? To proceed with any attempt to grow something within the soil without first understanding and appreciating the receptivity of the soil is foolishness.

Jesus speaks directly to this query in the parable of the sower, the seed, and the soils. Or, as I prefer to call it, the parable of the soul. Matthew 13 is a treasure trove of Jesus's parables, beginning with this one. Sitting by a lake, large crowds accompany Jesus, eager to learn what he has to say.

Jesus's parables illustrate a style of teaching that prioritizes context by drawing on situations and settings that would be familiar to the hearers. Parables were about everyday things: gardens and vineyards, common objects and common tasks. He taught in parables so those who had eyes to see, ears to hear, and hearts to respond would have greater clarity about the kingdom of heaven. Jesus's top priority for all his followers was for them to enter and remain in the kingdom.

Explaining to his disciples why he teaches in parables, Jesus quotes the prophet Isaiah:

> You will be ever hearing but never understanding; you will be ever seeing but never perceiving. For this people's heart has become calloused; they hardly hear with their ears, and they have closed their eyes. Otherwise, they might see with their eyes, hear with their ears, understand with their hearts and turn, and I would heal them. (Matt. 13:14–15, quoting Isa. 6:9–10).

Jesus frequently used parables, simple stories of common life used to illustrate spiritual lessons of eternal life. He knew his audience well and realized that the best way in his immediate context to keep truths memorable was to tell stories that encapsulated important biblical teachings. His compassionate empathy toward his followers resulted in the receptivity of his teachings among those with hearts ready to receive his wisdom. Blessed were the eyes, ears, and hearts of all who received his presence and the profound words of comfort and challenge that came from his lips.

The parable of the sower goes like this:

> A farmer went out to sow his seed. As he was scattering the seed, some fell along the path, and the birds came and ate it up. Some fell on rocky places, where it did not have much soil. It sprang up quickly, because the soil was shallow. But when the sun came up, the plants were scorched, and they withered because they had no root. Other seed fell among thorns, which grew up and choked the plants. Still other seed fell on good soil, where it produced a crop—a hundred, sixty or thirty times what was sown. Whoever has ears, let him hear. (Matt. 13:3–9)

This parable is about receptivity-challenged soils: the hard path, the rocky place, and the thorny patch. None of the seeds scattered on them took root because the soil hindered their reception and growth. But not so for the good soil. There, the seed was received, and life was birthed and multiplied a hundred, sixty, or thirty times what was sown.

Jesus explains that the hard path represents people (not groups of people—each of us carries these types of soil in our hearts) who hear the message about the kingdom and do not understand it because the evil one comes and snatches the truth away. The rocky place refers to those who receive the word with fleeting joy. Without roots, their joy doesn't last long. "When trouble or persecution comes because of the word, they quickly fall away" (v. 21). The thorny patch refers to people who hear "the word, but the worries of this life and the deceitfulness of wealth choke the word, making it unfruitful" (v. 22). Finally, Jesus describes the soil we should emulate: "But the seed falling on good soil refers to someone who hears the word and understands it. This is the one who produces a crop, yielding a hundred, sixty or thirty times what was sown" (v. 23).

Jesus warns his disciples and followers to notice their own receptivity to the riveting teachings of the kingdom. The *hard path* of resistance becomes such because of the work of the enemy of our soul, snatching away what God wants to offer. On the *rocky place* of shallowness we are crushed by the weight of fear, depression, or discouragement. The *thorny patch* of wandering seduces us through the worries of this world and the lure of riches. This leads to apathy toward God and distance from him. Over time the soul among thorns gets choked and dies.

The invitation here is to be like humus, *good earth*, open to receive the seed of faith from the hand of the sower. In this soil resides a noble and good heart. Here, the word is heard, received, retained, and through perseverance it produces a fruitful crop. Humus is the fertile ground of humility, where deep within the soul there is openness and preparedness for the seeds of truth to reside.

Jesus invites his hearers into a context of humility and grace, receptivity and faithfulness. All other contexts would lead them into pathways of distraction, depression, and destruction. This is the wake-up call of this parable. What path are you on today?

The Soul: Sower, Seed, and Soil

The soul is the deepest place within us, where God and God alone seeks to reside. The soul is the essence of our personhood, the eternal part of our lives. God delights to inhabit our souls and transform us from the inside out. The soul is fed by the sower, who scatters the seed into its soil, regardless of how ready the soil may be. The sower is extravagant with his seed and delights to see it received so that it can bear eternal fruit for his glory.

We either have a penetrable, permeable, pliable soul that's open to the ongoing work of God or a closed-off soul, defending, protecting, hardening, deafening, and warding off the dynamic work of the Spirit. This is the one choice we have that's optional on a daily, moment-by-moment basis. Will I remain open to preferring God in every situation of my life? Or will I choose to stiff-arm God and keep him at bay, turning a deaf ear or a defiantly resistent heart against his desire to occupy my soul?

In the biblical text, the English translation of "soul" is used in parallel to the words *spirit* and *heart*. Each word works well to describe the soul, but the word *spirit* can be confused with the Holy Spirit, and the word *heart* can be used to describe both our vertical relationship with God (having a "heart" for God) and our horizontal relationship with others (expressing a "heart" for others). Thus, I prefer to use the word *soul* here, which is also dominant in the Scriptures, particularly in the Psalms.

A few notable examples throughout the Psalms for your reflection include:

- "The law of the LORD is perfect, refreshing the soul" (Ps. 19:7).
- "He refreshes my soul. He guides me along the right paths" (Ps. 23:3).
- "Then my soul will rejoice in the LORD and delight in his salvation" (Ps. 35:9).
- "As the deer pants for streams of water, so my soul pants for you, my God. My soul thirsts for God, for the living God. When can I go and meet with God?" (Ps. 42:1–2).

- "Why, my soul, are you downcast? Why so disturbed within me? Put your hope in God" (Pss. 42:11; 43:5).
- "Truly my soul finds rest in God; my salvation comes from him" (Ps. 62:1).
- "My soul yearns, even faints, for the courts of the LORD" (Ps. 84:2).
- "Praise the LORD, my soul; all my inmost being, praise his holy name. Praise the LORD, my soul, and forget not all his benefits" (Ps. 103:1–2).
- "Return to your rest, my soul, for the LORD has been good to you" (Ps. 116:7).
- "My soul faints with longing for your salvation, but I have put my hope in your word" (Ps. 119:81).
- "Praise the LORD. Praise the LORD, my soul" (Ps. 146:1).

Although he doesn't use the word *soul* here, that's exactly what Jesus urges his followers to consider, and his teaching is clear: The soil of the soul is the context of receptivity (or not). The seed is the Word of God. The sower is Jesus himself.

A *satisfied soul* knows we are dearly loved by God despite our deeply sinful tendencies. We are daily in the ongoing process of redemption, sanctification, and transformation.

A *fruitful soul* chooses to be humus in the hand of God, is ready to receive all that God seeks to offer, is open to being shaped by his presence, is willing to be grown up for his purposes, and is responsive to his ongoing transformation every step of the way.

A *contented soul* is forgiven, healed, redeemed, crowned with love and compassion, and satisfied with the good gifts that come from the hands of a good God.

All of these are wrapped up in the words of the psalmist as he praises the Lord from the depth of his soul and as he recounts the many blessings derived from how God cares for our souls.

> Praise the LORD, my soul;
>> all my inmost being, praise his holy name.
> Praise the LORD, my soul,
>> and forget not all his benefits—
> who forgives all your sins
>> and heals all your diseases,
> who redeems your life from the pit
>> and crowns you with love and compassion,
> who satisfies your desires with good things
>> so that your youth is renewed like the eagle's.
>> (Ps. 103:1–5)

The formative work of God in the heart and soul of a disciple of Jesus begins with our full receptivity to God's unfailing love. My definition of the spiritual formation process is this:

Spiritual formation is the lifelong journey of being transformed by the love of the Father into the image of Jesus by the gracious movement of God's Spirit, in order to live an abundant life of trust, rest, hope, and joy, accompanied by suffering and sorrow, for the sake of God's kingdom and glory and the fulfillment of his mission of grace, justice, mercy, and peace for all.

This journey with God lasts a lifetime. It commences with the transformation we experience daily as recipients of the Father's affection for us. He wants us to look and act and sound and feel more and more like Jesus every single day. This is only possible when we surrender our hearts into the fresh movement of the Holy Spirit. Then we experience the fullness of the abundant life, which includes rest, trust, hope, and joy, all within the mix of our sufferings and sorrows, which, as the psalmist declares, God delights to forgive, heal, and redeem. All of this is for his kingdom and glory and the fulfillment of God's mission here on earth. To this, our souls should cry out with a hearty, "Praise the Lord!"

The care of the soul is to be the disciple's daily priority, so that we remain pliable in the hands of God. God delights to satisfy our soul in our context. Are we open to receive his gifts of love? Simply put, the care of the SOUL includes the priorities of:

- *Spacious* times to meet with God—where we breathe deep and notice with clarity the presence and power, peace and provision of God
- *Open* attentiveness to hear from God—where we listen well and attend to our yearning for clarity and unity of spirit that comes only from God
- *Unhurried* receptivity to the love of God—where we prioritize uncluttered, unhindered, unhurried openness to the fresh move of God's Spirit
- *Lifestyle* of transformation in the service of God—where we commit to the advancement of the kingdom of heaven in our lifetime, our soul, and our contexts of life and service

In essence, the care of the soul includes a **S**pacious, **O**pen, **U**nhurried **L**ifestyle that leads us into practicing a preference for God.

As we've been saying all along, the discerning life is soul-centric. We discern God when we are as attentive as possible to his presence.

The only place where it's legitimate to be selfish in this world is in the care of one's soul and in healthy, life-giving efforts of self-care (physical, mental, relational, material, and missional). This requires saying no to other demands for our time and affection in order to say yes to spacious, open, unhurried, life-giving encounters with God that feed the soil of our souls, so that the Sower can continually plant seeds of truth to grow from within and cultivate in us a kingdom-oriented lifestyle in Jesus.

From the well-nurtured soil condition of our souls, we learn what it truly means to become selfless in the service of others. Without the nourished soul, we remain manipulative in our service to others. God invites us to continually come home to his loving embrace and open our souls to his deep and abiding work, fostered in the crevices of our souls. This is the seedbed for revival and renewal in our souls.

Our Cultural Context

The discerning life is hospitable to the movement of the Spirit in the depths of our souls. A hospitable soul knows the Sower intimately, welcomes the seeds of truth receptively, and enriches the soil of the soul with a generous spirit of grace. Soul hospitality is and remains the priority.

However, the cultural context in which we live is rarely a contributor to the softening of the soul and the redeeming work of the Spirit that Jesus speaks of with such clarity. We live in this world, surrounded by influences that often discourage and dishearten the soul work we cry out for as disciples of Jesus.

Our wider cultural contexts often do not promote a spiritually discerning lifestyle. Quite the contrary. It's never been secular culture's focus or design. But it certainly impacts our discernment. Noticing and understanding the cultural trends of our time and place is essential for discerning God and his way forward.

One of the most distressing aspects of contemporary culture is how we've powered over the weak and vulnerable, mistreated women, and oppressed people of color. Living a discerning life opens our eyes to a growing awareness of the systemic problems of our day. And it invites us to lean courageously and boldly into empathetic awareness of and advocacy for anyone who's been pushed aside because of their gender, race, ethnicity, or socioeconomic status.

We don't live in secular cultural contexts where the values we espouse as Christians are widely embraced and upheld. Instead, a lifestyle of following Jesus and his ways of justice, honor, and *shalom*—the rightful ordering of relationships and actions—is being threatened and thwarted at every turn. Thus, there is a need for discerning lives by the thousands to be raised up for such a time as this.

We find ourselves influenced by our secular culture in a variety of ways. We can be . . .

- *enveloped* by our culture, smothered by the fumes of secular thought; when it feels like the gospel we present is constantly being extinguished;
- *encroached* upon by our culture, where the evil motives of others threaten our livelihood and bring decay to our faith communities;
- *enraged* by our culture, standing in total opposition to the ways of this world, and discounting anything positive to be gained by it as Christians;

- *enlivened* by our culture, modeling ourselves in alignment with secular cultural norms and practices, ultimately watering down our faith and witness.

Regardless of our current response to the culture within which we reside, we cannot rely on our secular culture to embrace Christian character and virtues found in the Scriptures. When we allow secular culture to infiltrate our Christian communities, we are no longer distinguishable as a distinct or "peculiar" people of God. Instead, it's incumbent on us to look with thoughtful hearts on our cultural context, with a critical eye as necessary, and always with the empathy of Christ, who came to live and die so our world could be transformed by his gospel of grace, mercy, compassion, forgiveness, and love. In what ways is the wider culture impacting your life with God today?

For the good of the gospel, we can indeed find ourselves enriched by the challenges of living a discerning life within our wider cultural context. Daily we need to return home to the heart of God, where we are equipped by the Spirit to embrace the ways of Jesus together as his disciples. Here we find ourselves in a place of *distinction* from our culture, living within it but seeking to transform it from the inside out. We are called to be a God-fearing people living within the culture but not being absorbed or subdued by it in unhealthy, soul-wrenching ways.

As Christians, we seek to be salt and light in our dark and needy world, hoping to transform our wider culture with our peculiar presence as the beloved children of God, the church, "a chosen people, a royal priesthood, a holy nation, God's special possession" (1 Pet. 2:9). This may indeed require us to stand up against that which is in opposition to a biblical worldview and at other times stand in solidarity with that which upholds the truth of God's Word and contributes to *shalom*. Living a discerning life is one clear step in that challenging direction toward reformation and transformation.

Our Christian Context

Anyone who follows Jesus as Lord and Savior resides within the context of the worldwide Christian church, a denominational or theological or regional context, as well as a local church context. As individual believers and as faith-based congregations, we need to be aware of the influences of our wider culture in ever-increasing ways. But more importantly, we need to ask God to clarify for us how we are to live with distinction as disciples of Jesus and as transformers of the culture in which we reside in an unapologetically Christian way.

Living as faith communities within this worldly context allows us to grow in our relationships with God and one another. In our specific contexts, we have the privilege of making the discerning life our daily priority. Here we practice a preference for God together, noticing God, pointing him out to one another, over and over again. Our marriages and families, our ministries, churches, marketplaces, and communities can indeed be strikingly distinct with and by the ways of Jesus.

When this happens, we are no longer crushed by the culture of polarity, where we are forced to take sides. When we live as "us" versus "them," it becomes nearly impossible to be united in our approach. This is the fruit of the divisive political climate in which we reside today. Jesus, however, invites us to be one with him and friends with one another. When the people of God yearn for a culture of friendship, hospitality, discernment, and grace, their uniqueness is a wonder to behold.

What will it take for us to become transformational within our Christian context? We need formational leaders who embrace discernment as a way of life and are humble enough to attend to the voice and movement of God's Spirit. All the while, the winds and storms of our wider culture bombard us with temptation to become more bullish in our posture. Summarily, what we need more than anything is to love and honor one another above ourselves by relinquishing our personal demands and empowering others rather than powering over them.

Over the past 500 years since the Protestant Reformation, our various faith movements have multiplied. More than 45,000 Protestant denominations and networks have emerged to date. We splinter, divide, and multiply mostly because of theological conviction that leads to practical application. When we differ with one another, we often depart and start something new. This has been the way of the "people of protest" for hundreds of years. Therefore, knowledge of one's own faith context helps to navigate the discerning life in community. To ignore this reality is ultimately to our detriment.

The global church is diverse in every significant way: theologically, relationally, ethnically, geographically. It's wide and long. Within the global church are theological or denominational networks where most churches reside. But when it comes to being a local church, we need to pay attention to our theological beliefs, leadership structures, missional priorities, evangelistic fervor, worship styles, discipleship of all ages, and fellowship among the flock. At Leadership Transformations, we encourage leaders to listen to their congregations and communities, and have an excellent tool for doing so (CHAT: Church Health Assessment Tool).[1]

There is always a better way than feeding the tensions that divide us, one which leads others into a more redemptive life together in Jesus. This begins when we are compassionately empathetic toward one another as Christ followers, despite our differences and united around that which matters most – the love of God, Father, Son, and Holy Spirit. When the voices all around us are shouting at us to embrace and be enthralled by the secular culture, we must seek a creative alternative together as the people of God. Perhaps it's time for us to be awakened by our reality, listen to the exhortations of our Lord, and embrace a new way of living, loving, and serving in his name.

Our Group Context

Our group context—our marriage and family life, our ministry team,[2] our small group, our elder board—is where we reside on a daily or semi-regular basis. Understanding the nuances of our group is helpful for those seeking to live a discerning life. We need to know our group well, identify the key defining markers of our context, and work well within our group to impact prayerful attentiveness and discernment-based transformation.

Our immediate context will either promote or deny the priority of discernment. Some contexts are easier to practice a preference for God in than others. Creating a healthy context for meaningful relationships and fruitful mission is the goal. But the barriers to a lifestyle of discernment within group contexts are pretty common:

- *Distraction.* When the effort of the group is all-consuming and there's no time given for cultivating a life of discerning God together.

- *Disharmony.* When the group is filled with unresolved tension and there's little attention given to grace, mercy, compassion, forgiveness, and reconciliation.
- *Disillusionment.* When the value of the group is diminished and there's less and less interest in making necessary changes from the way it's always been.
- *Disinterest.* When the passion of the group is waning and there are fewer and fewer reasons to celebrate the impact of the mission.
- *Dismay.* When the soul of the group is dying and there's diminishing interest in keeping things going and minimal desire for times together.

The ways in which we spend time with our groups, as well as the manner in which these groups are facilitated, are also important to consider. Charles Olsen and Danny Morris in their helpful book, *Discerning God's Will Together*,[3] help us understand the most common decision-making cultures within our church and ministry groups.

Olsen and Morris outline several leadership contexts that contribute to the culture of our groups. Many of these are represented in today's Christian community, some are rooted in our religious traditions, and others have been imported from education, business, social science, politics, or business. Notice below how they are similar yet distinct in approach.

Which of the following are you most familiar with, and which do you find most fruitful, especially when promoting the practice of a preference for God?

1. *Autocratic.* The group is led by the strongest voice with unchallenged power.

2. *Conciliar.* Leaders are elected or appointed, and they deliberate and decide as equals.

3. *Consensus.* The group patiently deliberates to a conclusion everyone can support.

4. *Debate.* The group follows an ancient classical debate format of for/against followed by resolution.

5. *Delegation.* A smaller group is charged with collaboration and implementation of decisions.

6. *Democratic.* The people are trusted to make best-informed decisions.

7. *Emotional.* The group makes decisions based on feelings alone.

8. *Mystical.* The group believes they act on direct knowledge of God and God's ways, prompted by inner light.

9. *Lottery.* The group casts lots in order to make choices or determine outcomes.

10. *Mediation.* Decisions grow out of conflict resolution.

11. *Parliamentary.* The group follows a well-developed process based on rules and procedures.

12. *Political.* Decisions are made in the interplay of influence and pressure from others.

13. *Strategic planning.* Success is based on goals, objectives, tactics, and time frames.

Many of these cultures can exist in any group context: family, church, ministry, or marketplace. Taking time to note the group context helps one engage with a discerning presence and priority. Inviting others into the discerning life will be either easy or challenging depending on the ways in which such a life together is presented and received.

Those who seek to live a discerning life in the context of their faith community context often stand against the current group context. Taking the time to influence a new way of living together as brothers and sisters in Christ requires patience and perseverance. This will not happen overnight.

It's challenging, if not impossible, to pour new wine into old wineskins. It's easier to just start fresh: new wine into new wineskins. But that's not always our reality. We need to learn how to grow together in our group contexts and to honor one another above ourselves every step of the way. How do we do so?

First, by listening to one another's stories, placing value on each other by appreciating the presence of another in our group. We all live complex lives with histories that matter.

Second, by empathizing with one another's joy and celebration, pain and heartache. We rejoice with those who rejoice and weep with those who weep.

Third, by verbally affirming the image of God in one another and celebrating the beautiful creation God is bringing to abundant life in our midst. We respect and honor one another.

Fourth, through reconciliation and any need for confession, forgiveness, grace, mercy, and peace. Learn to say redemptive phrases such as "I'm sorry," "I was wrong," "Please forgive me," and "I love you." Imagine how different our world would look if these were continually on our lips.

Know with clarity that our group context begins and continues onward with fresh awareness of the unique stories of each member. Start each meeting with questions of interest, love, and concern to help break the ice and keep the group on a level field of mutuality and trust. Ask each other, "How is it with your soul today?" or "Where have you noticed God recently?" or "What is your latest disappointment or joy that you'd be willing to share?" Inquire about individual group members' personal journeys to greatly enhance the discerning presence and context your group shares. To ignore such stories will keep your group in a more functional role, when the group could accomplish great things together from the central priority of healthy relationships around the circle. Is that your group's earnest desire?

By praying for wisdom and insight, courage and grace, we will be guided, sustained, and empowered to become God-centered friends who honor Jesus by honoring one another. Choose to be a reconciling influence in each of your various groups. This will ultimately lead to the discerning way of life we yearn for in Christ.

Our Personal Context

Our personal lives are the most obvious place to maintain the priority of a discerning life, but they are often the most neglected.

Your story matters? Taking stock of your personal identity is a great starting point. Prayerfully acknowledge the main chapters of your ongoing story development. Note the ways in which you've been significantly influenced over the years by crafting a personal autobiography and considering your personal co-cultures. These will help you recognize the formation of your true identity in Christ as well as the false claims on our character development over the years.

You can craft a *personal and spiritual autobiography* on your own, regardless of whether it's ever shared with others. It's designed to provide you with an opportunity to reflect deeply on your life to date. As you write, consider the various chapters of your life, the specific experiences that have shaped you to date, the themes that have defined you, the core beliefs and practices that provide nourishment and growth, and the relationships that God has given to you that have either positively or negatively impacted the development of your identity, character, and vocation.

Writing an autobiography takes effort and time. It's not something you can whip up overnight. Choose a season, a retreat, or even a full day set apart for this task. Consider organizing it into "chapters" of a book, starting with family of origin, childhood memories, youth and young adult, and adulthood. Or you might organize it into "seasons" and note the times in your life when it felt like you were in winter, spring, summer, or fall, with parallels to the natural seasons of creation. Or consider your awareness of God—his presence, his power, his protection, and perhaps even times when you sensed his absence. Or organize it by highlights, heroes, hurts, and hurdles. Perhaps you aren't inclined to writing and prefer something more creative; if so, you could draw out your autobiography using color, design, photos, images, or timelines, charts, graphs, and more.

We can also look at our lives through the lens of our *co-cultures*. Rather than noting them as "sub-cultures" (which assumes some are inferior or superior to others), it's best to call them co-cultures, seeing our lives alongside others as equals rather than above or below them. We've done this at LTI of late and found it to be a helpful exercise for both self-awareness and enhancing group unity. In noting our co-cultures, we discover transformational insights about who we are and how we've been shaped by others. You can begin by noting the particulars of your personal story development through the lens of the following:

- Gender and marital status
- Race and ethnicity

- Socioeconomic situation
- Educational pursuits
- Family system and structure
- Geography—home and travels
- Health status
- Hobbies and interests
- Vocational expertise
- Position on various topics
- Theological convictions
- Social media and technology preferences
- News outlets watched
- Community life and service
- Church involvement

Considering your co-cultures will enhance your ability to practice a preference for God. Take time to listen to others describe their co-cultures as well. This will expand your ability to recognize and honor the differences and similarities you share with those in your wider contexts of life and service to others. Moreover, it will lead to deeper compassion and empathy among your friends and community.

When we grow in self-awareness through tools like a spiritual autobiography, our co-cultural experiences, and others such as the Enneagram, Myers-Briggs, and Strengths Finder, we see with greater clarity how our immediate personal context will either promote or deny the priority of discernment. We bring our true selves into any and all group experiences. Nothing of us is left outside the group context, and it's far better for individuals and groups large and small to recognize this reality.

Showing earnest interest and compassionate concern for one

another's stories is essential to the quality of group life. Listen up. Listen in. Listen first. Listen always.

By empathically considering our cultural, Christian, group, and individual contexts, we discover the joys and challenges we face each and every day. God knows how difficult it will be for us to navigate each of these contexts as we seek to live a discerning life.

What, therefore, are you empathetic toward within each context? What do you long for, desire, and hope to see occur in each? What is God inviting you to consider as you engage compassionately in each context as one of God's ambassadors of grace? Pay close attention to the longings of your heart, identify them, and pray into them. This will hopefully lead to the fulfillment of each yearning in your lifetime and for generations to come.

Choose compassion and empathy always. Your personal story matters. Our collective story matters. Our contextual story matters. God's story matters most of all.

PRACTICING A PREFERENCE FOR GOD

In this chapter, we have been invited to consider the state of our souls within the contexts of our secular culture, our Christian community, our various groups, and our personal lives. Jesus's teaching on the parable of the soul reminds us that our hearts impact our context, whether on the hard path, rocky place, thorny patch, or in good soil. God is generously scattering the seeds of his truth regardless of the context, and it's our responsibility to help create humus for the seeds to be more readily received.

All of our contexts bring about the same yearning: for more of God's active presence to be noticed, celebrated, and affirmed in our midst. But we need to learn how to pay attention to God and one another, knowing that all of our various contexts and our personal stories are in need of ongoing discernment of his presence, power, and peace. In community, we strive to create a discerning culture within our contexts. This will only occur as we remain mindful of God, attuned to his empowering presence together.

Here are a few spiritual exercises to put into practice as you reflect on this chapter:

- **Context:** What context of yours is most hurting today and how will you be fully present to it? Do you believe Christ can transform that culture, as hurt as it is? Why or why not? What will your role be in that contextual transformation?
- **Co-cultures:** List your personal co-cultures. Note the ways in which your life is enriched as a result of these cultures. Share your co-cultures with a friend or trusted group. Listen attentively and empathically as others share theirs with you.
- **Autobiography:** Take a first step toward writing your spiritual autobiography. Think about how you might organize it—in chapters; seasons; or highlights, heroes, hurts, and hurdles? Or would you prefer to take a more visual approach—a timeline, collage, picture album, or something else?

CHAPTER 7

Focus

Spiritual Discernment Is Intentional

"Therefore, I urge you, brothers and sisters, in view of God's mercy, to offer your bodies as a living sacrifice, holy and pleasing to God—this is your true and proper worship. Do not conform to the pattern of this world, but be transformed by the renewing of your mind. Then you will be able to test and approve what God's will is—his good, pleasing and perfect will."

Romans 12:1–2

L iving a discerning life is an intentional choice of the will. It's a new awareness of the present that is essential for understanding the past and the future. It's a way of being tested in the daily fray of a full to overflowing life, when it's all too tempting to want to control all of our decisions, directions, inclinations, and outcomes.

Eugene Peterson paraphrases Romans 12:1–2 in *The Message* as follows:

So here's what I want you to do, God helping you: Take your everyday, ordinary life—your sleeping, eating, going-to-work, and walking-around life—and place it before God as an offering. Embracing what God does for you is the best thing you can do for him. Don't become so well-adjusted to your culture that you fit into it without even thinking. Instead, fix your attention on God. You'll be changed from the inside out. Readily recognize what he wants from you, and quickly respond to it. Unlike the culture around you, always dragging you down to its level of immaturity, God brings the best out of you, develops well-formed maturity in you.

Take your everyday, ordinary life. Place it before God. Embrace what God does for you. Fix your attention on God. You'll be changed from the inside out. Recognize what he wants. Respond.

That's the discerning life in summary.

And in keeping with our house-care motif, we are invited to do the same with our home: place it before God, recognize what's calling for attention, and respond. Regardless of how long you've lived there, home care never ends. Whether it's the daily grind of household chores or the desire to upgrade, fix, or replace, our homes always call for our attention.

Throughout our many years in our home, a variety of needs have called out for our response. As we were able, we would either address these things or leave them alone until a more appropriate time to reconsider. I like to categorize the house-care issues we've faced based on their level of scope and need:

Level 1: Chores. These are the day-to-day disciplines and necessities of house care, such as keeping the kitchen and bathroom clean, changing and laundering sheets and towels, dusting, scrubbing, vacuuming, mowing, digging, planting, and trimming.

Level 2: Maintenance. Included here are the small repairs and general upkeep of the home, like fixing a leaking faucet, strengthening a wobbly chair, gluing a splintered drawer, and repairing broken appliances. These seem like endless tasks calling for our attention.

Level 3: Emergencies. Here are the unexpected projects that emerge unpredictably in our house care and require immediate attention, such as vacuuming a flooding basement, replacing a leaking water heater, repairing rotting wood due to an ant infestation, and repairing hail or wind damage.

Level 4: Redecorating. This is when the restorative, creative house-care desires emerge. For example, this includes applying a fresh coat of paint, choosing wallpaper to accent the look of a room, selecting and hanging artwork, purchasing new furnishings, and buying throw pillows and accessories.

Level 5: Upgrading. These include somewhat larger projects chosen or needed for longer-term house care, such as pulling up carpet and replacing it with hardwood floors, upgrading heating and air-conditioning systems to meet current standards, purchasing new appliances, and replanting shrubbery.

Level 6: Renovating. This level requires the most energy and usually the biggest budget because it involves totally redoing major portions of your structures that lead to more radical house care. It includes building an addition, adding a bathroom, reconstructing the deck, digging up and planting a whole new garden, and transforming the design and look of all or part of the house.

In our quirky home, we've performed all levels of house care over the years. It simply never ends. It might feel like an endless money pit, but it's better to see these projects as a series of investments in your greatest earthly asset. To be a wise steward of the place you call home, regardless of how simple or complex it may be, is to treat your home with prayerful, careful, and discerning care.

Living in our homes and caring for them in both small and large ways can be paralleled to the care and nurture of our own bodies, minds, hearts, and souls. Some days life requires just simple maintenance. Other days we deal with an emergency. Still other seasons require the effort and resources to do a total renovation from the inside out.

So it is with our entire Christian life and our role in serving the needs of others in our church and community. Our goal is to live a discerning life amidst the scope of daily demands, noting when a more routine effort is required, versus something more dramatic in breadth and depth.

What is the level of need in your soul today? Let's chart our spiritual needs onto a similar series of scope-and-need-based levels:

Level 1: Chores. Do you need to pay greater attention to your daily spiritual practices?

Level 2: Maintenance. Is it time for some seasonal cleansing and maintenance, perhaps engaging prayerfully in an *Examen* of the past few months?

Level 3: Emergencies. Do you need to attend to an emergency in your soul, where you have been jolted by recent circumstances?

Level 4: Redecorating. Are you noticing the need to reconfigure or restore certain priorities?

Level 5: Upgrading. Should you consider upgrading what's seemed tired or passé about your prayer life?

Level 6: Renovating. Are you in need of a total renovation of your heart, changing the course of your spiritual life in major ways?

Perhaps as you attend to your house needs and lean intentionally into the appropriate level of care, even today there might be something to notice about the care and nurture of your soul. The discerning life is one of intentionality, which is fed and fostered by attentiveness.

The Intentionality of Jesus

Turning our focus back to Jesus, it's remarkable to consider the attentive and intentional way Jesus lived his earthly life and how he came alongside his beloved friends and followers regardless of the condition of the houses of their souls. From the earliest of days, he confounded the religious leaders with his wisdom, insight, and ministry in their midst. Their spiritual houses were an absolute train wreck, but they simply refused his entry.

His was a fruitful three years of ministry to the hurting, the outcast, the hungry, the abandoned, the thirsty, the lonely, and all who were lacking a home for their heart. He offered the abundant life to all who heard his voice and came in contact with him. Many responded with openness and receptivity, knowing he would enter their messy houses and bring order out of their internal chaos.

He did this up to the very end, even as he was rejected by his followers. He was put on trial for his humility. He suffered at the hands of those who were confused. He was tormented by the crowds who fed the insurrection. Even to those who planned his ultimate and humiliating demise, he remained true to his posture of grace. Many received his blessing, his empowering presence, and his gift of unmerited favor and transformational salvation.

It was all and always for love's sake. Regardless of the level of

147

approval or disapproval he experienced by others, he held fast to his daily priorities: forgive, restore, renew. He offered the gift of salvation and ushered in the kingdom of God.

He knew his destiny from the beginning. His intimate fellowship with the Father confirmed it repeatedly. His was the way of the cross. He humbly received by emptying himself of all that human beings think matter most and expressed love every single day of his life, as recorded for us in the Gospel record.

His faithful life was a discerning life, even on the cross. His outstretched arms of love were the demonstration of his complete submission.

The seven final words of Jesus are filled with attentiveness and intentionality. There was no question about the purpose for which he suffered and experienced such a horrific death. He knew it and articulated it even amidst the most severe suffering.

Consider the power of each of the following seven last words of Jesus as we continue to learn how to heed his voice and respond like him. Yes, even in the crucible of our own lives, often held captive by the challenging conditions we face, nothing we suffer compares to what Jesus endured, and thus we can find solace in his final words.

1. *Jesus speaks to the Father.* He grants forgiveness to his executors and his enemies. Jesus says, "Father, forgive them, for they do not know what they are doing" (Luke 23:34). In the midst of his excruciating suffering, Jesus focuses on others rather than himself. Here we see the nature of his love, unconditional and divine.

2. *Jesus speaks to the criminal on the cross.* He offers forgiveness and salvation to the repentant. "Truly I tell you, today you will be with me in paradise" (Luke 23:43). One of the

criminals who is crucified with Christ had recognized who Jesus was and expressed faith in him as his Savior. Here we see God's grace poured out through faith, as Jesus assured the dying man of his forgiveness and eternal salvation.

3. *Jesus speaks to Mary and John.* His care for his beloved ones is expressed with loving intimacy. "When Jesus saw his mother there, and the disciple whom he loved standing nearby, he said to her, 'Woman, here is your son,' and to the disciple, 'Here is your mother'" (John 19:26–27). Jesus, looking down from the cross, is filled with the concerns of a son for the earthly needs of his mother. None of his brothers are there to care for her, so he gives this task to the beloved disciple, John.

4. *Jesus cries out to the Father.* He expresses profound honesty to his Father. "About three in the afternoon Jesus cried out in a loud voice, *'Eli, Eli, lema sabachthani?'* (which means, 'My God, my God, why have you forsaken me?')" (Matt. 27:46). In the darkest hour of his suffering, Jesus cries out the opening words of Psalm 22. And although much has been suggested regarding the meaning of this phrase, his agony is apparent as he expresses a feeling of separation from God, bearing the full weight of our sin. He is attentive to his own suffering.

5. *Jesus is thirsty.* His humanness is being transformed by his divinity. "Later, knowing that everything had now been finished, and so that Scripture would be fulfilled, Jesus said, 'I am thirsty'" (John 19:28). Jesus refused the initial drink of vinegar, gall, and myrrh that was offered to alleviate his suffering (Matt. 27:34; Mark 15:23). But here, several hours later, we see Jesus fulfilling the messianic prophecy found in Psalm 69:21. He is fully aware of his suffering.

6. *It is finished.* His pre-resurrection life on earth is completed. He says, "It is finished." (John 19:30). Jesus knows he is suffering the crucifixion for a purpose. Earlier, in John 10:18, he had said of his life, "No one takes it from me, but I lay it down of my own accord. I have authority to lay it down and authority to take it up again. This command I received from my Father." The three words he utters from the cross—"It is finished"—are packed with meaning. Not only is his earthly ministry finished, not only his suffering and death, not only his payment for sin and redemption for the world, but also—and most importantly—his final act of obedience is complete. The Scriptures have been fulfilled with unparalleled intentionality.

7. *Jesus's final words.* His full submission, obedience, and glorification is declared. "Jesus called out with a loud voice, 'Father, into your hands I commit my spirit.' When he had said this, he breathed his last" (Luke 23:46). Here Jesus closes with the words of Psalm 31:5, speaking directly to the Father. Jesus enters death in the same way he lived each day of his life, offering up his life as the perfect sacrifice and placing himself in God's hands. His loving obedience opens the door to eternal life for all.

In the final words of Jesus from the cross, his soul care goes from the forgiveness of his adversaries and the repentant, to the compassionate care for his mother, to his own heart cries toward the heavenly Father. His final words are of total and complete submission, similar to the "not my will, but yours be done" he prayed in anguish on the Mount of Olives prior to his arrest (Luke 22:42). They are also reminiscent of the prayer he taught his disciples to pray many months prior: "Your will be done, on earth as it is in heaven" (Matt. 6:10).

His is a discerning life to the very end. Jesus models for us the full submission he invites us to consider for ourselves.

Reverential Indifference

The holy and reverential obedience of Jesus is demonstrated for all who follow him in his act of complete submission on the cross. Most of us don't like to keep Jesus on the cross in our minds for very long. We generally prefer to talk about his triumphant resurrection than to ponder the significance of his suffering. We choose to focus more on the empty tomb than on the suffering that led him there.

But the contemplative in us calls for a more concerted reflection on the cruciform nature of his obedience—and ours. Ironically, this starts with our openness to the deeper life, marked by our awakening to the presence and power of God. Knowing this life will be filled with sorrow and suffering, a discerning life clings first to the suffering Christ who willingly offered his life for the sake of ours.

This requires that we hold life with a much looser grip. When we allow God to reign ever more supreme in our heart and soul, our mind and strength, we grow in faith. Jesus was full of trust in the Father's word, will, and way of living. His was a life of gracious contentment, deep humility, contagious grace, and heightened hope. He came to offer peace to all who called him "Lord." He offers the same to us as his discerning followers.

This requires a willingness to let go of the reins of a self-empowered life and let God carry you forward into a God-empowered life. Choosing to "let go and let God" is the way of holy indifference, caring deeply about a life of intentional obedience that grows out of an ever-deepening awareness of the powerful presence of God.

As in the song by Horatio Spafford (1876), the affirmation "It is well with my soul" is the result of one's holy indifference. Regardless of the circumstances and situations of life, "When peace like a river attendeth my way, when sorrows like sea billows roll; whatever my lot, Thou hast taught me to say, 'It is well, it is well with my soul.'" Pay attention to your soul and notice if you are grasping, clinging, or anxious. Or are you open-hearted, peaceful, and trusting? The latter is the fruit of reverential indifference, the result of a life with growing awareness of God and his myriad gifts of grace, mercy, joy, and peace.

As we raised our children in our quirky home, we reminded them every day of two important words for life, abbreviated "O.K.": obedience and kindness. We knew they would be influenced by others to respond protectively, reactively, and thoughtlessly amid the stresses they faced. We wanted something much bigger for them. But we knew it would require a daily decision to live counterculturally as people seeking to follow Jesus more obediently. And we hoped their lifestyle would embody kindness to all who crossed their path.

The way of Jesus is our continual objective. But it takes daily practice to live life open-handedly in submission to the Father, to learn how to breathe deep, receive humbly, release indiscriminately, and respond intentionally in the power of the Spirt. The slow and daily drip, drip, drip of steady faithfulness is what produces a life that grows in the discerning of God's remarkable presence, power, protection, and peace.

Intentionality in Community

Choosing to live a discerning life begins with a mind and heart change, especially when we seek to live this way together in community. Living in a discerning posture toward God and one another runs counter to the ways of the world. Therefore, we need the reinforcement of such ideals with family and friends who share our conviction. How is it possible for this to occur, when most of us have been living a non-discerning life of inattentiveness for so long?

A slow shift toward a discerning community can indeed take place if everyone on the team or in the group is open to consider this new way of being present to God and one another. Creating such a community takes time, but the transformation it produces is noticeable, beautiful, insightful, and wonderful. Going back to a pseudo-community experience simply won't suffice.

Here are a few suggestions for individuals and groups to prayerfully consider.

1. Noticing God

Where do we see God expressing his unconditional love toward us?

God makes himself readily accessible to us in the biblical text, in the created world, in our personal lives, in our prayers, and in our shared experiences of worship, fellowship, and witness. We just need to train our eyes to see, ears to hear, and hearts to notice God.

Point God out as we reflect on the Scriptures and listen for his gentle voice of love speaking to us in our prayer closet or around the discernment table. Celebrate him as we walk along the shoreline or traverse a hillside. See him in the eyes of one who's joyful or tearful. Notice him when our hearts are aflame with joy in worship, prayer, Bible study, fellowship, or in service to others in need. Attend to his activity in our lives as we practice *Examen*.

God is everywhere. He is always active; he is there to be noticed, appreciated, celebrated, and thanked. Taking the time to point him out requires us to slow down long enough to hop off the bullet train of our lives and savor his gracious presence, his abiding love, his thoughtful grace, and his enduring peace. Our God-sightings are the beginning, middle, and end of our noticing. Add this to your routines and watch how your souls are fed.

2. Releasing Our Attachments

What is standing in the way of you and God?

Sometimes we become attached in an unhealthy way to an idea, a desire, or a person that limits our freedom to respond to God's invitation in our lives. For example:

- People might be overly attached to a desire for wealth, success, or power in a way that interferes with their ability to open themselves to God's invitation (e.g., the rich young man in Mark 10:17–22).
- People might become overly attached to another person in a way that clouds their judgment (e.g., David's obsession with Bathsheba in 2 Samuel 11).
- People can be overly attached to things and to the acquisition of material possessions in a way that causes them to lose their focus on living for God.
- People can become inordinately attached to being popular or being liked by another person or group of people, so much so that their decision-making is clouded by how this other person or group might perceive the choice.
- People may be attached to a certain idea or philosophy and miss out on expanding their knowledge or insight, or cling to an attitude that may come across as needing to be right, strong, central, or in control.

Basically, an attachment becomes disordered and unhealthy when we convince ourselves that we *must* have this person or thing to be happy, and we set our minds on attaining it and holding onto it at all costs. As a result, the person, thing, or desire begins to control our choices, and we lose the freedom to answer God's call when it comes because we are so overly consumed with our attachment.

Learning how to let go or detach from these attachments is absolutely necessary in order to reattach to the living God—yes, even if they are good things. Releasing the fullness of our attachments is profitable for the soul. A healthy dependence on God's Spirit to define and refine you as an individual and as a group will lead you into a posture of releasing. Letting go is what defines most of our spirituality and our maturity. Clinging to, holding firm, or clenching selfishly is a damaging-to-the-soul way of being present to others, God, and ourselves as beloved disciples of Jesus.

3. Holy Indifference

What is God inviting you to hold more open-handedly?

Reordering our affections opens us to the life transformation exhibited most clearly in the priority of remaining open-handed in all things. Even on the cross, Jesus cared for the needs of others. In his suffering, he offered the abundant life with generous hospitality and tons of grace. "Not my will, but yours be done" (Luke 22:42), "What you meant for evil God meant for good" (paraphrase of Gen. 50:20), and "Let go and let God" define the posture of holy indifference. In the same way as Jesus, we are invited to live with a more "care-less" attitude. We shouldn't go so far as to become careless or carefree, but we must become far more care-full in our desire to hold things (people, possessions, attitudes, actions) more loosely and with a much lighter grip (if any).

Caring less means that we are actually caring more appropriately. When we care more appropriately, we are doing so as . . .

- *good listeners*, receiving words and sentiments without needing to correct, convince, compare, or even cajole.
- *good ponderers*, holding what we're hearing with prayerfulness and grace.
- *good discerners*, noticing what's happening in, through, and all around the circumstance.
- *good servants*, offering ourselves to another in ways that feed and foster healthy growth and maturity in Christ.

Learn how to live more open-handedly to discover the joy of dying to self in order for another to flourish.

4. Decision-Making

What decisions do you need to act on, hold, or discern together?

St. Ignatius of Loyola (1491–1556), in his paramount work on discernment, talks about how discernment happens in three main time frames: The First Time, The Second Time, and The Third Time.[1] I've modernized and summarized these three as follows.

Obvious Time. This is when it's apparent beyond a shadow of a doubt what needs to be done. It's crystal clear what the decision is before us. If there's a fire in the building, our next step is obvious: find the nearest exit and get out fast. This is like the blinding light in the eyes of Saul when he fell to the ground on the road to Damascus, put his trust in God, and was converted from hater of the church to its champion. In this story, God revealed himself, his word, and his ways without any mystery or uncertainty. It was obvious and revelatory.

Many daily discernments are obvious and agreed on without any debate or reconsideration. At these times, we don't question the logic or meaning behind the action. We know it's simply the right thing to do, and we move forward with intentionality. Most of the time, we don't even notice how frequent this discernment is; it happens naturally, organically, and rhythmically all the time. Noticing these obvious discernments will aid in your pursuit of a discerning life.

Deliberating Time. This is when we have options in front of us to discover and then discern the best way forward, requiring new ways of prayerfulness, consideration, and determination. In our personal lives and in our collective community experiences, we seek to discern God's choice for us, but his will and his way forward are not always as clear as we'd prefer. When faced with various options, we tend to look at our decisions from a human perspective: weigh the pros and cons and come up with the best solution.

In all times of spiritual discernment and decision-making, we are invited to prayerfully choose God's intentions for us. This requires hearts that are inclined in God's direction, practicing a preference for him in all matters great and small, at all times and in every season of life. From that prayerful posture we can look at new ways of discerning God, his Word, his will, and his way. (That is the topic we will discuss in chapter 8. There we will review a trustworthy deliberative process that has worked for centuries and is still relevant today.)

Waiting Time. This is when it's not at all obvious which way to go, and the best option is simply to wait. Think of this time like a sailboat out on the lake with no wind. There's always the option to put in the oars and begin to row with human strength and fortitude or to turn on the outboard motor and putter forward by the strength of a mechanical device.

But God might be inviting you to slow everything down to wait for the fresh wind of God's Spirit. This is usually the toughest time of discernment, as it requires a willingness to do nothing and simply wait. This can be productive time for individuals and groups to learn how to trust instead of always leaning on human strength and wisdom. Still, it's also a difficult posture to embrace, since we are all most closely affiliated with the decide-and-do model that's espoused nearly everywhere in our fast-paced world.

5. Consolation and Desolation

Which options seem most hopeful and which appear more harmful?

St. Ignatius also described the interior movements we will undoubtedly experience throughout our discerning life, especially during times of specific discernment. This is most relevant when multiple options are in front of us and we are looking at every angle of discernment.

The movement of *consolation* is best described using words such as light, peace, energy, life, spaciousness, freedom, joy, hope, faith, trust, God's presence—maybe even risk, but also safety.

In order to notice consolation, my colleague Susan Currie encourages us ask questions such as:

- What about this option seems most life-giving?
- What about this option appears most light-filled?
- Is there energy and passion expressed in this option?
- Does it seem right to us?
- If we head in this direction, are we focusing our attention on staying attuned to the love of God, the affection of Christ, and the movement of the Spirit?

If you feel a sense of joy and amen, encouragement and hope, and if the possibility before you provides feelings of equilibrium and deeper communion with God, then the invitation in consolation is to find peace, joy, faith, and love as a result.

It's important, however, to realize that in discernment we may be facing a difficult choice or challenge and still have a deep sense of consolation. This can be confirmation from God that the hard step is the right step. Sometimes a choice doesn't make sense to family or friends, but we still feel consolation about the choice and that gives us courage to move forward.

At times the enemy of our souls can give us a false sense of consolation, so we always have to be careful to discern whether the consolation we feel is from God or from the enemy. For example, a person having an affair outside of marriage may feel lots of consolation: *This person really understands me. We are true soul mates. How can something that feels so right be wrong?* This is not the consolation that comes from God, because the choice violates a previous commitment made to a spouse. Even though consolation teaches us to pay attention to our emotions, we need to guard against being tricked by them.

The movement of *desolation* is best described by words such as darkness, turmoil, unrest, unease, sloth, acedia, despair, despondency, depression, fear, feeling closed in, unsafe, absent from God, and perhaps even evil.

In order to observe desolation, ask questions such as these (also from Susan Currie):

- What about this option feels off kilter, not right, filled with a draining sense of awareness?
- Are we feeling more distant from God in this consideration?

- Would we feel distracted from our primary objective if we went in this direction?
- Would there be a shift, even subtly, away from God's purposes for us if we headed here?

In the midst of desolation, we are holding back the essential ingredients of faith, hope, and trust. We are allowing our negative emotions to take center stage. We are more reactionary than intentional. And most likely, we are responding from anxiety or fear, worried about the past, or not trusting ourselves for the way forward. In desolation we let shame, guilt, blaming, and covetousness into our hearts and minds, which in turn can ruin the discernment.

According to St. Ignatius, it's best to never make an important choice during times of desolation. Desolation is the red flag warning you that you haven't completed the process and there's more work to be explored. Spiritually healthy individuals and groups will press the pause button in times of desolation and only move forward when called to reengage in the prayerful process of discernment.

Any disordered attachments that are revealed in this time may in fact point to one's idolatry. A firm footing in Christ will reveal these disordered attachments and lead you out of desolation by the tender mercies of God. Testing our desolations with Scripture and within community will reveal what God is inviting us to in trustworthy ways.

By taking the time to recognize, repent of, and release our desolations before God, they will in time be redeemed and returned to us in the form of consolation. Trust God to do his deep inner work and wait patiently for consolation to return before moving ahead in the discernment process.

6. Abundant Life

How will you know when the discerning life is abundant?

The most appealing aspect of a discerning life is abundance—not as the health and wealth proponents would espouse, but for those who know with great certainty that this is God's clear desire. Our triune God—Father, Son, and Holy Spirit—yearns to be gracious to us (Isa. 30:18). In his graciousness, his delight is that we know him intimately and affectionately, that we trust him implicitly and wholeheartedly, and that we share his cruciform salvation message with all who are within our orbit, inviting them into the kingdom of light.

Life with God is meant to be lived abundantly.

Yet our own sinful tendencies, our broken relationships, and our dark world bring us down. They tear us apart. All of us know about the darkness that looms and lurks and is ready to lunge toward us. And the evil one, the devil himself, knows all of our soft spots and our propensities to look away from God and in the direction of lesser gods.

Those lesser gods—our own sinfulness, the sinfulness of others, the memories of sinful experiences and relationships, the shame and guilt associated therewith, and the voices that represent all this crud—keep us from the abundant life. Phooey on the evil one. Spit in his face. Turn away from his voice. Say no to his temptations. To follow him is to live in the realm of darkness and despair. Too many around us have said yes to either his glaring or his cunning ways—even in the church today.

You will know you are living the abundant life when you consistently say yes to God's invitation to love, to trust, to follow, to obey, to serve, to know, and to give. Choose to live abundantly. Make daily choices to open your ears, your hands, and your heart to receive the gifts God delights to freely offer. And then choose to give yourself away in abundance.

When we live our daily lives with outstretched arms of love, our inner and exterior world is abundant. There's nothing scarce about it. Posture yourself in this way—yes, physically stand up and stretch out your arms as wide as possible—and you'll feel the radiance of abundance. Live this way and you'll never be the same again.

Creating a Discerning Culture

Choosing to live together with intentionality and a growing awareness of the presence, power, protection, and peace of God demands a culture change. This is layered over the heart-and-mind transformation noted above. To create a culture of discernment, a major shift needs to emerge.

It begins with leadership. We say at LTI, "As the leader goes, so goes the organization. . . . More importantly, as the soul of the leader goes, so goes the leader."[2] In order to create a discerning culture, leadership must embrace this priority. Without leadership buy-in to the discerning life, you won't have a discerning culture.

Leaders are called by God to follow the example of Jesus, who was a servant (Mark 10:45), a shepherd (John 10:11), and a steward of all that was entrusted to him (John 8:28–29). This model of leadership is worthy of our following, but it's a challenge to fulfill in this secular age. Yet it's essential to the discerning culture we are seeking to create in local churches, Christian nonprofits, and Christian-led organizations and businesses today. Here's my definition of the kind of leadership needed to create a culture of discernment:

Spiritual leadership provides hospitality for the soul to dwell and flourish in God, facilitates community cooperation and collaborative partnership with God's people, and ensures God's glorious and gracious kingdom is preserved and advanced in our lifetimes.

Spiritual leadership is the essential ingredient that must be prioritized for disciples of Jesus to embrace with gusto the discerning life and practicing a preference for God.

A discerning culture is created only by those who choose to make the following adaptations:

1. *Shift from human-engineered to Spirit-empowered.* Instead of relying on your own strength, choose deliberately to become more empowered by the Holy Spirit. Depend on God more than yourself or others. This shift will impact every other aspect of your life.

2. *Shift from prayer-less to prayer-full.* Instead of believing the lie that you can live without concerted, united prayer, choose instead to cloak your life in prayer. Spend large blocks of time in silence and solitude and in intentional prayer for every aspect of your individual and shared life in Christ. Interview the Holy Spirit continuously, "What do you desire, God?"

3. *Shift from fast-paced to God-paced.* Instead of figuring out how best to move fast, deliberately practice moving slowly. Pace your strides according to the 3 mph that Jesus walked when he was here among us. Become comfortable with the notion that God is at ease with his will taking forty days, forty years, or even a whole generation to complete. Learn to love the God who is grace-paced and trust-paced.

4. *Shift from strategic to systemic.* Instead of always leaning on the business-minded, bold-faced, decisive-blinded individuals that surround you, look at life and decision-making from a more systemic approach. Notice what's above, around, beneath, and ahead of you as you prayerfully discern the way forward. It's always worth the risk and the time invested. The layers of understanding are worth plummeting.

5. *Shift from successful to faithful.* Instead of believing in the god of success, trust the Lord of the faithful. Don't simply measure your outcomes and monitor your success. Instead, see God's faithfulness, his daily, ordinary provision, and the gifts and blessings of the present. Your response of faithfulness usually looks quite different from success. Training your eyesight around God's faithfulness is the best way to see and live by faith.

6. *Shift from coerced to organic.* Instead of letting the loudest voice or the most powerful person rule the day, look for the humble, gracious, prayerful, and gentle among you. When we feel manipulated, we need to learn how to knee-jerk toward the organic. Trees, animals, and people grow naturally over time. None of them respond well to forced existence or growth. In fact, most die from such treatment. Consider that truth the next time you feel forced to act before adequate time of prayerful consideration.

7. *Shift from static to agile.* Instead of believing the seven last words of fallen people—"We've never done it that way before"—choose to remain agile and open to change. Nothing about this life is static, nor should we look at our discernment in static terms. God is consistent and faithful, never changing from season to season. But we and our

worlds do change, and we must learn to adapt, pivot, and respond in ways that honor and please God. Remaining agile means that we are tender, prayerful, and gracious.

Such a discerning culture doesn't necessarily stand over or against the various cultures created by others. In fact, the creation of a discerning culture may incorporate some of the good of what others have to offer. For example, there is a lot of human energy and insight included in a discerning culture that cries out for more Spirit-empowerment. As we grow in understanding systems and pivot toward agility, we will need to become more strategic in our output and resource allocation.

Once we learn how to be a discerning culture, we become organic (comfortable with how we grow naturally, over time, and without force), systemic (aware of the underlying systems that are pervasive and ingrained within our life together), *and* systematic (choosing a plan and following it toward desired ends). This both/and approach, with emphasis on the natural order of things, includes the sharp minds and leadership abilities of those called to that approach. Healthy things grow by natural and organic means, not by manipulation or coercion. We need to model natural growth and empower one another to fulfill God's will and way in and through us, and not necessarily how others have done it in the past.

Eventually every group will need to make plans, activate resources, establish goals, and assess outcomes. But these things are always done in submission to the way of discernment. Ultimately, we are not in control of our destinies. We're not even in charge of others to create that destiny. Instead, as a community of Christ-followers we're called to hold hands and stick together, to look both ways before crossing the street, to believe together that the best is yet to come, and to prayerfully, organically, lovingly, relationally, and with agility and flexibility, shift and let God bring forth whatever growth he so desires.

Leaders and learners must become more focused on discernment in our various contexts. It's essential for individual leaders and group participants to engage with a common desire: to discern God together, and from that place of intentional awareness, to live and learn and lead for the glory of God and the sake of his kingdom.

PRACTICING A PREFERENCE FOR GOD

Before we get into the specifics of a process to incorporate in your discerning life in the coming pages, there's much to absorb here about intentionality. What do you need to consider prayerfully and attentively as it relates to the state of your soul? What is God inviting you to notice about choosing to live intentionally as an individual and within the groups you are involved in: your marriage and family, work, friends, church, group, or community? Are you aware of your own consolation and desolation, and could you describe those feelings today? Is there something specific here that you feel led to encourage among the groups where you offer yourselves in service to others, particularly related to creating a discerning culture? Take some time to notice what's going on within and around you and prayerfully offer your heartfelt ideas and concerns to God.

Here are a few spiritual exercises to put into practice as you reflect on this chapter:

- **Indifference:** What aspect of your life is God inviting you to hold more loosely? What steps can you take to adopt a "holy indifference" toward that need/thing/issue that grips your heart today?

- **Consolation:** Notice your feelings of consolation. (Flip back a few pages if you need a refresher on what this means.) Based on those feelings, where is God fully present in you?

- **Intentionality:** On a scale of 1 (low) and 10 (high), how intentional are you about attending to the state of your soul? What are some of your reasons for choosing that number? What is one practical step you could take to increase that number a few points?

Pray for a wise discerning heart

Ask for wisdom, he will give it.

CHAPTER 8

Process

Spiritual Discernment Is Practical

> *"'Give your servant a discerning heart to govern your people and to distinguish between right and wrong.'... The LORD was pleased that Solomon had asked for this. So God said to him, '... I will do what you have asked. I will give you a wise and discerning heart.'"*
>
> 1 Kings 3:9–12

A wise and discerning heart. This was a great request from Solomon, and it's a wonderful plea for us today.

Wisdom for wisdom's sake can become pontification and exposition. Wisdom for discernment's sake leads to a lifestyle of distinguishing the difference between right and wrong, better and best, forward and sideways, yes and no, later and now—and living differently as a result.

Wisdom granted by God leads to hearts strangely warmed and

lives generously transformed. Wisdom in the daily, the routine, and the mundane leads us toward a life of faithfulness and fruitfulness. But we don't get there overnight.

There is a process to every aspect of discernment. At times the process is measured, but often it's random and completely Spirit-led, only seen with clarity in retrospect. Sometimes the process is immediate, swift, and hardly given much thought due to the simplicity and directness required. But most of the time, especially when the questions are harder to answer, the practicality of the Spirit-empowered process becomes all the more important.

It's best to be intentional about your discernment, present in the now, waiting and wondering in stillness if necessary, looking forward with anticipation, and taking steps that lead you to the discernment you require through the lens of the wisdom you desire.

For the person who believes they have the spiritual gift of discernment, this chapter may feel redundant or irrelevant. But, from one who believes he has the gift, I also trust the importance of a well-articulated and facilitated process. Both gift and process lead us to the same end: discerning God, his Word, his will, his way. And both gift and process should be compatible and complementary to one another in the spiritual practice of discernment.

In caring for our house, my wife and I have used both types of discernment over the years. Sometimes it's totally random and only seen clearly in the rearview mirror. Often, however, Ruth and I have been deliberate about asking the questions and methodically searching for answers. But in both cases, we've used some form of process, and we've always done so in the hopes of being led by God.

Recently I discovered a hole in the back of our house that had been dug out by an unknown critter. It led under our back room, which has a low-to-zero crawl space within the boundary walls of the foundation. We added this small room on top of what was once our deck. Since we had the appropriate cement pilings for support, we were granted permission to add the room.

Over the years, we've edged the room outdoors with a handful of small shrubs to adorn the perimeter, sitting on a gravel rock base. When I discovered a hole in the ground adjacent to one of the pilings, I was surprised any critter could find entry into that space.

In typical nuisance avoidance, I simply raked the rocks back into place and hoped it would become a one-off mishap. But the next time I went outside, the hole was back. I knew I couldn't ignore it anymore, so I did some reading about possible culprits. Squirrels, chipmunks, rats, and groundhogs were all on the list. I bought some critter-deterring, non-poisonous granules and placed them in the area, closing off the hole again. That didn't work.

I read an article that said these critters don't like light at night, so I purchased some cheap solar-powered outdoor lights. They seemed to work for a couple days, but soon the hole was dug once more.

I heard that mothballs could be effective but perhaps not great for the environment. Nor would they detract all possible invaders. I mischievously went to the local hardware store and bought a box of mothballs, threw them into the hole, and then covered it again with the rocks. The next day the hole was recreated, and the mothballs were scattered about.

One more attempt: orange peels. I went to the grocery store, purchased a handful of juicy oranges, and peeled them as the article suggested. I placed them around the hole. Nope. It was just another failed attempt to solve my problem.

In utter frustration, I tried to cover the hole with bigger rocks to deter entry, knowing the animal would get through them, and gave up for a while. I was losing my patience with the process, so for a while I decided to just let it be—until Ruth said she heard rustling sounds underneath our back room. Would this random critter make entry into our home, or become a family of critters, or possibly destroy what was underneath the hardwood flooring in the back room? I succumbed and called the critter control professionals.

Their diagnosis was a skunk or groundhog. Their plan was to dig a foot down around the perimeter of the foundation and install wire meshing and to put a one-way exit door of mesh at the site of the hole. This would allow safe exit but no reentry for any trapped critters (perhaps already a family of critters) still inside. Then, after waiting a handful of days for safe exit, they would secure the wire mesh and enclose the foundation.

This (much more expensive) solution worked. As the critter control specialist completed his work on our property, he pointed out the culprit: our neighbor's open trash barrels. These were a haven for hungry critters, a magnet for future critter homes, and a frustration for yours truly.

Should I let it go or speak to my neighbor? This was yet another layer of discernment. Wisdom told me to wait it out. No need to ruffle the feathers of our neighbor. Best to just keep cleaning up the foil wrappers, the donut crumbs, and random garbage pieces that weren't secured inside the barrel and landed in our backyard.

When I eventually mentioned this to my neighbor, let's just say it didn't go well and leave it there. Wisdom was needed once more.

What Would Jesus Be?

Discernment is often best done through an intentional process of discovering the Word, the will, and the way of God. Left to the random approach, we may be surprisingly and mysteriously attuned to the Spirit and granted wisdom without even asking—which would be marvelous. But more likely, we will get lost along the way, as my countless attempts to stop the critter unfortunately demonstrate.

Jesus maintained a consistent, faithful posture toward teaching his disciples about gaining wisdom and living lovingly. His instructions were in sharp contrast to the leaders of his day. The way of Jesus is often counter to the culture, and his economy is based on kingdom values. So, the will and the way of Jesus will always upset the establishment and the norms of the day.

In Matthew's Gospel, chapters 5, 6, and 7, we have recorded for us a treasure trove of wise teachings of Jesus. Those who hear him are "amazed at his teaching, because he taught as one who had authority, and not as their teachers of the law" (Matt. 7:28–29).

Beginning with the Beatitudes, Jesus makes his Word, his will, and his way crystal clear for his disciples, to whom he would entrust his message and mission. He contrasts his views with those in religious authority, who were powering over the people of his day with restrictions, obligations, and regulations. Jesus wants to set them free to consider a new way of living and to help them discern the way forward with heavenly wisdom.

First up is how Jesus invites them *to be*.

> Blessed are the poor in spirit,
> > for theirs is the kingdom of heaven.
> Blessed are those who mourn,
> > for they will be comforted.
> Blessed are the meek,
> > for they will inherit the earth.

> Blessed are those who hunger and thirst for
> > righteousness,
> > > for they will be filled.
> Blessed are the merciful,
> > for they will be shown mercy.
> Blessed are the pure in heart,
> > for they will see God.
> Blessed are the peacemakers,
> > for they will be called children of God.
> Blessed are those who are persecuted because of
> > righteousness,
> > > for theirs is the kingdom of heaven.

Blessed are you when people insult you, persecute you and falsely say all kinds of evil against you because of me. Rejoice and be glad, because great is your reward in heaven, for in the same way they persecuted the prophets who were before you. (Matt. 5:3–12)

The Beatitudes are Jesus's clarion call for how he wants his disciples to live out their relationship with him. It is quite the contrarian approach in the culture of their day. The way of Jesus is defined by choosing to be poor in spirit, mournful, meek, hungry for righteousness, merciful, pure, peacemaking, and willing to be persecuted and insulted for righteousness' sake. These qualities show that his followers look like him, and doing otherwise would be legalistic, bowing in submission to a false and lesser god.

Pause and reflect afresh on the power of the Beatitudes. Read the passage several times over before moving forward in this book. There's something fresh in that living text for your personal life today. Sit with it. Absorb it. Reflect on it. Pray it. Choose it. Live it.

What are you noticing as you reflect prayerfully and attentively today? Perhaps there's one or more of the Beatitudes specific to your discernment today. Don't miss it.

After the Beatitudes, Jesus teaches them how *to live*. The wisdom of Solomon doesn't compare with the wisdom of Jesus.

First to consider: "You are the salt of the earth" and "the light of the world" (Matt. 5:13–16). Don't grow dull, but instead be spiced up for flavor, healing, and preservation of life. Share your saltiness everywhere you go. Don't hide the light of Jesus that shines in dark places. Instead, let your light shine.

Next up: Don't even think that Jesus came to abolish the Law and the Prophets, as the Pharisees accused him of doing (Matt. 5:17–20). Instead, notice the many ways the Law and the Prophets' words are fulfilled in Jesus. Practice and teach things that point others to the kingdom of heaven, Jesus's favorite topic.

For example: What follows is a healthy handful of teachings on seventeen critical topics that demonstrate how the teachings of Jesus fulfill this new way of living. One issue after another is taught with practical, particular, and prayerful intentionality. There is method to his wisdom, and he speaks directly into their hearts.

1. *Murder* (5:21–26)
2. *Adultery* (vv. 27–30)
3. *Divorce* (vv. 31–32)
4. *Oaths* (vv. 33–37)
5. *Revenge* (vv. 38–42)
6. *Love for enemies* (vv. 43–48)
7. *Giving to the needy* (6:1–4)
8. *Prayer* (vv. 5–15)
9. *Fasting* (vv. 16–18)

10. *Treasures* (vv. 19–24)
11. *Worry* (vv. 25–34)
12. *Judging others* (7:1–6)
13. *Asking, seeking, and knocking* (vv. 7–12)
14. *The narrow gate* (vv. 13–14)
15. *True and false prophets* (vv. 15–20)
16. *True and false disciples* (vv. 21–23)
17. *Wise and foolish builders* (vv. 24–27)

Teaching with such authority, Jesus makes his will and way perfectly clear. The kingdom of heaven is the endgame, and every aspect of one's personal life should lead to that purpose. To disregard his simple-yet-divine intentionality is to risk your soul. The expectations for Jesus's disciples are in juxtaposition to the ways of the world, including the directives of well-intentioned (or harmful and evil-intentioned) leaders in the body of Christ.

Be warned. The kingdom of heaven belongs to those who follow fervently the will and the ways of Jesus. The Sermon on the Mount is the place from which we launch and land, over and over again.

What Are the Questions?

Living our lives around kingdom values is hard to do. In so many respects, the teachings of Jesus get lost in the cacophony of voices calling out much louder for our attention. The political arena shouts at us, encouraging us to take sides against one another. The business sector challenges us to organize around its competitive and commercial advantage. The academic community is wide open to debate just about every possible mindset and methodology created by humans.

Even the religious community continues to dispute and divide around subpoints of theology, some of great theological magnitude and others of tactical minutiae.

The questions you're facing today are important to monitor and explore, hopefully within a prayerful process of spiritual discernment. Listen intently for the voice of Jesus within the ever-swirling voices of the day. Keep coming back home to the heart of God and incline the ears of your heart toward the clarity Jesus offers. The teachings of Jesus in the Sermon on the Mount are identity markers from which we should make every decision. This foundation for life and service will ultimately lead us homeward to heaven.

In the meantime, while we are still this side of heaven, what are the questions we need to address if we're practicing a preference for God within our discerning life?

The most difficult yet important question to ask is *why?* Throughout your entire discerning life, you will be confronted by the *why* question. Virtually every question comes back to the *why*. And the layers of *why* go deep. One answer to *why* may lead to yet another *why*. In fact, you may have to ask *why* several times before getting to the real root reason. Don't grow weary of asking *why* and you'll stay fresh and vibrant as a result.

Asking *who* or *what* or *when* or *where* or *how* should always come from the *why*, not vice versa. *Why* is first and foremost, never to be undermined by any other question. To know why with certainty will lead naturally into all other relevant questions. For example, when considering the possibility of a new ministry program, instead of jumping to *what* and *how*, linger with the *why* first. When leaders start with the *why*, the *what* and *how* follow, perhaps in surprising ways. When LTI pivoted all our programs online, the *why* was obvious: we were in a pandemic, and we couldn't be together in person.

The *what* and *how* ended up looking like online workshops and retreats, as well as a podcast—a time- and energy-intensive project I'm not sure we would have considered without first asking *why.*

Look back on the Sermon on the Mount. Jesus has one big idea in mind: the kingdom of heaven. Everything was built around and toward the kingdom of heaven. The Beatitudes were to be lived out—*why?* Because they expressed the kingdom of heaven on earth. Be salt and light—*why?* Because that's how the kingdom of heaven is multiplied.

Repeatedly, Jesus teaches about murder and the subtlety of anger, adultery and its cousin lust, divorce, oaths, revenge, even love for enemies—*why?* Because it's in the face of darkness that the kingdom's light is lived out. Give to those in need, pray, fast, value what God values, don't worry or judge, and offer others the same generosity God offers you—*why?* Because each of these are central to the inverted and untidy nature of the kingdom of heaven.

Jesus's final instructions on the Sermon on the Mount involve leaders: prophets, disciples, and builders—*why?* Because he knows that leaders will either invite followers to embrace his way, or they will foolishly entice them their own way. And for Jesus, the religious leaders are his target. Be careful who you follow—*why?* Because wisdom will always outstrip foolishness.

Ask *why* as often as possible, for every decision, large and small: "Why do we exist?" "Why is this so important?" "Why should we consider each option?" "Why?" "Why?" "Why?"

Our ministry, Leadership Transformations, serves many churches and organizations who are engaged in meaningful discernment processes. Getting them to wrestle with *why* is often the greatest challenge, mostly because they believe the *why* is assumed or previously agreed upon and therefore owned by all around the

discernment table. But in most cases, there are at least slight variations to the answer to the *why* question, and usually there is quite a
chasm among the members of the group. Writing down the answer
to *why* and agreeing to it together is a great starting point.

Never tire of the *why*. It will inevitably lead you to the *who, what,
when, where,* and *how.* Those are much simpler questions to answer,
but only after the *why* is firmly rooted and established. Don't flirt
too quickly with any other question until you've done due diligence
and prayerful reflection on the *why*.

What Are the Principles?

Pastor Dave and First Church (friends we will follow for the rest of
this chapter) found themselves engaged in a discernment process.
They were running out of space in their sanctuary and needed to
make some decisions about their future. The first and most important question needed to be addressed: *Why* were they entering this
discernment process?

Pastor Dave and the leaders of the church were concerned about
reaching their community for Christ. There had been an influx
of people arriving at their doorstep and calling First Church their
spiritual home. The worship and fellowship and witness of their
church had experienced some healthy growth. The *why* was obvious:
because God was growing a kingdom-minded congregation in their
midst, and more people were arriving than they could handle. Space
and staff and programs were all being taxed beyond their capacity.
It was time to commence a prayerful discernment process using the
following seven principles.

   1. Ask why before asking who, what, when, where, or how.

Principles come from the *why*; practices follow suit and are encapsulated in the *who, what, when, where,* and *how.* Keep *why* first and all the others will follow one step at a time. Pastor Dave and First Church kept coming back to the *why*: we need more space to accommodate the growing number of congregants and to fulfill God's call on our community.

Many times, the questions that need asking and answering in ministry settings begin with what we call the Ministry Platform, the foundation on which you stand. This includes the following:

Statement of Faith: What do we believe (creeds, faith
statements, etc.)?
Philosophy of Ministry: How do we function together
(principles and priorities)?
Covenant: What relational and practical commitments are we
making to one another?
Vision: Where is God leading us in the future (our preferred
future)?
Mission: What are we doing today that leads us toward that
preferred future?
Ministry: What are we currently doing to serve others
(programs and initiatives)?

2. Strive to hear God's voice over the world's loudest shouts.
Listening is skill number one for any healthy discernment process. Pastor Dave and the leadership team at First Church began their process in the Word and prayer. They reflected on the material found in appendix B of this book and spent the first forty days of their shared discernment experience reading and praying through the same readings, listening for God's voice, and encouraging the

group to do the same throughout the process. And it paid off in both specific and mysterious ways.

3. *Press the pause button often throughout the process for prayerful reflection, reevaluation, and renewal.* The reflective process must be affirmed and celebrated and given its due time and effort. Pastor Dave and the leadership team chose to meet regularly as a team, but they also included some retreat days for themselves and a wider circle of leaders from other ministries in the church. The focus of their retreats was to worship, pray, sing, read, share, and reflect together on what they were noticing about God's movement in their midst. This concerted reflection led to continual elasticity in their shared process. Ultimately, the decisions they made together led to their own spiritual renewal and to the growth and maturity of their congregation.

4. *Rigorously pursue the disciplines of the spiritual life.* Committing to a life of daily and weekly spiritual habits will contribute positively to each person's involvement in the discernment process. From the beginning of their process, the leaders of First Church pledged to one another a holy pursuit after God in their personal prayer closets. They committed to one another an earnest desire and follow-through in their own spiritual development.

They knew they needed to be "prayed up" and ready to engage with the others on the team from a prayerful perspective. Each meeting began in prayer, in the sharing from their readings the prior week (some of which are provided for you in appendix B), discussion about what they were learning about discernment, and a recommitment to continue forward in a discerning posture. To do otherwise would be to totter toward lesser ways of decision-making based on political or business acumen, falling toward the ways of the world rather than the kingdom of heaven.

5. Interdependently serve one another as a foundation for ministry together during and after the discernment is achieved. Learning how to love one another throughout the process will provide the foundation for all the "one another" passages in Scripture to be fulfilled then and thereafter. Practicing sacrificial love for each other enhances the "honoring one another" and "serving one another" and "praying for one another" and all the others. Pastor Dave and the leadership team were stretched in this regard, with various leaders from the congregation involved in the discernment but holding loosely their own ministry's agenda. Learning how to work as "us and we" rather than "I and me" leads to healthier interdependence.

6. Be willing to wait on God and trust him to guide, uphold, empower, and fulfill his good and perfect will. In his time. His way. For his glory. And his name's sake. Waiting is often difficult, especially for those who get antsy, anxious, frustrated, or flippant about the entire exercise of discernment. When processes were slowing down, this was hard for Pastor Dave. He was a decisive leader and became impatient at times. His community helped slow him down to the speed of trust. There will be times in your discernment when there's forward motion, but there will also be lag times when the best option is to pray and wait on God. Since he's a God of clarity and not confusion, we can trust that he will make the way clear in his time.

7. Follow a proven discernment process. Read widely and be open to how the Scriptures and the history of the church unfold for us a different way to discern together. What follows is a process that has worked in a variety of settings and among diverse groups. Each time, it has been slightly modified according to the needs of the group, but overall, it has become a tried-and-true process. There are other processes worthy of your consideration, but I have come to appreciate the fruit that's borne as a result of what follows. By taking the discernment process one practical step at a time, bathed in prayer, trusting the work of God's Spirit, working in harmony with others on your team, you will uncover the riches of God's Word, will, and way—guaranteed.

What Is the Process?

The discernment process described below was first introduced to me by Brother David Vryhof, a member of The Society of St. John the Evangelist (SSJE), a religious order for men in the Episcopal/ Anglican Church. Brother David and his community have long appreciated and practiced the principles for spiritual discernment outlined by St. Ignatius in his *Spiritual Exercises*. Although the *Exercises* are designed primarily for individuals making life choices in the context of a thirty-day retreat, the principles can also be applied to a group discernment process. In fact, Ignatius and his companions went through a careful discernment process as a group before applying to become a religious order in the church. The Ignatian way of "finding God in all things" informs the discerning life we have been describing as practicing a preference for God—particularly when that requires a careful, balanced process for reaching a clear decision.

I have taken the liberty of revising this process even further, mostly as a result of the experiences I've had with groups like Pastor Dave and First Church. The discernment process outlined below also works for individuals in discernment about questions that affect one's personal life, vocational calling, relational health, and more.

Adopting an attitude of prayerful freedom and indifference and utilizing the central concepts of consolation and desolation we touched on in chapter 7, the way forward is held loosely and prayerfully. Thereby, the process becomes akin to decision-making but with a loving heart for God, one another, and those whom we're called to serve. It's the coming together of healthy reasoning, a vibrant inner life, and a desire to abide in Jesus's way—better known as wisdom—that makes for a Spirit-empowered discernment process.

Phase 1: Frame the Question

What is the question we are discerning together?

Make time up front to frame the question and agree to it as a team before moving into the process. Perhaps it's one specific question, or maybe it's a few (if so, take them one at a time). Clarity on the discernment question is essential for an effective process. Write it down and agree on the wording. Don't start your process with ambiguity about the specific question for which you are seeking clarity.

Pastor Dave and the First Church leadership team were asking, "How do we handle our church's growth?" Their predetermined sub-question focused on options: "Should we stay on property and maximize our space here, relocate to a new property, or plant churches?" Clarifying the best and most important questions will keep you and the team focused appropriately.

Phase 2: Gather the Team

Who are the appropriate members of the discernment team?

Once the discernment question(s) are identified, then choose the right people to serve on the team. Not everyone is fit for the task, although everyone can be equipped for the role (if they are invited and willing to be taught). Pastor Dave and the First Church leadership team determined that a mix of leaders was preferred for the discernment of their question. So, they assembled a team of staff, elders, and key ministry representatives to oversee this endeavor.

I LOVE YOU

Diverse voices, backgrounds, ages, ethnicities, vocations, and interests make for a lively process.

Write a short covenant of guiding principles (e.g., timeliness of meetings, follow-through on tasks, praying together each meeting, willingness to listen well, confidentiality as appropriate, and positive contribution) to enhance the shared experience. Include how final decisions will be made. Will you need to be unanimous, accept a simple majority, or lean into consensus? Taking the time to create this covenant together can be a great team-building experience. Hold one another to the covenantal agreement to enhance your shared experience from start to finish.

Phase 3: Release All Biases, Preconceived Conclusions, and Predetermined Assumptions

Are you willing to release or hold loosely your preconceived ideas for the outcome?

Each member of the team will have ideas about how best to approach and answer their discernment question, so it's important that all are willing to die to that notion early on in the process. The team needs to value prayerfulness, openness, flexibility, and creativity, which begins with a spirit of holy indifference.

In the early meetings of Pastor Dave's discernment team, Dave kept floating the same option with slightly different slants each time he spoke. One meeting he finally realized what he was doing and sought the forgiveness of the group. We granted him our grace, and then I invited him to write out his bias on a 3x5 card, rip it up, and place it in a bowl. I then asked each team member to write out their preconceived idea of what they thought would be the outcome of the discernment process, rip it up, and place it in the same bowl.

YOU ARE LOVED

YOU ARE FORGIVEN

185

That bowl became our centerpiece for the rest of the process. Learning to let go is hard for many. But when we do it, we become more pliable to the movement of God's Spirit and the discernment that results.

And PRAY

How is God inviting you to pray?

In between each of the subsequent phases in the discernment process, you will find a specific invitation to pray. Keep praying. Pray again. Stop and pray. Notice and pray. A spiritually healthy discernment process should be bathed in prayer—not just punctuated by an opening and closing prayer, but permeated by prayer throughout, during, and in between meetings and phases of the process.

If you take discernment seriously, then you will continually return to God's Word, his voice, his direction, his empowerment, and his way. With Pastor Dave and the team, we kept reading through the biblical texts and materials from *A Guide to Spiritual Discernment* (which is summarized in appendix B), discussing elements of discernment together, bathing our times together in prayer, and setting apart special times to go on retreat together at the beginning and the end of the discernment process. We knew that our prayerfulness would impact our ability to discern God and his will together.

Phase 4: Assemble the Facts

What are the facts as we currently know them?

All good discernment processes begin with the now, the present. It's a superb indicator for the future. It's the secret to what's next. Unpacking the now gets the group in touch with their current reality. Teams are best served by defining their reality with unfiltered honesty and clarity. All members of the team must have access to all the facts. When one individual or a handful of people hold on to a portion of the data, the process will short-circuit.

Pastor Dave and the team began with a full assessment of their circumstances. They looked at the size and occupancy of their current structure. They reviewed attendance charts, financial reports, membership stats, program participation, and parking capacity. They interviewed staff and lay leaders and began to catalog the facts as they could best assess.

They spoke to community leaders, interviewed unchurched neighbors, talked with the church's prayer warriors (mostly the older members of the church), and listened to as many key voices as possible. They used Leadership Transformations' Church Health Assessment Tool (CHAT, based on the ten traits of a healthy church as expressed in my first book, *Becoming a Healthy Church*, and found at www.healthychurch.net) to listen attentively to their congregation and assess the spiritual health of their church.

This was quite invigorating for the team as they noticed together how God had blessed their ministry and multiplied their effectiveness over the years. It was especially affirming for Pastor Dave, who had been serving as senior pastor for more than three decades. The fruit that emerged from his faithfulness was a testimony to his leadership, and the team recognized it with joy.

After listing and reviewing the facts, *prioritize* them. What facts are more important than others? Be diligent in this regard. The weight of each major data point matters as the team moves forward in discerning God's will by answering the question at hand.

And PRAY

How is God inviting you to pray?

187

Phase 5: Critique and Review Options

What are the options as we know them today?

Once the facts are outlined and prioritized, the team returns to the discernment question and begins to review their options. All options are noted and then prioritized to keep the team properly focused and not derailed by options not worth consideration. This too is discernment for the team; too many options may curtail an effective conclusion. Pastor Dave and the First Church team originally thought they had three options: max out their current property, build a new facility elsewhere, or plant churches.

Interestingly, during this phase they unlocked a fourth option: keep the main campus as is and plant satellite congregations in various sites surrounding their town. From their prayers and early conversations about options, this fourth option emerged and brought about curiosity and enthusiasm from the team. They were all overjoyed with how God was shaping their thought process and aligning their dreams for the future of their church. A healthy handful of options for prayerful consideration brought new life and energy to the entire experience.

And PRAY

How is God inviting you to pray?

Phase 6: State Reasons Why NOT

One option at a time—why should we NOT pursue it?

Taking one option at a time, the group prayerfully considers the reasons why it would *not* be wise to move forward with this concept. St. Ignatius believed that each member of the discernment team (or the individual involved in personal discernment) needs to look attentively at the reasons why each option is not to be preferred. No option is ever perfect. We are searching for the better of two or more options, one of which will emerge as best, recognizing there will be flaws or questions that remain no matter the choice.

Looking at *why not* before considering *why yes* will bring discipline to the entire discernment process. It will lead to certainty and a profound settled-ness when final decisions are made. Also important in this phase is to prioritize the options according to what seems to be weighted more toward *why not*, and then to the lesser options not to be considered. The goal is to find unity around the discernment team, discovering that which seems to be emerging as "good to the Holy Spirit and to us" (Acts 15:28).

This was extremely helpful for Pastor Dave and First Church, as each team member was kindly required to speak to the *why not* for each option. No one was exempt from coming up with reasons why not, which was especially important for the voices around the table who were known to favor the option they now had to speak against. This is hard but profitable for all involved.

And PRAY

How is God inviting you to pray?

Phase 7: State Reasons Why YES

One option at a time—why SHOULD we pursue it?

On the flip side to phase 6, each member is invited to voice reasons why we should say yes to each option. Affirming the value of each option being prayerfully considered is also essential to the process. And when each person around the discernment table must make arguments for an option they may not prefer, it disciplines the team to stay honest, humble, and wide open to the Spirit's movement in their midst.

This was a liberating, creative, and life-giving exercise for Pastor Dave and the team. We noticed around the circle how surprising insights arose from members who had previously been quieter than others. We affirmed and celebrated one another for stepping up to the plate and speaking positively for options we may not have been excited about. Prioritizing the options that seemed most viable became even easier after getting both the *why not* and the *why yes* in front for the group to notice and discern.

And PRAY

How is God inviting you to pray?

Phase 8: Deliberate Openly, Honestly, without Judgment or Conclusion

Taking one option at a time—which ones stay, and which ones go away?

By the time the group gets to phase 8, there's been a lot covered in prayer and conversation. Now is the time to deliberate and comment on the various options still on the table for discernment. But hold off on a decision. Here, it's helpful to see each option with clarity, preferably in written form. You can use large sheets of paper outlining the reasons *why not* and *why yes* visible for all to see, or you can put these in digital shared documents that allow each member to review the material together.

Taking one option at a time and vetting it together will begin to bring clarity, without judgment or conclusion. Pastor Dave and the team did a great job looking at each of the four options on the table. They spoke honestly with one another about what seemed to be the strengths of each option. They were earnest in their deliberation and withheld their final decision until they spent a bit more time in prayer, together and apart. They held this process open-handedly, lovingly, and graciously. They knew they were close to making a decision that would dramatically impact their shared life together as a spiritually healthy church.

[handwritten: Christ died when for you were at you your worst.]

And PRAY

How is God inviting you to pray?

Phase 9: Decide and Proceed

What is our final decision—which of these choices is for the greater glory to God, and what are the steps to achieve what we've discerned together?

A unified conclusion will emerge from the time spent learning about spiritual discernment, praying together as a team, discussing options from a negative and positive perspective, and deciding the best way forward. When Pastor Dave and the team reached this phase, it had become clear what God was leading them into as a church. Pastor Dave had initially wanted to build a new facility outside of town. But through this process, he and the rest of the team realized their church had been strategically placed in the center of town. To leave that behind felt like abandoning a huge part of their history—and future—as a church. Therefore, staying put at their current location and adding satellite campuses in surrounding communities seemed like the best of all options. This option wasn't on their radar at the beginning; it emerged as a viable option midstream.

The God-led story, shared with the congregation, unified the church and propelled them into a fabulous next chapter. The team was glad to let all other options go in order to receive the clarity of God's discerning presence and protection, which led them forward into the fullness of his will.

In phase 9, it's important to have predetermined as a team whether your decisions will be made via simple majority, consensus, or unanimous vote. I have found over the years that simple majority isn't quite enough for large decisions, and unanimous puts too much power into the hands of a single holdout. In my experience, coming to consensus is the best option to pursue. For example, if your group has eight members, then a consensus would preferably be six. Always consider what's best for the whole group (e.g., the entire congregation for Pastor Dave and the team). This should outweigh personal preference, which can be detrimental to the overall process.

Most importantly, however, is for the group to assess, as St. Ignatius would query his discernment followers, "Which of these choices is for the greater glory to God?" And finally, what steps do we need to take to implement each aspect of the decision(s) made together? Mapping out the details helps everyone to implement what's been decided.

And PRAY

How is God inviting you to pray?

Phase 10: Review, Evaluate, and Start Again

What have we learned, what's working well, what needs our attention, and/or when will discernment recommence?

No discernment process is perfect, nor are the decisions we make, even after praying and pleading with God for his will. Therefore, it's best to remain open to ongoing review of the decisions made. Then you can tweak them as needed in order to remain focused on God's way for the future. It's totally fine to adjust your plans; as soon as decisions are made, there are possibilities for change.

Keep your planning documents as living white papers. Don't

make them too pretty or permanent. Keep your plans in front of you, but hold them loosely, pliably, and lean ahead to fulfill them with agility. Determine when and how to provide ongoing evaluation and review. And start the discernment process all over again when needed.

After coming to their decision, Pastor Dave and the team kept meeting and determined together their action plan, next steps, communication, and execution timetable. Then, as the plans came together, particularly for their satellite congregations, new teams of leaders were assembled, new staff hired, new leadership structures emerged, and everything new coming forth was attended to with diligence and vigilance. The season ahead of them as a church family was filled with anticipation and joy. It's been fun to watch them flourish as a result of this process.

And PRAY

How is God inviting you to pray?

The conclusion to your discernment process will likely be filled with joy and deep satisfaction. Knowing that you've prayerfully engaged in each of these phases gives you greater contentment and willingness to hold all with an open-handed posture of discerning grace. Offer that freely to all who are involved, every step of the way.

As previously noted, there are many available variations to the above process. All are fallible at one point or another, especially since they are led by imperfect human beings. But each process is worth consideration.

Some processes have great historical significance. If you are interested in pursuing other noteworthy processes, consider the following:

- Ignatius of Loyola's *Spiritual Exercises*
- John Cassian's *Conferences*
- Thomas à Kempis's *Imitation of Christ*
- John Calvin's *Institutes of the Christian Religion*
- Frances de Sales's *Finding God's Will for You*
- The Benedictines' discernment through a patterned life of prayer
- The Augustinians' discernment through desire
- The Franciscans' discernment through availability
- The Quakers' Clearness Committee process (with an emphasis on silence and prayer, waiting together for the Holy Spirit to speak and offer direction)
- The Wesleyan Quadrilateral (which includes a careful weighing of Scripture, reason, tradition, and experience, relying heavily on practical judgment)[1]

Blending these voices together makes for a great discernment symphony within and among the body of Christ. Praise God for the generations who have gone before us in pursuit of the discerning life.

What Are You Noticing?

In all good discernment processes, the participants are invited to continuously notice the handiwork of God. This will occur in a variety of ways as the group focuses on listening intently and intentionally to the voice of God. Every step of the way will inevitably be dotted by consolation and desolation, and with the invitation to trust God implicitly no matter the state of your soul or your emotional well-being. This will include lots of calls for indifference on the part of each member of the team, holding loosely that which we believe are the must-haves or the must-dos of our discernment.

Noticing God, pointing him out to one another, and leaning in his direction to listen attentively will lead us home to God's heart and to an awareness of his will—nothing more, nothing less. Jesus knows all about you, including the skunks or groundhogs living under the surface attempting to foil your discernment, and his invitation is for you to fully engage in building up the kingdom of heaven.

Like the dawning of a new day and the rising of the sun, each layer unfolds with breathtaking beauty. So it is with the discernment process, revealed to the people of God one phase at a time. "Therefore," Jesus says, "everyone who hears these words of mine and puts them into practice is like a wise man who built his house on the rock" (Matt. 7:24). May it be so for all who desire to live the discerning life.

PRACTICING A PREFERENCE FOR GOD

Some have the spiritual gift of discernment. For them, the key word is *stewardship*: practicing a preference for God and prayerfully, lovingly, and obediently giving voice to what you see, hear, feel, and understand to be true. It's like the gift of the prophet, who sees in advance and is called to offer words that predict and protect. For the rest of us who do not possess the gift, there are practical processes available to us that are trustworthy because they've stood the test of time.

The ten-phase process outlined in this chapter, with modifications and variations, has been used by individuals and groups for hundreds of years. As you pause and notice what's emerging inside you as you ponder this process for yourself and for those with whom you love and serve, ask God for his abiding peace. Celebrate what you are seeing and hearing from God as you reflect on his Word, particularly the Beatitudes and the Sermon on the Mount. Follow Jesus with ever-deepening intimacy, and trust him to lead you forward in whatever you are discerning about the future. Notice the now, for it truly is the secret to discovering what's next.

Here are a few spiritual exercises to put into practice as you reflect on this chapter:

- **Process:** Consider the ways in which people tend to make big, important decisions—individually and in groups. Which phase of the discernment process is most needed today?
- **Why:** Think about a decision you're currently thinking through—again, individually or in a group. Have you considered the *why* before moving on to the *what*, the *how*, and other questions? If not, spend some time writing out a clear *why*.
- **Pray:** This may seem simple, but unfortunately, it's easy to forget. Bathe your discernment in prayer before, during, and after a decision is sought. If you're currently working through a discernment process, stop reading right now and pray—to discern God and his will.

never question that + he loves me.

CHAPTER 9

Lifestyle

Spiritual Discernment Is Radical

"Though the fig tree does not bud
and there are no grapes on the vines,
though the olive crop fails
and the fields produce no food,
though there are no sheep in the pen
and no cattle in the stalls,
yet I will rejoice in the LORD,
I will be joyful in God my Savior.
The Sovereign LORD is my strength;
he makes my feet like the feet of a deer,
he enables me to tread on the heights."

Habakkuk 3:17–19

There's no place like home—when my home is Christ's heart and Christ's home is mine.

No matter the house you were raised in or how good or hard

it was to reside there, we are always welcomed home by God. No matter the condition of our quirky houses and the state of our souls, their order or disorder, God seeks to dwell in our midst.

That's remarkable and radical. Just give it a ponder. Reread these simple phrases again and again.

There's no place like home.

When my home is Christ's heart.

And Christ's home is my heart.

The prophet Habakkuk reminds us that even though there are no buds on the fig tree, no grapes on the vine; if the olive crop fails, and the fields produce no food; if there are no sheep in the pen or cattle in the stalls, I will still rejoice in the Lord. The Sovereign Lord is my strength.

Despite the circumstances of our lives, we can rejoice. This is only possible because of God and the work he desires to do in our hearts each new day. And only when we are in a trusting space, accepting the will of the Father's heart for us regardless of how well things are going.

Life isn't always neat and clean, bright and shining, easygoing, upbeat, and positive. Life is hard. It's filled with challenges and difficulties, twists and turns, disappointments, heartaches, suffering, and sadness. Perseverance tests our character and challenges our well-being. But nothing we face isn't first known by God. If God allowed Job to suffer and empowered him to survive, so too will he come alongside us in all our times of need.

When Ruth and I first moved into our house, we were told by the previous owner that "occasionally" we might get water in the basement. Thus, the washer, dryer, freezer, water heater, oil burner, and any perishable or important items stored there were all placed on blocks, bricks, or wooden pallets. We thought, *We can live with an occasional inconvenience.*

But what we were told was "occasional" soon became "frequent" and ultimately "always." After our first couple of early spring seasons in the house, when the likelihood of flooding most often occurs, we knew we were in trouble. Water trickled in along the edges of the foundation, in between the crevices of the tile flooring, and even along the concrete block walls. If we didn't keep up with it with our water vacuum, it would seep everywhere and require more attention.

Ruth kept a pair of boots at the bottom of the basement stairs. She could slip them on to trudge through an inch or more of water over to the laundry space—in tears. Her Dutch cleanliness heritage was seriously put to the test. Sometimes I think I even heard a bad word come from her mouth when it was simply too much to endure. I didn't blame her. I was equally frustrated.

When we were searching for homes that we could afford in our town, we looked at houses with dirt basements. We were appalled. Who could live in such conditions? Well, apparently many do. They only use their basements for storage and the essential heating, electric, and water mains, many of which were hanging from the ceiling or side walls. Some had low ceilings, where you had to duck to avoid bumping your head. These basements served more as crawl spaces. And perhaps for good reason: just let the water seep in as it must, and over time it will be absorbed by the dirt.

Having lived with a flooded basement, I'm not sure it's better than a dirt one. But what were our options? We could have packed up and moved. Or we could have lived with it as it was, as our previous owners had for more than a decade. Ultimately, we decided on option number three: fixing the problem once and for all.

We hired the local "basement flood busters" and did radical surgery on our basement. We cleared it as best as possible to prepare for their arrival. They proceeded to break up the cement flooring all around the inside perimeter of the basement walls, where they placed a permeable tubing with rocks around it for easy water flow. Then, they found the lowest point of the basement, dug a deeper hole there, and placed in it a submersible sump pump for removing the water before it could seep up into the floor.

This did the trick—until one early spring about twenty years later, when the water table outside overran the inside perimeter drainage system and overwhelmed the sump pump. But this one blip on the screen fit the original owner's "occasional" diagnosis, and we found it to be endurable. We haven't regretted the investment in our basement. It allowed us to stay in our home. In Habakkuk's style, "Though the water had once overwhelmed our basement, yet we can rejoice in God."

I've noted throughout this journey that discernment comes in various shapes, sizes, and forms. Yet it always begins with our relationship with God, noticing him in everything. He is our Rock and our Redeemer, the One in whom we can put our complete trust. Sometimes we see him with crystal clarity. Other times we search for him amidst the rubble of our lives. At times we need a detailed process to discover him and his will for us.

As in the story above, at times we need to consider a radical digging up of our past and present in order to look by faith to the future. Did we set out to contend with a flooded basement? No, but it became our reality, and we needed to step up to the plate and take care of it once and for all. The cost was high, the mess was worth it, and the result ended our sleepless nights and worries about when the floods would start again. So it is with our pilgrimage of faith in Christ. Sometimes the reality is hard, frustrating, disappointing, and costly, but in God we can survive and even thrive.

When life gets hard, I turn to Habakkuk and join his refrain, "*yet* I will rejoice in the LORD." That's a radical posture for discernment amidst difficult circumstances—one I heartily recommend.

There's No Place Like Home

Throughout this book, I've described discerning God as noticing God's generous and gracious hospitality to us while seeking to be hospitable to him. Our awareness of God is our discerning life, in that we are continually noticing him and doing what we can to make our home (and our heart) a safe and hospitable space where God and others, including ourselves, can reside. It's daily and constant and worth noticing now, in the present, because tomorrow will be here before we know it. It's best to practice a preference for God amidst the life we're invited to life fully and abundantly and graciously with God today.

I've likened spiritual discernment to home ownership and stewardship. Our house, apartment, or dwelling place is always in need of attention. We must stay attentive to discern what's needed now in order to maintain its safety, health, cleanliness, and wellbeing for all who enter our space and live among us. So it is with spiritual discernment, both alone and with others. It's all about how well we notice and how well we attend to the invitations from God in our homes and in our hearts, as we practice a preference for God in all aspects of our personal journeys, relationships, leadership, and service to others.

Spiritual discernment is an everyday practice, just like making our beds and clearing the table after a meal. It's as rhythmic as weekly laundry and trash day. It's as cyclical as monthly bill payments, as seasonal as spring cleaning and fall yard work. It's as sudden as attending to emergencies that propel us into action. Just as we pay attention to the needs of our personal house care, so too must we perceive our own soul care and notice God in the dailyness of life as well as in those special times that require more attention.

Discernment is a lifestyle, as foreboding as major refurbishment or as common as daily house care. And amid our quirky homes and lives, God delights to show up and make himself known. He's as accessible as a light switch or the generous water flowing from our faucets. God is visible to the naked eye as well as invisible and mysterious. He's present everywhere. God is hospitable to us, and he loves it when we are hospitable to him and then to others.

As I've mentioned before in brief, Psalm 139 is the great "omni" psalm. Here we discover some amazing truths about God. In the first six verses we learn about his *omniscience*: he knows all.

> You have searched me, LORD,
>> and you know me.
> You know when I sit and when I rise;
>> you perceive my thoughts from afar.
> You discern my going out and my lying down;
>> you are familiar with all my ways.
> Before a word is on my tongue
>> you, LORD, know it completely.
> You hem me in behind and before,
>> and you lay your hand upon me.
> Such knowledge is too wonderful for me,
>> too lofty for me to attain (vv. 1–6).

Next, the psalmist reminds us of God's *omnipresence*: he is everywhere present.

> Where can I go from your Spirit?
>> Where can I flee from your presence?
> If I go up to the heavens, you are there;
>> if I make my bed in the depths, you are there.

If I rise on the wings of the dawn,
> if I settle on the far side of the sea,
even there your hand will guide me,
> your right hand will hold me fast.
If I say, "Surely the darkness will hide me
> and the light become night around me,"
even the darkness will not be dark to you;
> the night will shine like the day,
> for darkness is as light to you. (vv. 7–12)

And in the next verses, we discover the truth of God's *omnipotence*: he is all powerful.

For you created my inmost being;
> you knit me together in my mother's womb.
I praise you because I am fearfully and
> wonderfully made;
> your works are wonderful,
> I know that full well.
My frame was not hidden from you
> when I was made in the secret place,
> when I was woven together in the depths of
> > the earth.
Your eyes saw my unformed body;
> all the days ordained for me were written in
> > your book
> before one of them came to be.
How precious to me are your thoughts, God!
> How vast is the sum of them!
Were I to count them,

> they would outnumber the grains of sand—
> when I awake, I am still with you. (vv. 13–18)

There is no other god like our God. Our lifestyle of discernment is designed to posture ourselves to notice him as such in every aspect of our lives. Like the psalmist, we can continually cry out "Search me, God, and know my heart" (v. 23) while we pursue God and desire his heart to remain in us.

Discernment as a lifestyle is in the searching for and being found by God, the One who is all-knowing, always present, and all-powerful. It's the "coming to our senses" that the prodigal son exhibited, and more significantly, it's the prodigal God's loving response. God delivers to us extravagant love, grace, forgiveness, kindness, and unnumbered blessings and gifts, simply because that's who he is. To discern his loving presence and then to receive it fully is our radical response. There's no place like home when it's the heart of God for you, your loved ones, and the world we occupy together. To live this way is to embrace the transformational, radical, and eternal life we're invited to live.

A Kingdom Lifestyle

The unconditional love of God is the foundation for our discerning life. We must recall and continually remember that we are dearly loved sinners, beloved children of God. Our identity in Christ is secure when we know we are his beloved. Reminding ourselves of this reality is a daily endeavor of the soul, and it's best expressed to one another in the context of our spiritual communities and households of faith. Do you know you are dearly loved by God? Reflecting on passages such as Psalm 139 keep us focused on this reality.

The underpinnings of Jesus's life and teaching are his uncon-ditional love for all who crossed his path—the lost, the least, the little, and the left behind. Even to his enemies, especially the reli-gious leaders of his day, his affection was love—albeit tough love. As the Gospels recount the growing tensions between Jesus and the Scribes and Pharisees, his admonitions ascend to a crescendo. And as we read the accounts between Jesus and his opposition, we see with clarity his passion for the kingdom of heaven and his protection of his sheep, the people he loved and served with radical extravagance.

In Matthew's Gospel, one of the grand transitions in his text is the pivot in chapter 22, when the frustrated leaders seek once more to corner Jesus. After Jesus silenced the Sadducees, the Pharisees get together, and an expert of the law tests him with the question, "Teacher, which is the greatest commandment in the Law?" Jesus replies, "'Love the Lord your God with all your heart and with all your soul and with all your mind.' This is the first and great-est commandment. And the second is like it: 'Love your neighbor as yourself.' All the Law and the Prophets hang on these two com-mandments" (Matt. 22:34–40).

The radical nature of Jesus's teaching continually confounded the religious leaders, but it was a balm for the soul of his devoted followers, who felt seen, known, and protected by his humble presence in their midst. His teachings remain to this day an invitation to live a discern-ing life in a radical, upside-down way. The world around us is not keen to Jesus—never has been, never will be. To be accused of being a "Jesus freak" or to hear "there you go again with your Jesus talk" is a badge of honor to those who walk with the radical Jesus, seeking first and foremost to walk in love for God and for our neighbors as ourselves.

Matthew 23 is a stinging rebuke of the hypocrisy of the teach-ers and leaders who keep pulling the people away from Jesus's earlier teachings in the Sermon on the Mount and his many parables. His teachings emanate from the faithful life he lives among them. But what irks Jesus is the lack of humility among the teachers of his day. Jesus warns, "Do not do what they do, for they do not practice what they preach." Instead, "the greatest among you will be your servant. For those who exalt themselves will be humbled, and those who humble themselves will be exalted" (Matt. 23:3, 11–12).

Jesus's litany of woes proclaimed over the teachers of the Law and the Pharisees is stunning to read. "Woe to you, teachers of the law and Pharisees, you hypocrites!" or "you blind guides!" or "you blind fools!" is repeated seven times and with equal number of rebukes:

1. "You shut the door of the kingdom of heaven in people's faces" (v. 13).
2. "You travel over land and sea to win a single convert, and when you have succeeded, you make them twice as much a child of hell as you are" (v. 15).
3. You confuse swearing by the temple and by gold, not knowing which is more sacred to offer as a gift to God (vv. 16–22).
4. "You give a tenth of your spices—mint, dill and cumin. But you have neglected the more important matters of the law—justice, mercy and faithfulness" (v. 23).
5. "You clean the outside of the cup and dish, but inside they are full of greed and self-indulgence" (v. 25).
6. "You are like whitewashed tombs, which look beautiful on the outside but on the inside are full of the bones of the dead and everything unclean" (v. 27).
7. "You testify against yourselves that you are the descendants of those who murdered the prophets" (v. 31).

Does this sound like the Jesus you love and serve? "You snakes! You brood of vipers! How will you escape being condemned to hell?" (v. 33). It is! For his is a radical gospel, and he takes his mission and mandate seriously. He's willing to speak truth into hard hearts who seek to destroy his work. He does so for love's sake, loving them enough to be honest with them. He never stops loving his enemies or the religious leaders of his day. His unrelenting critique is meant to grab their attention and turn them in a new direction. So should we love, even with truth-telling that may seem harsh in the moment.

Living a life of discernment is radical because its focus is on the kingdom of heaven, not the kingdom of this earth. And because the day and the hour of his return is unknown to all of us, the urgency for living a radical life of discernment is growing in importance each new day. Who will stand up for the radical teachings of Jesus and withstand and persevere the trials, tribulations, and persecution that will undoubtedly result? This is a difficult question for most of us to answer honestly and faithfully.

A Radical Preference for God

Matthew 25 includes three parables about the kingdom of heaven. Each is a primer for us as children of King Jesus who are called to build up the King's kingdom here on earth. Each is worth our prayerful reflection, especially as we become more discerning and practice a preference for God.

The parable of the ten virgins (vv. 1–13): Jesus likens the kingdom of heaven to "ten virgins who took their lamps and went out to meet the bridegroom" (v. 1). Five of them are foolish, taking their lamps without oil. Five of them are wise, taking oil in jars along with their lamps. When the bridegroom arrives at midnight, the foolish realize they have no oil for their lamps. The wise trim their lamps and fill them with oil, awaiting the bridegroom's arrival, and are welcomed into the wedding banquet. The door is shut, and when the foolish return with oil for their lamps, they have to stay outside. "Therefore keep watch, because you do not know the day or the hour" (v. 13).

The parable of the talents (vv. 14–30): Here, Jesus likens the kingdom of heaven to "a man going on a journey, who called his servants and entrusted his wealth to them. To one he gave five bags of gold, to another two bags, and to another one bag, each according to his ability. Then he went on his journey" (vv. 14–15). At once, the man who received five bags of gold invests them and gains five more in return. The same happens to the one with two bags of gold. "But the man who had received one bag went off, dug a hole in the ground and hid his master's money" (v. 18).

Upon his return, the man summons his servants to account. The one with the five bags and the one with two bags return to the master double. This pleases the master and he replies, "Well done, good and faithful servant! You have been faithful with a few things; I will put you in charge of many things. Come and share your master's happiness" (v. 21). But the man with one bag simply returns what had been given to him originally. The master is greatly displeased and says,

> You wicked, lazy servant! So you knew that I harvest where I have not sown and gather where I have not scattered seed? Well then, you should have put my money on deposit with the bankers, so that when I returned I would have received it back with interest.
>
> So take the bag of gold from him and give it to the one who has ten bags. For whoever has will be given more, and they will have an abundance.... And throw that worthless servant outside,

into the darkness, where there will be weeping and gnashing of teeth. (vv. 26–30)

The parable of the sheep and goats (vv. 31–46): In the third parable, Jesus says,

When the Son of Man comes in his glory, and all the angels with him, he will sit on his glorious throne. All the nations will be gathered before him, and he will separate the people one from another as a shepherd separates the sheep from the goats. He will put the sheep on his right and the goats on his left.

Then the King will say to those on his right, "Come, you who are blessed by my Father; take your inheritance, the kingdom prepared for you since the creation of the world. For I was hungry and you gave me something to eat, I was thirsty and you gave me something to drink, I was a stranger and you invited me in, I needed clothes and you clothed me, I was sick and you looked after me, I was in prison and you came to visit me." (vv. 31–36)

When questioned by the sheep as to when he saw them do this, the king replies,

"Truly I tell you, whatever you did for one of the least of these brothers and sisters of mine, you did for me." Then he will say to those on his left, "Depart from me, you who are cursed, into the eternal fire prepared for the devil and his angels. . . . Whatever you did not do for one of the least of these, you did not do for me." (vv. 40–41, 45)

No matter how you digest these parables, the message is clear. The kingdom of heaven is for those who open the home of their hearts to Jesus. But to those who close off the home of their hearts from Jesus, there are dire consequences. Notice how the foolish virgins are kept outside the wedding banquet. The lazy servant who hides the bag of gold is thrown "outside, into the darkness." And the goats are denounced: "depart from me, you who are cursed" for your unfaithfulness to provide for the hungry, thirsty, stranger, naked, sick, and imprisoned. The state of their soul is dire, void of God, absent of an awareness of Jesus as their long-awaited Messiah. Their foolishness, greed, and lack of compassion cost them their lives.

Those who know Jesus intimately, who find themselves desperate for more of Jesus each new day, and who have put their hope and trust in his hands are the faithful ones. Those who claim to know Jesus but who live in houses built on sand are the foolish ones who can often lead the faithful astray. Walk with Jesus, trust him implicitly, notice him actively engaged in your daily life, and then point him out to others. Let's follow Jesus, no matter the circumstances of our existence, and in him find our joy.

Repatterning Our Life with God

I have a vivid childhood memory of a season when my mother invited me to join her on an adventure that is difficult to fully absorb even today. But its significance remains fresh in my heart.

There was a young boy in our neighborhood who lived on a street adjacent to the elementary school I attended. He was born with physical and mental challenges; I do not recall the exact diagnosis, nor do I remember many of the specifics of his prognosis. However, I do remember that he was a part of my elementary school's special needs class, and he would appear among my peers on the playground and in the lunchroom. And as a member of the safety patrol, I would see him get dropped off for school near the front entrance.

My mom was part of a group of adults who for several months helped this boy's parents "pattern" his legs, arms, and head by moving them rhythmically in more natural, organic, physiologically appropriate ways. I would walk with her to the boy's house and either sit in another room or be invited to join the group and assist them in the repatterning experience. As I look back on it, I'm struck by how this shaped my view of and compassion for people with disabilities for the rest of my life.

Although I don't know if our efforts made a difference for the boy from my childhood, "neuromuscular reeducation" is a proven form of physical therapy that can help people such as stroke victims achieve functional mobility. The purpose of this therapy is to re-educate the brain to move muscles and limbs in a way conducive to how God ordained when he created our complex bodies. To unlearn and then relearn seems to be the pattern of our lives, not just our physicality.

We need to "reeducate" or "repattern" our lives around the purposes and priorities of God. That includes our awareness of God's all-powerful, all-knowing, ever-present way of being near to us and our corresponding desire to walk with him into the kingdom lifestyle he invites. But none of this comes to us naturally.

The repatterning of our lives can be summarized in the following nine simple truths:

- *We know the true God of the Scriptures* by regularly, prayerfully, and reflectively spending time in the Word, alone and in community. **Discerning God is biblical.**
- *We know the true God as Father, Son, and Holy Spirit and*

proclaim his trinitarian presence: the unconditional love of the Father, the redeeming grace of the Son, and the empowering presence of the Spirit. **Discerning God is trinitarian.**

- *We know our true selves with honesty* by acknowledging the ways God has created us for his purposes, fashioned us in his likeness, gives us our identity in Christ, and uniquely designed us with gifts, temperament, and passion. **Discerning God is prayerful.**

- *We know our true selves in our belovedness*, and as Jesus was declared by the Father at his baptism (Matt. 3:13–17), so we too are known by God in a life-transforming way as dearly loved people in whom God is well pleased. **Discerning God is personal.**

- *We know our true selves in our brokenness*, and like Jesus, who was tested in the wilderness but never succumbed (Matt. 4:1–11), we too struggle with temptations. **Discerning God is humbling.**

- *We know our true selves in our blessedness*, and like Jesus, who affirmed the fulfillment of his calling in the synagogue (Luke 4:14–30), we declare to the world our identity and calling in Christ. **Discerning God is missional.**

- *We know the needs of others* by discerning the heart cries of those who surround us in our families, neighborhoods, communities, churches, and culture. **Discerning God is relational.**

- *We know the best way to serve* is with generous love and compassion, for it was Jesus who modeled for us the fullness of generosity on the cross, where he gave his all and commissioned us to do likewise in every generation. **Discerning God is loving.**

- *We know we are setting others free* to fully live as God's image bearers when we graciously share the gospel, invite them into the cleansing work of redemption, welcome them into the kingdom, affirm and encourage their calling, and empower them to thrive. **Discerning God is transformational.**

When we come to grips with the reality of God's unique thumbprint on our lives, one of the ways we can express this is by writing out a "rule of life," an ancient practice that helps us articulate and then lean more fully into our unique self and the well-ordered way.[1]

The repatterning of our lives starts when we come to grips with the radical call on our lives as children of God. We are to look peculiar in this world. The eyes of our hearts need to be fixed on God and his intentionality for us. His way is the way of love, and love is the key to the radical lifestyle of the discerning life. Will you walk this way, friend?

Learning to Say No and Yes

The repatterning of our lives includes our learning when to say yes and when to say no on a daily, moment-by-moment basis, as we practice a preference for God in all aspects of our personal lives, our relationships, our leadership, and our service to others.

What do we say no to in order to say yes to something greater?

In our discerning life, we cannot say yes to everything. In fact, as we grow in our ability to discern God in all things large and small, we develop the heart muscle to affirm or deny ourselves according to God's greater desires.

The discerning life is *countercultural* in that we are called to live as salt and light in this world, not being swayed by the stronger influences of our day that pull us away from God.

The discerning life is also *counterintuitive* in that, as we grow in Christlikeness, we are repatterning our hearts and minds around kingdom priorities of humbly serving Jesus instead of responding to the loudest and strongest voices that surround and envelop us.

The discerning life is also quite often *counterproductive* in that we no longer share the metrics the world uses to evaluate effectiveness and success. In a discerning life, it's okay to "waste" a normally productive hour and repurpose it for godly pursuit, even if that means giving it up for silence and solitude, reflection on the biblical text, and a prayerful and deeper focus on God.

The discerning life is *transformational* for all who embrace and embody it within the Christian community. Today we need formational leaders and learners who espouse discernment as a way of life. They are the ones who will be humble enough to attend to the voice and movement of God's Spirit. All the while, the storms of our culture bombard us on every side and nearly force us to bend to their more bullish practices. We must make a radical choice to say no to forces that pull us away from a discerning life. Here are four things we should consistently reject, alongside four things we should consistently embrace.

Say no to *complacency* about God and yes to *communion* with God. When we are complacent toward God, we tend to take him for granted. We assume God will give us the provisions he delights to offer his beloved regardless of the state of their soul, but we fail to notice those gifts and continually forget to give him proper thanks. We disregard the need to spend time deepening our intimacy with him in our prayer closets and in public worship.

We ignore the suffering and sadness of our lives and look instead for health and wealth at all costs. We become consumers of blessings rather than worshiping God in spirit and truth. Complacency can lead us into sloth, and such laziness over time leads us into pride and self-absorption. God delights in the returning to and reordering of our affections toward him, which in turn will lead us outward to a deeper union with others.

Individuals and groups can become complacent about God. Notice this tendency in yourself and then note this possibility among those with whom you live and serve in Jesus's name. How is God beckoning you into greater communion today?

Say no to *compulsions* within ourselves and yes to *companionship* with God. We live in a world awash with striving. We want the bigger, better, bolder, new, next, now; and we will push and shove our way toward such ends. Growing out of a deep restlessness, we assume that more of everything will lead us into a fuller life, all the while becoming even more restless and unfulfilled.

Our compulsions are fed by our addictions to adrenaline rushes, which are fed by 24/7 access to technology, days filled with constant noise and perpetual activity, and a pace of life that keeps us from noticing the slow work of God. He desires our companionship, and when we abide in him and grow in our trust of him, we can believe with certainty that he will lead us gently by the hand without the need to repeatedly strive and struggle for more.

Individuals and groups can become compulsive about their striving. Notice what you are striving for today and note how the groups you are involved with are striving too. How is God reaching out his hand of love and inviting you to more intimate companionship today?

Say no to *comparisons* with others and yes to *community* with others. When we compare ourselves with others, we are ultimately choosing some form of self-loathing. Be careful not to constantly look over your shoulder toward those you feel are better looking, better off, smarter, stronger, wittier, wiser, or wealthier than you. Instead, God invites you to look in the mirror and acknowledge who you are, what you look like, where you've come from, what you offer to this world today, and where you're heading tomorrow. Saying no to comparisons allows you to more fully engage in community with others. We are better when we freely recognize our uniqueness and our diversity and then pursue unity and oneness together. Such joy!

Both individuals and groups can compare themselves with others. Notice this tendency in yourself and among those with whom you are seeking to build community. How is God expressing his unconditional love toward you and your community today?

Say no to *competition* with others and yes to *cooperation* with others. Healthy competition belongs on the playing field, the political arena, in the marketplace, and perhaps even in places like education and the arts. But it simply doesn't belong in the church. There are no biblical texts that espouse the values of spiritual competition. We only have one enemy with whom to compete; the devil is our single and common adversary. Instead, in the Christian community, we are called to pursue virtuous cooperation.

A competitive spirit is always divisive in the body of Christ. When we allow competition to exist among churches, organizations, teams, and individuals, we are letting the enemy have a field day in our midst. The enemy of our souls loves it when we speak ill of another, ridicule, shame, offend, and judgmentally critique each other. A cooperative spirit in the body of Christ is exhibited when we want the best for others, as God would have it for them, even if it lessens our own image (or mirage) of greatness in the eyes of others.

Cooperation is our higher calling. Individuals and groups can become competitive with others. Notice this tendency in yourself and note this possibility among those with whom you desire greater cooperation. How is God inviting you to cooperate with a friend or another group toward a kingdom priority?

Learning to Discern God

The discerning life, practicing a preference for God, is completely unlike the ways of this world. It's certainly not complacent toward God. Nor is it a compulsive, comparative, or competitive life. It's not designed to be void of God or destructive to relationships. It's not self-focused or rude. Instead, it's to be a radiant reflection and beautiful fulfillment of the kingdom of heaven here on earth. With Jesus as our anchor and guide, his invitation is always toward communal, constructive, and cooperative ways of living.

Each of Jesus's instructions is transformational. We are called into this life because of his generosity and grace. Learning how to discern God begins and ends with our radical need for God's grace. We cannot live a discerning life without a tonnage of grace.

Grace is a gift from God. It's offered to all, and never because we deserve it. It's given because without it we die. And it's the glue that holds together members of the body of Christ. Void of it among others, we limp along, splinter, or crumble. Absence of grace calls out for even more. To offer it is to enhance life for all, to deny it is to invite conflict among all, to restore it is to humbly ask for it from all, and to live it discerningly is to generously grant it to all.

There are far too many lives and teams struggling to learn how to discern God. They've often jumped ahead of themselves by testing their ability to discern around decision-making. The discerning life isn't all about decision-making, and it's not summarized exclusively by the will of God for a particular purpose. As we've explored together, the discerning life is first and foremost about noticing God and preferring him, individually and collectively. As we see God, we can't help but see his grace poured out upon his people and his world, over and over again.

Our response to seeing God in all things, even in our waiting on God, is the beginning, end, and everything in between for a discerning life. From what we discover about God in his everlasting and historical Word and in his eternal and biblical ways, we lean into his current and future will as members of his family and participants in his kingdom. But when all we're about each day is surviving the day, managing the hours, and even strategizing about the way forward, we can miss so much of what God loves to share with us as his beloved ones.

What does God want us to remember as we lean fully into a discerning life? Here are a handful of radical truths from our trustworthy God:

- **I am with you always.** You can trust my presence.
- **I am here to provide all that you need.** You can trust my power.
- **I am true to my word.** You can trust my promises.
- **I am here for you, with you, and in you.** You can trust my peace.
- **I am going to provide for you, as I always have.** You can trust my provision.
- **I am offering myself for you now and eternally.** You can trust my passion.

- **I am holding your future and am aware of your heart.** You can trust my plans.
- **I am watching over you and covering your soul.** You can trust my protection.

In these truths about God, you can rest and trust. His grace is always sufficient to meet your every need. His hope and joy will come from that place of love that only God can provide. When you walk with God, notice him, point him out to others, and then rest in God each day, you are living a discerning life. From that prayerful vantage point, there is life and freedom in Jesus.

There's no place like home.

When my home is Christ's heart.

And Christ's home is my heart.

PRACTICING A PREFERENCE FOR GOD

Throughout this book, you have been invited to consider your own quirky home as I've shared about mine. We've looked at house care as a metaphor for discernment, noticing the needs around us and responding to them appropriately. Sometimes discernment is sudden, brought upon us by emergencies like the explosion of a rotten jar of tomato sauce. Other times it needs greater attention, such as the replacement of a new water main. Still more, discernment may bring us back in time; as expressed in the story about letters of our last name appearing under layers of paint and wallpaper, our discernment process is historical.

As you consider the state of your own soul (your soul's home), where is God inviting you to trust him more deeply for today and into the future? How is he inviting you to practice a preference for him, seeing him with greater clarity in the midst of the questions you carry? Will you put your heart in his and keep the eyes of your heart wide open to his extravagant love? Perhaps your answers to these questions will invite you into the radical choice of practicing a preference for God.

Here are a few spiritual exercises to put into practice as you reflect on this chapter:

- **Home:** Think about the many experiences you've had in your own home. It is filled with metaphors for the discerning life. What is one story from your home that might lead to a revelation about discerning God?
- **Repattern:** What is one way in which you could "repattern" or "reeducate" your spiritual life? Look back at the nine simple truths about discerning God. Pick one you sometimes have trouble believing and think of a way to live out that truth over and over again until your soul is repatterned to believe it completely.
- **Yes and No:** Read back through the four pairs of things we should reject and embrace—complacency versus communion, compulsions versus companionship, comparisons versus community, and competition versus cooperation. Is there one pair on which you need to focus? Which of these things do you most need to reject? Which do you most need to embrace?

Epilogue

Trust

Spiritual Discernment Is Restful

> *"Truly my soul finds rest in God;*
>   *my salvation comes from him.*
> *Truly he is my rock and my salvation;*
>   *he is my fortress, I will never be shaken."*
>
> Psalm 62:1–2

Trust in him at all times. Find rest in God alone. Pour out your hearts to him. God is our rock, our refuge, and our salvation. With the Lord is unfailing love. Yes, my soul, find rest in God; my hope comes from him. He is my fortress; I will not be shaken. These are awesome words, all of which pop off the page of Psalm 62. King David, the psalmist, reminds us poignantly that our journey in life is best lived in a trusting and loving relationship with God. To miss that leads to an empty and unfulfilled life.

Throughout this book, I have encouraged you to discern God's presence, power, and peace, by practicing a preference for him—each and every day; in matters great and small; alone and in community; with hospitality granted, received, and shared with others.

Spiritual discernment is not for the faint of heart. It's for those who courageously desire to walk a different way than the world espouses and seek the profound intimacy offered generously by God alone.

The discerning life is liberating. It's a life lived under the shadow of God's wings, safely trusting and resting in his presence. We are set free to keep coming back home to the heart of God, regardless of how quirky our homes may be or how peculiar our lives may look. We come to our senses and return daily to the eyes and heart of the Father who is waiting with open arms. Pure delight.

It's almost as if we are surrounded by a plexiglass shield of protection by the Spirit, keeping us fully present in our world but impenetrable to the fiery darts of the evil one. The enemy of our souls wants nothing for us that appears to be godly, God-fearing, or God-focused.

But God, in his infinite wisdom and matchless grace, invites us to notice him showing up over and over again. He beckons us to find our rest solely in him and to trust him implicitly together as his people and alone as his dearly loved child.

Our journey together began in the biblical text as we unpacked the various ways God has made himself known throughout the generations. We looked at our life of prayer and how to listen attentively to the voice of God so as not to miss his presence and peace, his compassion, and his direction.

We talked about the relational character of spiritual discernment and the great need for us to be fully present with one another. We focused on hospitality as the gift to offer to one another in community. We reviewed the various contexts for the discerning life and how important it is to empathize and fully comprehend their complexity.

We then looked at the intentionality required for clarity in discernment and the process we can consider using or adapt to our contexts, especially during times of desire to know and follow his will. Finally, we considered how radical it is to live a discerning life in this day and age, especially if the kingdom of God matters to us.

Below, in the appendixes, you fill find an outline of the discernment process discussed in chapter 8 and *Practicing a Preference for God*, a practical guide for sealing and solidifying these transforming principles in a forty-day window, enhancing our shared experience of the discerning life.

Trust in God. Rest in God. Entrust the fullness of your life into God's hands. All that you are, all that you've been given, all that you are becoming, place before God. And invite him to reign supreme in your heart and life, to receive all the honor and glory and dignity and worship and joy that he deserves.

For we are mere mortals, sinners saved by grace, learning how to rest and trust, and then courageously, faithfully, and obediently to hope and bless, create *shalom*, and share this way of being with all who have ears to hear.

May it be so. Amen.

Gamboa
Rainforest
Reserve

Westin
Playa

APPENDIX A

The Discernment Process

Ten Questions for Leaders and Teams

Stephen A. Macchia

Phase 1. Frame the question.

> *What is the question we are discerning together?*

Phase 2. Gather the team.

> *Who are the appropriate members of the discernment team?*

Phase 3. Release all biases, preconceived conclusions, and predetermined assumptions.

> *Are you willing to release or hold loosely your preconceived ideas for the outcome?*

And PRAY

> *How is God inviting you to pray?*

Phase 4. Assemble the facts.

> *What are the facts as we currently know them?*

And PRAY

> *How is God inviting you to pray?*

Phase 5. Critique and review options.

What are the options as we know them today?

And PRAY

How is God inviting you to pray?

Phase 6. State reasons why NOT.

One option at a time—why should we NOT pursue it?

And PRAY

How is God inviting you to pray?

Phase 7. State reasons why YES.

One option at a time—why SHOULD we pursue it?

And PRAY

How is God inviting you to pray?

Phase 8. Deliberate openly, honestly, without judgment or conclusion.

Taking one option at a time—which ones stay, and which ones go away?

And PRAY

How is God inviting you to pray?

Phase 9. Decide and proceed.

What is our final decision—which of these choices is for the greater glory to God, and what are the steps to achieve what we've discerned together?

And PRAY

How is God inviting you to pray?

Phase 10. Review, evaluate, and start again.

What have we learned, what's working well, what needs our attention, and/or when will discernment recommence?

And PRAY

How is God inviting you to pray?

Practicing a Preference for God

A Forty-Day Prayer and Reflection
Resource Based on *A Guide to Spiritual
Discernment* by Rueben P. Job

Overview, Edits, and Compilation by Stephen A. Macchia

*"Oh, the depth of the riches of the wisdom and
knowledge of God!*
    *How unsearchable his judgments,
    and his paths beyond tracing out!*
Who has known the mind of the Lord?
    Or who has been his counselor?
*Who has ever given to God,
    that God should repay them?*
*For from him and through him and for him are
        all things.*
    To him be the glory forever! Amen."

                    Romans 11:33–36

> *"Holy, holy, holy*
> *is the Lord God Almighty,'*
> *Who was, and is, and is to come."*
>
> Revelation 4:8

As was mentioned at the outset of the book, this appendix is devoted to a soul-care exercise for individuals and teams. Taking forty days to reflect alone or together on the meaning of spiritual discernment over a six-week time frame will deepen your practice of a preference for God.

A good part of the following material was originally published in *A Guide to Spiritual Discernment*, which was written and compiled by one of my spiritual mentors, Rueben P. Job, and published in 1996 by Upper Room Publications. Rueben has since gone home to be with the Lord, but in his incredible lifetime was a devoted husband, father, grandfather, Methodist pastor (and later, Methodist bishop), and was one of the most gracious, kind, and humble men I've ever met.

Over the years, Rueben and his friend Norman Shawchuck compiled four incredibly rich, yearlong, Christian-calendar-adhering prayer books. They originally sought to compile some of their favorite readings on various spiritual-formation topics for a group of friends. Rueben firmly believed that as spiritual friends engage in a common reading and prayer practice, their walks with God and one another will deepen. This has proven to be true for thousands of their readers over the years. I've been reading their *Guides to Prayer* since the mid-1980s, when I was first introduced to *A Guide to Prayer for Ministers and Other Servants.* For nearly two decades, our Leadership Transformations team and ministry associates have been reading through the yearlong *Guides to Prayer* as an ongoing spiritual practice for our ministry community.

When Leadership Transformations was formed in 2003, I invited our founding board to read and pray through Rueben's forty-day guide, *A Guide to Spiritual Discernment.* Our team received a rich understanding of spiritual discernment, the heartbeat of our ministry to leaders and teams. As a result, I'm convinced that our foundational years of flourishing came from our board's commitment to become more prayerfully discerning about our shared ministry to leaders and teams. Over the years, I've invited several leadership teams to do likewise, with similar results.

May these Scripture passages, prayerful readings, and meditative reflections usher you into God's presence, deepen your understanding of spiritual discernment, and renew your soul. All the daily Scripture passages are newly collected as "Fifty Biblical Reflections for Noticing God." What follows also includes short excerpts from a handful of the meditations that were republished with permission in *A Guide to Spiritual Discernment,* and their original sources are duly noted in the endnotes.

A Guide to Follow

This appendix is designed to give an individual, a small group, a leadership team, or a congregation a useful tool to assist in the process of understanding and living out spiritual discernment. All persons of faith want to know God and do God's will. Yet in our busy and noisy world, it is often hard to hear God's voice. While we all walk by faith, we desire some special means of listening to God. Perhaps the greatest work any person of faith is called to is to learn to pay attention to God. To learn how to see God at work in the everyday events of life and to hear God's voice in the sacred Scriptures and the life of another is of enormous significance to the person who seeks to live a life of faithfulness. This simple yet profound process is designed to slowly and prayerfully transform us into the image of God.

The guide below is designed to be used every day as a way of listening and noticing God more intimately, and to perhaps prepare you for a discernment process and decision-making that will come near the end of this forty-day period. The resource includes a structure for daily prayers, a liturgy for covenant groups in which you may gather for discernment and support, and a handful of readings for each week. In each case, you will need a Bible and your hymnal to make the most of this resource. Since busyness is one of our most persistent problems, it will be important for you to determine the time and place for this forty-day experience. Set aside some time every day to listen to God's voice, to ask for God's guidance, and to offer your life to God in fidelity, trust, and love.

Each of the liturgies in this guide offers suggested Scripture readings and hymns to be sung or read. You may wish to select additional or other hymns or Scripture passages for your time of prayer and praise. Feel free to adapt this resource to your individual or corporate needs. Listed below are some brief suggestions and comments about the liturgy for Daily Prayer and Praise.

Prayer of Invitation. Begin this time of prayer and praise by giving full attention to God and by inviting God into your life anew. Use the prayer daily as one way in which you become present to God and invite God to be present to you.

Hymn of Praise. You will need a hymnal for this portion (or the internet to look up the words and music). Sing or read the hymn every day. Next to the Bible, our hymnbooks are our most helpful resource in listening to and hearing God speak.

Scripture Reading. Read the Scripture at least once, and always listen for what God is saying to you during the reading. Perhaps follow the *lectio divina* practice introduced earlier in this book. We will walk through the Old and New Testament, noticing God's initiatives toward his beloved family of followers.

Reflection and Response. Keep a time of silence to permit the Scripture to be God's message for you and for your life for this day. Ask frequently, "What is God saying to me through this passage? What response is he calling for from me?" Use a journal to record your insights and questions.

Sacred Reading. Use one or more of the readings in this resource, your hymnbook, or some other source for spiritual reading. There are a plethora of options to consider here. Don't feel like you have to read extensively. Instead, read meditatively and prayerfully.

Reflection and Response. Once again seek to listen to the material as a letter from God to you seeking to give guidance to your process of discernment. Record your findings for later reference. Writing down your insights and questions often brings clarity to your thought.

Prayer. Each week, there are suggestions for your prayers of gratitude and your prayers of petition or intercession. Again, you will want to make this list more specific and add to the list those special areas of thanksgiving and petition that you bring to this time of prayer. Be sure to offer your prayers and spend time listening to God's Spirit as you pray.

The Lord's Prayer. To pray this prayer is to remember that we are not alone. When we come into the presence of God, we come into the presence of God's people. This prayer that Jesus taught us saves us from simply praying selfish prayers, gives us a glimpse of a reality larger than our own concerns, and binds us once more to God's vision for all creation.

Closing Prayer of Consecration. In this prayer, we declare our willingness to be led by God throughout the activities of the day. It is a time of surrender on the one hand and of picking up our directions and promised sustenance for the day on the other.

Many are praying with you and for you as you prepare to be an instrument in God's hand in the deliberation and decision-making of your congregation, which always begins with *practicing a preference for God* in your personal life. If you are using this resource as a guide to personal discernment and decision-making, ask others to join in prayer with you. May God's grace and peace be yours in abundance as you seek to know God and do his will.

Introduction: Discerning God's Vision

Forty Days of Preparation and Reflection
By Rueben P. Job

The time frame of forty days has special significance for Christians. We remember Moses and the children of Israel wandering in the wilderness for forty years in search of the promised land. We are especially aware of the forty days Jesus spent in the wilderness facing the subtle and yet hard decisions of life. And we annually complete the forty-day Lenten journey from Ash Wednesday to Easter and then from Easter to Pentecost. Exodus and promised land are a part of the reality of the church year and of each of our lives.

Thus, it is fitting that as Christians seeking to know God and do God's will we spend forty days in watching, listening, and reflecting as we seek to discern God's way for us. Our relationship with Jesus Christ can grow stronger and our responsibility to Jesus Christ can grow clearer as we practice methods of discernment as old as Christianity. We will also discover that our relationship to one another is strengthened as together we seek God's will above all else. Congregations often discover a new unity, faith, vitality, mission, and sense of God's nearness as they fervently seek God and God's will.

The exodus we are called to make is to leave the land of self-centered and self-serving living and decision-making for the promised land of seeking and finding and preferring God, and doing God's will in all things. To enter the promised land of living in the center of God's will, we must leave behind the sin that so easily captures and controls us; that is, the desire for our will to be done. Instead we are invited to reach out for the "upward call of God in Christ Jesus" (Phil. 3:14 ESV). This requires a radical renunciation of sin and a radical declaration of faith in the God for whom all things are possible. For when our faith in this God without limits is strong, we begin to recognize that our way may not be the best way and God's way is always the best way.

We as the children of Israel have embarked on a journey toward the promised land of God's will in the affairs of our lives and within our congregation. Our faith is not in our prayers, our process of discernment, or a forty-day time frame. Our faith is in the living God who comes to guide and companion those who seek to walk in God's way. While there may be many ways to the promised land of God's full and complete reign, and we as individuals and as a congrega-tion may face many options, we can be sure that there is one most desirable way for us to follow. What is it? Which way is God call-ing us to go? What is the right decision for us to make? How will we decide the important questions before us? How will we face the temptations of the wilderness and remain faithful and true? With God's help we can be led to discover answers to these and other questions that confront us as we move toward decision-making as an individual or as a community of faith from a context of preferring God in all things and at all times.

The people of God are always on the way to the promised land. To be a follower of Jesus is to be a pilgrim, and it is to be on a journey that always leads us toward God and God's goodness. The Scriptures remind us that God loves us and seeks to sustain us in all of life. Therefore, we can ask for guidance in the confidence that God's way, the very best way, will be made known to us.

The vision of the promised land comes from God. The direc-tion and strength to get there also come from God. But if we are to see the vision and to make the journey, we must be willing to give up what we have for that which is not yet fully realized. We need a willingness and openness to discern, to see God's way, and finally, a yearning to be led in that way alone.

"If you love me, you will keep my commandments. And I will pray the Father, and he will give you another Counselor, to be with you for ever, even the Spirit of truth, whom the world cannot receive, because it neither sees him nor knows him; you know him, for he dwells with you, and will be in you" (John 14:15–17 RSV).

This is the road of spiritual discernment, practicing a prefer-ence for God.

234

Week 1: Discernment: A Listening Community

Prayer of Invitation

Almighty God, you who have made yourself known to all humankind and to us in times past, make yourself and your way known to us in this time of prayer and reflection. In the name and Spirit of Christ. Amen.

Hymn of Praise

"Great Is Thy Faithfulness"

Scripture Reading

Sunday — Genesis 1:1–31, God creates

Monday — Genesis 2:1–3, God rests

Tuesday — Genesis 2:4-25, God forms man and woman

Wednesday — Genesis 6:9–22, God calls Noah

Thursday — Genesis 12:1–9, God calls Abram

Friday — Genesis 18:1–15, God appears to Abraham and Sarah

Saturday — Genesis 22:1–18, God tests and blesses Abraham

Reflection and Response

Sacred Reading

Reflection and Response

Prayer

Thanksgiving for God's sustaining grace and goodness. Petitions for the following:

Peace in the world, especially . . .

All the churches of God, especially . . .

> Our pastors and congregational leaders, especially . . .
>
> All who suffer and are oppressed, especially . . .

All who are prisoners of addiction, especially . . .

All who seek to walk in faithfulness, justice, and righteousness, especially . . .

My own life and witness and for those in my care, especially . . .

The Lord's Prayer

Closing Prayer of Consecration

> *Loving Creator, we place our lives into your hands with confidence in your love and fidelity. We know that you will lead us into your will and so we ask in confidence, do with us what you will and lead us this day in truth and righteousness. We offer our prayers and our lives in the name of Jesus. Amen.*

READINGS FOR REFLECTION

A Listening Community

Christians at their best are good listeners, and the Christian church, when most faithful, is a listening community. To live with God in this world that God loves requires some intense and intentional listening. So many competing voices are calling for our attention that without concentrated effort and determination we may easily miss what God is saying to us. We may even miss the way and will into which God is trying to lead us.

I wear two hearing aids, and even with them discover that I often mistake one word or phrase for another and often answer questions never asked and take directions never given! Sometimes, even when I remember to listen carefully, have both hearing aids on, and take my time, I still need to ask someone for clarity on the message that I am trying to understand. We all need help to hear clearly and completely the truth of God for our lives and for our world. The Christian community is one of those helps or aids to our hearing clearly the voice and direction of God. The events of the world around us, the events of our lives, the natural world, the Scriptures, prayer, worship, sacred reading, a spiritual guide or friend, all can help us to hear.

Faithful guides who have gone before us have suggested that there are several prerequisites to hearing clearly the voice and direction of God. First of all is faith in a God who communicates with us. Our willingness and our effort to listen will be conditioned by our faith in a God who speaks and gives guidance. The wise and faithful leaders of the past also believed that we listen for and to God's voice and direction only when we are intensely dissatisfied with things as they are. It is unlikely that we will hear God's voice calling us to risk, to move out in new mission or with new vision, if we are very comfortable and settled with things the way they are. And perhaps the most important of all is a great love for God and a passion for God's will. When these elements of faith in God, desire for God's way (dissatisfaction with our way), and great love for God and God's will are present in a solitary life or a community, the possibility of one hearing God's voice of guidance is greatly multiplied.

I used to believe that everyone mumbled. My family, my friends, telephone callers, even radio personalities seemed to have lost the ability to speak clearly. Then I was fitted with hearing aids. What a surprise! Everyone spoke with clarity. What had changed? I had accepted help in hearing. Trying to listen and hear clearly the voice of God is not an easy task nor a casual undertaking. Ask God to guide you today and always to the help you need so that you may hear clearly even the slightest whisper of the One who spoke you into being.

—Rueben P. Job[1]

True discernment calls us beyond the well-tended gardens of conventional religious wisdom to the margin between the known and the unknown, the domesticated and the wild. We incur risk any time we place ourselves in the presence of that which exists beyond our control. How crucial, then, that our efforts to sift and sort the forces shaping our spiritual life be undertaken with some bedrock assurances. King David provides one which cannot be surpassed. We are guided through narrow paths and led to spacious vistas because God delights in us. Deep in the layers of history, beneath the great upheavals of infidelity that reshape the landscape of our life with God, there abides a divine pleasure in the human creature. In the fullness of time this delight overflowed the bounds of worldly prudence and swept God into our very midst, one with us in suffering and hope. It is always in the gladsome company of this God that our discernment occurs.

—John S. Mogabgab[2]

O God, by whom the meek are guided in judgment, and light riseth up in darkness for the godly: Grant us, in all our doubts and uncertainties, the grace to ask what thou wouldest have us to do, that the Spirit of wisdom may save us from all false choices, and that in thy light we may see light, and in thy straight path may not stumble; through Jesus Christ our Lord. Amen.

—The Book of Common Prayer

Watching and waiting have been observed by the church from the most ancient times down to the present. The purpose of vigil, the purpose of watching, is to bring us to reconciliation with God and with all creation, allowing us to be ready for the coming of Christ. Daily contact with the word of God guides us in keeping watch. With openness of heart, with obedience to the deepest call of God in our spirit, we listen to what God is saying to us, through others and through the church, about how to be born and brought back to the fullness of the image of God.

—Timothy Kelly[3]

In his gentle way Jesus comes into the company of two walking to Emmaus. He presumes nothing, but simply joins them since safety in numbers was common for travelers. When occasion presents itself, Jesus shares his good news. At village edge, he hints at going on but accepts their offer of hospitality. Luke gives no indication that Jesus is yet recognized (see Luke 24:13–35).

The economy of details leaves a lot of the story to our imagining. We depend on studying translations and commentaries for details. J. B. Phillips translates the key event by giving this emphasis in verse 31: "Then it happened!" When Jesus was at table with them, he took bread, gave thanks, broke it, and handed it to them. In that most common of daily privileges—breaking bread—their eyes were opened.

Whatever the reason for their recognizing that Emmaus moment, Jesus became present. Then they understood why it had been like fire burning within them as he had explained the Scriptures to them.

—Robert K. Smyth[4]

Week 2: A Broken World

Prayer of Invitation

Tender shepherd, make your way and yourself known to me in this time of prayer and praise. Bring healing to the brokenness in my life and help me to be an answer to another's prayer for healing, mending, and reconciliation. In the Spirit of Jesus. Amen.

Hymn of Praise

"Holy, Holy, Holy"

Scripture Reading

Sunday — Genesis 28:10–22, God appears to Jacob in a dream
Monday — Genesis 32:22–32, God wrestles with Jacob
Tuesday — Genesis 41:1–40, God selects Joseph to interpret Pharaoh's dreams

Wednesday — Genesis 50:15–21, God protects Joseph from his
jealous brothers
Thursday — Exodus 3:1–15, God appears to Moses in a
burning bush
Friday — Exodus 5:22–6:12, God promises deliverance for his
people
Saturday — Exodus 20:1–17, God provides the Ten
Commandments

Reflection and Response

Sacred Reading

Reflection and Response

Prayer
Thanksgiving for God's lovingkindness and petitions for:

Those who suffer: the addicted, homeless, poor, hungry,
imprisoned, sick, despairing, sorrowing, and dying.
Those who work with the suffering: social workers, doctors, nurses,
counselors, chaplains, pastors, and volunteer workers.
The broken places in our community.
Faithful congregations and individuals who reach out to bring
healing and hope to the brokenness of our world;
My own life and witness as a follower of Jesus.

The Lord's Prayer

Closing Prayer of Consecration

Crucified One, we bind our lives once more to you with all of the faith and commitment we have to offer. We ask you to hold us close to yourself throughout this day and to lead us in faithfulness all day long. Show us your will and help us to walk in it. We offer our prayers and our lives in the name of Jesus. Amen.

READINGS FOR REFLECTION

Discernment in a Broken World

We live in a broken world. Even a casual survey of last week's headlines is enough to convince us of the fractured nature of our human family. The pain that many of our sisters and brothers bear seems almost unbearable. We want to reach out and help, but the need is so enormous that we find it easier to shut out the cries for help that come from every point of the compass, lest we ourselves be overcome with the burden of it all.

We need not look to the other side of the world or country or even the other side of our town to find signs of brokenness. Careful self-examination reveals the fractures deep in our own lives. These wounds, old and new, also cry out for healing.

The cries of the broken world are all around us and within us. How can these cries be heard as the voice of God? How can the world's brokenness be a sign of God's vision for a new heaven and a new earth?

Those who have gone before us along the pathway of discernment, seeking only God's will and way, remind us that *dissatisfaction with things as they are* is one essential element in discovering God's will. When we are settled and very comfortable, it is hard to listen for and respond to God's voice calling us to move out, over, up, beyond, or even to new ministry where we are.

The pain of our world is almost beyond our ability to bear. Because it is, we find ourselves more willing to face the possibility for radical and rapid change of things the way they are for things as they can be when God's reign is fully come. Dissatisfaction with things as they are is one of the ways that we invite the coming of God's reign in our midst.

A second characteristic of those who are able to discern God's will is *a passion for God's will.* Along with dissatisfaction with things as they are is the yearning for what can be. The vision of the reign of God is not yet complete. The vision is not altogether clear, but we believe that the One who is the truth and who promised to give us the truth will make God's vision known to each of us and to all of us together as we seek to listen and then respond in faithfulness. As followers of Jesus Christ we are all pilgrims on a journey toward God. To turn away from seeking this shared vision is to turn away from Christ.

Another quality of the person or community that is able to hear God's voice and to see God's vision is *the capacity to remain open to God.* To read the Scriptures, to listen to the cries of the world, including our own hearts, to immerse ourselves in prayer, and to act quickly when we sense God calling us to some simple or profound witness or service. Discerning God's vision for a denomination, congregation, organization, family, or solitary life is not a simple or easy endeavor. The One who promised never to leave us also promises to assist us, and therein is our hope.

—Rueben P. Job

Guide me, O thou great Jehovah, pilgrim through this
  barren land.
I am weak, but thou art mighty; hold me with thy
  powerful hand.
Bread of heaven, bread of heaven, feed me til I want
  no more;
Feed me til I want no more.

—William Williams, "Guide Me, O Thou
  Great Jehovah," 1745 (public domain)

There is a balm in Gilead to make the wounded whole;
There is a balm in Gilead to heal the sin-sick soul.
Sometimes I feel discouraged, and think my works
  in vain.
But then the Holy Spirit revives my soul again.
There is a balm in Gilead to make the wounded whole;
There is a balm in Gilead to heal the sin-sick soul.
Don't ever feel discouraged, for Jesus is your friend,
And if you look for knowledge he'll ne'er refuse
  to lend.
There is a balm in Gilead to make the wounded whole;

There is a balm in Gilead to heal the sin-sick soul.

If you can't preach like Peter, if you can't pray like Paul,

Just tell the love of Jesus, and say he died for all.

There is a balm in Gilead to make the wounded whole;

There is a balm in Gilead to heal the sin-sick soul.

—"There Is a Balm in Gilead," an African-American
spiritual based on Jer. 8:22 (public domain)

Down in the human heart, crushed by the tempter,

Feelings lie buried that grace can restore;

Touched by a loving heart, wakened by kindness,

Chords that were broken will vibrate once more.

Rescue the perishing, care for the dying;

Jesus is merciful, Jesus will save.

—Fanny J. Crosby, "Rescue the
Perishing," 1869 (public domain)

Christ has no body now on earth but yours; yours are the only hands with which he can do his work, yours are the only feet with which he can go about the world. Yours are the only eyes through which his compassion can shine forth upon a troubled world. Christ has no body now on earth but yours.

—Teresa of Avila (1515–1582)

Week 3: A Broken Body

Prayer of Invitation

God of healing and wholeness, I invite your presence into the midst of my own incompleteness. Show clearly the reality of my brokenness and lead me now and always into your way of healing and wholeness. In the name of Jesus. Amen.

Hymn of Praise

"Be Thou My Vision"

Scripture Reading

Sunday — Numbers 22:21–41, God speaks through
Balaam's donkey

Monday — Joshua 1:1–18, God selects Joshua as leader to
succeed Moses

Tuesday — Joshua 3:1–17, God parts the waters of the Jordan

Wednesday — Ruth 4:1–22, God provides a guardian-redeemer

Thursday — 1 Samuel 3:1–21, God calls Samuel

Friday — 1 Samuel 16:8–13; 17:1–58, God calls and
empowers David

Saturday — 1 Kings 3:1–15, God gives Solomon wisdom
and discernment

Reflection and Response

Sacred Reading

Reflection and Response

Prayer

Thanksgiving for God's redeeming and healing presence. Petitions for the following:

For all denominations and especially for the denomination where
    God has called me to live out my discipleship.
For the congregations, members, pastors, and all volunteer workers;
For boards and agencies, colleges and seminaries, hospitals, care
    centers, and all ministries that offer the healing love and justice
    of the risen Savior;
For my congregation and for burning desire to know God's will and
    for desire and faith to follow God's will alone.

The Lord's Prayer

Closing Prayer of Consecration

*Tender shepherd, we offer to you all that we are, aware of our
incompleteness, and ask for your healing presence in our lives
and in the life of this congregation and of every congregation.
We are ready to take the next step toward completeness. Show
us the way. In the name of Jesus Christ. Amen.*

READINGS FOR REFLECTION

Discernment in a Broken Body

The church is not perfect. Sometimes we wish it were. Sometimes we even think it is. There are those moments of Christ in action through the church that move us to joyous thanksgiving. There are also those moments that painfully remind us that the church is made up of persons like ourselves. We are the body of Christ, the church. And we are persons who are a mixture of motives, hopes, faith, fears, anxiety, and who have been shaped by family, culture, education, and the church itself. And we carry all of who we are into the church. So it should not be surprising to us that the body of Christ is broken and fractured. The conflicts, halting discipleship, fragile faith, timid witness, and qualified commitment are a natural outgrowth of who we are as individual Christians.

While we may look at the church in its various expressions with joy at times and dismay at others, we must remember that new life is possible. Transformation can begin today. Resurrection power is available to us and can be invested in the church this very moment. With God's help we can initiate change this very day!

This is true because our first line of defense against further brokenness is within each of us. My efforts to stop the brokenness and to take the first step to reform and transform the church must begin with me. My prayer for a holy church marked by righteousness and love can be answered only as I yield my life to the way of Jesus Christ and the power of the Holy Spirit. The transformation begins with me. What a liberating thought! I am not powerless and without options. With God's help I can surrender my life to the transforming, life-giving power of the Holy Spirit and in that very moment begin the journey toward the wholeness and faithfulness I want to see in the church.

Discernment for the Christian community begins with the individual Christian. Do I want to know God and God's will more than anything else? This question is the entryway into discernment. And it can be answered with affirmation only by those who love God and have learned to trust God. If we have any higher priority in our search for God's guidance, we will not be able to trust our discernment. I must spend enough time in prayer and faithful listening to the voice of God to be brought to that moment of trust and surrender when I can give up my preconceived ideas and become open to God's idea. My first concern is not my desired result. My first concern is always God and the fidelity of our relationship, and then the result of my discernment efforts will come quite naturally. We know that God is completely faithful, and we must be alert, prayerful, open, and ready to respond in obedience if we are to be led toward greater faithfulness on our part.

Obedience is the next essential step in seeking God's will. The word obedience has a bad reputation in our time but a very positive record in humankind's relationship with God. Those who were ready to follow God's direction received the guidance needed. The biblical record suggests God's desire to lead a faithful people. And yet it seems that God is reluctant to make clear the road to faithfulness to those who are not willing to walk along that road. Many who have gone before us have declared that we cannot know God's will unless we commit our way to that will, even before we ask for clarity on what that will is for us.

Can Christians know God's will? Can the church know God's will? Can our congregation know God's will? Nearly two thousand years of experience shout a resounding yes! But it will not be easy to know God's will because such knowledge begins with us. We first must offer our lives to God in all of the completeness we can bring and then listen in all the ways we know for the voice of the One who alone can transform our lives, our congregations, our denomination, the entire body of Christ, and even the world. As we listen, hear, and respond, we will discover transformation occurring within and around us, and perhaps even to our surprise, we will begin to see clearly God's will. May it be so!

—Rueben P. Job

Thanks be to thee, O Lord Jesus Christ, for all the benefits which thou hast given us; for all the pains and insults which thou hast borne for us O most merciful Redeemer, friend, and brother, may we know thee more clearly, love thee more dearly, and follow thee more nearly, for thine own sake. Amen.

—Richard of Chichester, 13th century

Read 1 Samuel 17:19–23, 32–49.

The army of Israel stood in despondent fear before the might of Goliath. The saying goes that it is darkest before the dawn. That is often the time when, at the end of our rope, God's deliverance surprises us. And what an unlikely source provided God's deliverance for Israel—a lad, a keeper of sheep. Young David faced Goliath with fuzz still on his cheeks and an innocent trust in God in his heart. Hearing the taunting of Goliath, he offers himself as Israel's champion. At first Saul rejects the offer as ridiculous. Then he listens and finally agrees. Perhaps something in the lad's passion, in his confidence in God, won Saul's consent.

So David goes to face the giant. He has no heavy armor, no great spear—only a sling and five smooth stones from the brook. The giant roars in disbelieving laughter, as David's sling begins to circle. Then the Philistine champion falls, and the rest is history.

—Ron James[5]

The discerning community of faith is undergoing God. God beckons. God draws forth. And as the community responds, even haltingly, God sustains. God permeates. God shapes. All this comes of God at once.

Such undergoing, as I have seen it, dawns where there is a gentle and graced willingness at the heart of the community of faith. This willingness is not wrapped in the expectations of instant change. It is not encased in tight mechanisms of control that would force a community in some direction already selected by its leaders. The willingness arises utterly unadorned. It is a modest, "Here we are." It is a "Let it be with us according to your will." It is a deep "Yes" to the new patterns of prayer, attentiveness, and communal understanding that emerge.

And the "Yes" to undergoing God invariably gives rise to patterns of living where love becomes incarnate. The changes are fresh and deep. A community of faith that consciously discerns the fresh beckonings of God is also a community that undergoes God.

—Stephen V. Doughty[6]

Direct us, O Lord, in all our doings with thy most gracious favor, and further us with thy continual help; that in all our works begun, continued, and ended in thee, we may glorify thy holy name, and finally by thy mercy, obtain everlasting life; through Jesus Christ our Lord. Amen.

—The Book of Common Prayer

Week 4: God Made Visible

Prayer of Invitation

God made known in the face of Jesus, come and reveal yourself to me in this time of prayer and reflection. Help me to come before you in openness so that I may receive you more fully into my life and to receive your guidance in all that I do and am. In the name of Jesus Christ. Amen.

Hymn of Praise

"Praise to the Lord, the Almighty"

Scripture Reading

Sunday — Psalm 1, God watches over the righteous
Monday — Psalm 16, God makes known the path of life
Tuesday — Psalm 23, God is our Shepherd

Wednesday — Psalm 42, God is our Rock
Thursday — Psalm 51, God forgives and restores
Friday — Psalm 62, God offers rest for our soul
Saturday — Psalm 103, God is compassionate and gracious

Reflection and Response

Sacred Reading

Reflection and Response

Prayer

Thanksgiving for God's presence and guidance in your life and in the church. Petitions for:

Leaders and all who join you in seeking only God's will;
All who this day face decisions that must be made;
The suffering and dying;
Those who long for the new life that only God can bring.

The Lord's Prayer

Closing Prayer of Consecration

Living and present God, we thank and praise you for your presence with us in all of the experiences of life. We seek your guidance in every decision of life, and even as we ask for your help, we offer our lives to you anew and ask you to do with us what you will. Our promise to you today is to follow wherever you may lead us. We are yours. Amen.

READINGS FOR REFLECTION

Hearing God's Voice: Seeing God's Way

We do not see God up close, face to face every day. Or do we? Could it be that God is with us at all times, seeking to be our guide and companion as well as our Lord and Savior? Our Scripture readings for the week suggest that the answer is yes. We are never outside the care and loving gaze of God, and we can learn how to live more fully in the awareness of and surrender to that presence. To do so is to open ourselves to guidance and direction in all of life.

You have been given responsibility for decision-making. It is a large responsibility, and the issues are complex and seldom clearly one way or the other. Even when we have gathered all the facts and looked at and listened to all the evidence, the answer may still be unclear. We bring our best thoughts and all of our previous experiences to the decision-making process, and still we find that prejudice, half-truths, insufficient evidence, and lack of wisdom leave us uncertain about God's way in the matter.

At times like this we long for the assurance of God's presence with us. We yearn to ask Jesus, who always reflected God's will, what our decision should be, what really is God's will in this matter. We would seek to know how we can discern that our decisions are not our own, not where the popular opinion is, not what is easy or cheap, not even what will please the most persons or defeat someone we don't like. Rather, one might ask, "What is God's will? What does God desire around this concern I have? What decision would I make if I were to block out all other interests and seek to please only God?"

To ask these primary questions is to begin to open ourselves to God's guidance and gradually to lower the volume of all the other competing voices that seek to influence our decision-making. It is to place ourselves in a position where we can receive God's guidance in our personal and corporate decision-making process.

Competing voices are always around us, and some of them loudly proclaim that they are hearing or have heard the voice of God, and consequently we should follow them. How to decide which voice to listen to is an essential step to discerning God's will. In other words, which voice are we to follow? Faithful Christians want to follow the way of and do the will of the God made known through Jesus Christ, the Scriptures, our own experiences, and the experiences of those faithful persons who have gone before us. In other words, preparation for decision-making began a long time ago, and we can bring the experience of a long-time companionship with God to our decision-making.

Added to our experience of walking with Jesus and daily seeking the guidance of the Holy Spirit is our listening to the Scriptures for God's voice addressing us in our daily reading and reflection. We can place ourselves under the Scriptures, and let them address us rather than placing ourselves over the Scriptures, seeking to use them to fortify our own position. Our time of prayer can become a time of listening for an answer to a simple petition of "show me your way." As a matter of fact, those who seek to walk with God in the world are always praying "show me your way" and face every event of their lives with the question, "What is God saying to me though this experience?"

The Gospels and book of Acts give a glimpse of the dependence upon God for guidance that marked every decision the early church was called upon to make. The promise to the individual Christian and to the church has always been that wisdom and guidance were available for the asking to those who sought only God's will. We have nearly two thousand years of testimony declaring that such an earnest request will be heard and answered. Therefore, you may ask for guidance with assurance and respond with confidence as God guides your decision-making.

—Rueben P. Job

Grant me, O Lord, to know what I ought to know, to love what I ought to love, to praise what delights you most, to value what is precious in your sight, to hate what is offensive to you. Do not allow me to judge according to the sight of my eyes, nor to pass sentence according to the hearing of my ears; but to discern with a true judgment between things visible and spiritual, and above all things, always to inquire what is the good pleasure of your will.

—Thomas à Kempis

Discernment is like the turning of the sunflower to the sun, or the intuitive hunch of the scientist seeking new and creative solutions for unexplainable, contradictory observations, or the restless seeking of a heart longing to find its way home to an estranged lover, or the artistry of the musician, sculptor, or

choreographer delineating in sound, stone, or the human body
the emergent, self-propellant, rightful line that says "yes."

Discernment is about feeling texture, assessing weight,
watching the plumb line, listening for overtones, feeling the
quickening, surrendering to love. It's being grasped in the Spirit's
arms and led in the rhythms of an unknown dance.

—Wendy M. Wright[7]

> God be in my head
> and in my understanding;
> God be in my eyes and in my looking;
> God be in my mouth and in my speaking;
> God be in my heart and in my thinking;
> God be at my end and at my departing.
>
> —Sarum Primer (1514)

I have certainly had those times in my life when I wanted to
make sure God heard me clearly—the times when I was in some
crisis, had a loved one very ill, or cared deeply about something. I
tried to figure out some way to let God know these requests were
especially urgent.

Yet as a parent, I want to listen carefully to all the joys, concerns, feelings, and requests of my own children in whatever state
they are. Surely God is even more attentive than I as a human
parent am able to be (though, of course, God has many more children than I). Perhaps the real issue here is my ability to trust that
God hears and responds appropriately. Sometimes what I need is

simply a chance to pull out feelings and thoughts and to look at them in God's presence.

—Susan Ruach[8]

Week 5: A Time of Hope

Prayer of Invitation

Loving teacher, come and make your home in my heart this day and always. Dwell within me to save me from error and foolish ways. Teach me how to avoid doing harm this day and how to be an answer to another's prayer and help me today to be one of your signs of hope in the world. Stay with me always I pray, in the name of Jesus. Amen.

Hymn of Praise

"A Mighty Fortress is Our God"

Scripture Reading

Sunday — Psalm 121, God watches over you

Monday — Psalm 139, God knows and loves his own

Tuesday — Ecclesiastes 3:1–22, God makes everything beautiful

Wednesday — Isaiah 6:1–13, God commissions Isaiah

Thursday — Jeremiah 1:4–19, God calls Jeremiah

Friday — Ezekiel 37:1–14, God brings dry bones to life

Saturday — Daniel 3:19–30, God protects his own in a fiery furnace

Reflection and Response

Sacred Reading

Reflection and Response

Prayer

Thanksgiving for the signs of hope in the world and in the church. Petitions for:

All leaders, especially those who seek to follow the path of
   righteousness, justice, and love;
Persons in all walks of life, young and old, in every part of the world
   who seek to be obedient to the vision of God's reign and the
   unity of all humankind.
Those in this congregation who seek only God's will in all the
   decisions we must make.

The Lord's Prayer

Closing Prayer of Consecration

*Gracious guide and giver of life and hope, I give you thanks
for your steadfast love that has sustained me from before my
birth and has brought me to this moment. I offer my life to you
this day and invite you to guide, direct, and uphold me all day
long. In the name of Jesus. Amen.*

READINGS FOR REFLECTION

A Time of Hope

Hope has always been a dominant quality in the life of the Christian community. From the time of the resurrection of Jesus until today, individual Christians and the Christian community have been full of hope. In the face of fierce opposition and persecution, followers of Jesus never lost hope. Even when failure interrupted their journey, hope was the undercurrent that swept them to repentance, forgiveness, and companionship with the living Lord once more.

The source of this resolute hope was never found in the surroundings or how things were going for the church. Rather, hope was found in God and the assurance that God was at work in the church and in the world. The disciples felt a calm confidence that God's work and will would ultimately be completed and fulfilled. And they were assured that every Christian was invited into a partnership with God that moved toward the fulfillment of God's grand design for all creation. Such assurance is fertile ground in which the seeds of hope can flourish and bear the fruit of faithful living.

This week's readings give evidence of God's active presence within the Christian community. The church is seen as the body of Christ in the world, and individual Christians are seen as essential members of Christ's body in the world. God is described as a near and present partner in all of life's experiences.

At times the near and present partner was rejected, and the

Practicing a Preference for God

church became the crucified body of Christ all over again. There were times in the past and may be times for each of us when we think it too risky to be in partnership with God. We don't want to be the body of Christ. We don't want to be too close to Jesus. Sometimes we are just too shy, and sometimes we are reluctant to ask God to enter our decision-making because we already know that our will must be surrendered to God's will. When we strongly hold a position that we think may not be God's will, we find difficulty asking God to enter our lives.

At times we may be like the child who wrote a letter to Jesus saying, "Please come to our house, we need you." Yet at other times we are not so sure we want to expose our motives, our desires, our wishes, and even our acts to the loving scrutiny of God. We quickly forget that God already knows and, even now, waits for our invitation to join with us in the work of personal and social transformation that leads to righteousness—righteousness that is a sign of God's reign and a sign of hope.

To remember that God's will shall be accomplished completely and that we are invited to be a part of the fulfillment of that will gives a new perspective to life. We lose some of our fear of the risk of seeking and doing God's will. We know that sometimes doing God's will does get us into trouble, and at other times it saves us from trouble. Most of all we know that, when we seek to know and do God's will, we have set our feet upon a pathway of companionship, joy, and fulfillment. Our journey becomes one that holds challenge, excitement, meaning, assurance, and deep peace. Our journey gets richer day by day and will never end. Our journey begins in this life and continues into the next. Our

261

journey is made possible by the One who walks with all those who are faithful.

A Christian or a Christian community eagerly and sincerely seeking God's companionship and direction is a wonderful sign of hope. With God's help and our desire, we can be that sign of hope to others today.

—Rueben P. Job

Some years ago a friend decided to take photography lessons. After several inquiries, she learned of a highly regarded teacher who was about to start a new class. Without hesitation, she signed up....

One day toward the conclusion of the course, I asked my friend what special tricks she had learned about lighting, filters, and printing. Much to my surprise, she replied that she had learned nothing about such things. Indeed, her teacher had spent no time on technical subjects.... The most important thing... was teaching his students to develop an eye for the picture.... Unless they learned to develop this "eye," no level of technical sophistication would make them good photographers.

Developing an eye for the "picture" calls us daily to accept the invitation offered by a gracious, surprising God: "I am about to do a new thing; now it springs forth, do you not perceive it?" (Isaiah 43:19).

—John S. Mogabgab[9]

My hope is built on nothing less than Jesus's blood and righteousness.

I dare not trust the sweetest frame, but wholly lean on
  Jesus's name.
On Christ the solid rock I stand, all other ground is
  sinking sand;
all other ground is sinking sand.
> —Edward Mote, "My Hope Is Built on
> Nothing Less," 1834 (public domain)

Read Psalm 139:7–12.

What a blessing it is to know that the discerning of God's presence is not left simply to our own ability to find God. I am painfully aware of moments in my own life when I felt that God was absent and nowhere to be found. But always there has been a creature of God's handiwork who has helped me in my times of disbelief, bringing God close to me. I recall . . . a bright sunlit morning that broke through the shadows of death with God's love, and a cool dusk that helped me to know God's presence. Sisters and brothers, sometimes unbeknownst to them, have also at important moments provided just the right word of expression of care to affirm God's presence in my life. Yes! In all things, in all places and spaces under God's creation, God is present!

> —Minerva G. Carcano[10]

Read Acts 4:32–35 and Psalm 133.

The risen Christ is never just for us to receive; we must also do our part by sharing with others out of the foundation of that experience. . . .

The internal component that motivated the sharing of

property was the sharing of themselves. When individuals gather with their identities based on individual achievements and possessions, the result is people hiding their needs or pretending to be something they are not. When a community gathers with its identity found in the well-being of the entire group, then people are more willing to share themselves, to be vulnerable, and to express their needs.

Christian communities are drawn together in the experience of the risen Christ. The risen Christ unites us heart and soul, enabling us to overcome our isolation as individuals and become the people of God.

—Phyllis R. Pleasants[11]

Week 6: A Living Companionship

Prayer of Invitation
God of all wisdom and truth, come to fill my life with your presence. Dispel the dark clouds of doubt and depression, reveal and remove that which is false from my life, help me to cast out all other gods and to live in loving companionship with you this day and always. Amen.

Hymn of Praise
"Spirit of God, Descend Upon My Heart"

Scripture Reading

Sunday — Luke 1:5–25, 67–79, God speaks to Zechariah

Monday — Luke 1:26–38, 46–55, God speaks to Mary

Tuesday — Matthew 1:18–25, God appears to Joseph in a dream

Wednesday — Luke 2:1–22, Jesus the Messiah is born

Thursday — Luke 4:13–22, 38–44, Jesus proclaims and fulfills his mission

Friday — Luke 11:1–13, Jesus teaches on prayer

Saturday — Luke 24:13–35, Jesus appears to his disciples

Reflection and Response

Sacred Reading

Reflection and Response

Prayer

Thanksgiving for God's leadership during all of life and especially during these past weeks of more intense efforts of discernment. Petitions for:

All who seek the light of Christ for their darkness;

All who suffer the evils of addiction, oppression, and injustice;

All who are this day making decisions, especially the leaders of the church and the world who this day seek your will;

All who suffer and those who are dying, that none will suffer or die alone;

All who seek to live out their prayers and live into a closer walk with God.

The Lord's Prayer

Closing Prayer of Consecration

Holy Spirit, guide and comforter of all who turn to you for help, thank you for your sustaining presence in the life of the church and in my own life. I offer my life once more to your direction this day. Lead me wherever you will and sustain me wherever you lead me. Grant to me the necessary strength to walk in faithfulness and to live in company with you all day long. In the name of Jesus. Amen.

READINGS FOR REFLECTION

A Living Companionship

Discernment at its best is the consequence of a daily and lifetime walk with God. A lifetime of such companionship produces profound results that range from guidance in decision-making to transformation of one's life. Living a life of discernment, then, is a simple process of staying attentive to and open to God in all of the active and contemplative times of our lives.

Practicing preference for God has always been the first commandment and the first step toward faithful living. From this stance we seek God and God's companionship first. And as we do so, we will learn how to surrender our will to God's will. We will learn that God's presence and direction can be trusted. From this vantage point we learn that God's will is good and to be desired. When these truths begin to become a part of our very lives, discernment becomes a natural consequence of our daily walk with God.

When our preference is for God and God's will alone, we can begin to see the possibility of "indifference" in our own decision-making. "Indifference" is the Ignatian term for the capacity to be free from prior commitments, to be genuinely open to God's will and God's leadership. This kind of freedom, essential to discernment and faithfulness, is very hard to discover in our own lives. We bring so many preconceived ideas and so many strongly held prejudices that must be removed before we can be open to receive some new word or direction from God. To further complicate our movement toward indifference is the constant bombardment of other views. Some are well intentioned, believed to be God's will by those who promote them. Others may have fallen into the unhealthy and unholy world of political power plays that result in winners and losers.

Therefore, to have a way of living with God that serves to remind us again and again who we are and who God is in our lives is important. Such a rhythm of life will include time and space for listening to the Word, periods of deep and intimate prayer, a sensitive listening to the cries of God's people, and an action cycle that leads to reconciling, healing, and saving deeds. This kind of living becomes an answer to our prayers.

Another reason a lifetime of companionship with the living God is the way to discernment is the time that it takes to develop relationships of trust. Time is necessary for such a relationship with God to develop and mature. We learn by practicing this life of companionship just as we learn how to seek and receive God's direction in all things. When small and seemingly insignificant decisions flow out of this companionship, we will find it natural for us to practice discernment and obedience to God's direction in the major decisions for our lives. "Whoever is faithful in a very little is faithful also in much; and whoever is dishonest in a very little is dishonest also in much" (Luke 16:10).

We know from experience that those who live together for long periods of time begin to think and act alike. Workers on an assembly line, team members of highly trained sports teams, or work teams with complex assignments often can anticipate the thoughts and actions of one another. We even learn to "read" our children, spouse, or siblings and know what they will do in any given situation. When we live with God in daily companionship and declare our first preference for God and God's will, we develop our natural capacity to know, live with, and follow God in all of life. Out of this kind of companionship true discernment arises most easily.

I suspect that your life, as mine, may not yet be at this ideal place of discernment. We may find lapses in our "indifference" and see our own will or that of another displace God as central in our lives. When we become aware of such lapses, we should not scold ourselves or give up on the concept of companionship with the living God. Rather, we must return once again to God, ask for help to walk faithfully, and go on confident that God understands our weakness, is pleased with our desire for companionship, and will offer assistance equal to our need.

Each of us has the capacity to discern God's will. The capacity to do God's will is developed as we practice a way of living that keeps us in companionship with God and faithful to God's direction in our daily lives. Gradually we learn to hear, see, and know God's direction more and more until our individual and corporate decision-making flows out of our companionship with and clear preference for God.

—Rueben P. Job

But when he leaves their sight, they wonder together why they had not recognized him earlier. "Were not our hearts burning within us while he was talking to us on the road?" (Luke 24:32).

As we study closely the [Emmaus Road] account, we see clearly delineated the nature of the fire that burned in their hearts. Peace was spoken in their midst. Authentic clarity was given. Redemptive meaning was given to pain. Fear was healed, and joy was released and increased. Empowerment from God was promised rather than demands for their will power. Above all, the whole encounter was drenched with the spirit of tenderness, the burning love which is released from fear. And this is the supreme sign, the authentic, unmistakable presence of the Spirit we call Holy.

—Flora S. Wuellner[12]

Beloved, let us love one another, because love is from God....

If we love one another, God lives in us, and his love is perfected in us.

By this we know that we abide in him and he in us, because he has given us of his Spirit....

There is no fear in love, but perfect love casts out fear; for fear has to do with punishment....
We love because he first loved us.

                                 I John 4:7, 12-13, 18-19

Spiritual discernment asks us to pay attention. We need to attend to both what goes on around us and within us. Ideally, this attentiveness goes on much of the time, a sort of low level, constant spiritual sifting of the data of our experience. But there are times when discernment becomes much more focused, when a crossroad is reached or a choice called for. At times like these the cumulative wisdom of tradition tells us to pay attention on many levels: to consult Scripture, to seek the advice of trusted advisors, to heed the collective sense of the faithful, to read widely and deeply the best ancient and contemporary thinking, to pray, to attend to the prick of conscience and to the yearnings and dreamings of our hearts, to watch, to wait, to listen.

—Wendy M. Wright[13]

O Master, let me walk with thee in lowly paths of
     service free;
          tell me thy secret;
help me to bear the strain of toil, the fret of care.
Teach me thy patience, still with thee in closer, dearer
     company,
in work that keeps faith sweet and strong, in trust that
     triumphs over wrong.

In hope that sends a shining ray far down the future's
broadening way,
in peace that only thou canst give, with thee,
O Master, let me live.
—Washington Gladden, "O Master, Let Me
Walk with Thee," 1879 (public domain)

A Liturgy for a Prayer or Covenant Group Meeting

Optional: for group use during the forty-day window or at the conclusion of a specified discernment season, as a way of living out collective discernment as an ongoing priority. Sharing in prayerful attentiveness with members of your team, ministry, community, or congregation enhances the practicing of a preference for God for all.

Prayer of Invitation

God of all holiness and love, we invite your presence into our lives and into our gathering. Knit us together in mind and heart and lead us in faithfulness always. We pray in the strong name of Jesus. Amen.

Hymn or Chorus

"Amazing Grace" and "Savior, Like a Shepherd Lead Us" or other selected song(s)

Scripture Reading

Choose from one or more of these Scriptures, or take time reading all of them together. They complete the readings through the Old and New Testament that were read throughout your forty days of prayerful reflection. Reading all or portions of the following passages bring to completion a summary of the whole counsel of God as we notice the Lord initiating lovingly toward his beloved disciples.

John 13:1–17, Jesus washes the feet of his disciples
John 17, Jesus prays for his disciples
John 19:17–30, Jesus dies for his disciples
John 20, Jesus is raised from the dead and appears to his disciples
Acts 2:1–47, God's Spirit comes at Pentecost
Acts 9:1–19, God converts Saul
Revelation 1:4–20, God gives John a vision

Silent Reflection

A time of silent reflection on the selection of the day. What is God saying to me/to us through this passage? What does this text prompt me/us to pray for? What does this text prompt me/us to do?

Mutual Sharing of Insights and Promptings

Make certain every person has an opportunity to share his or her individual insight. What common themes or promptings arise? Are there insights we should explore further? What action is suggested? What are the directions for prayer?

Mutual Sharing of Concerns and Joys

All of us carry joys and burdens. To share our joys is to multiply them. To share our concerns is to divide them as together we bear one another's burdens. My joy today is . . . My concern today is . . .

A Time of Mutual Prayer

This time of prayer may include confession, petition, offering, and thanksgiving.

Silent prayer.
Spoken prayer.
The Lord's Prayer.

Next Steps

What steps are we being led to take?

Prayer of Covenant

Loving God, who keeps covenant with us, we offer ourselves anew to you in this hour. Do with us what you will, lead us where you will, send us to the task you will, and grant us grace to follow you more faithfully every day. In the Name of Jesus. Amen.

Conclude or Remain in Fellowship

Acknowledgments

I'm indebted to many family members and spiritual friends who have accompanied me on the journey toward a discerning life and practicing a preference for God. There aren't pages enough to add the names and the impact their lives have had on mine. The Lord knows how grateful I am for his extravagant affection toward me, as evidenced in the richness of my relationships.

Specific to this book, I am first and foremost indebted to my beloved wife, Ruth. She has patiently, graciously, and enthusiastically supported me in this endeavor. She is my first and best editor, reading each and every page with her red pen, sharp mind, quick wit, and amazing heart. This one is dedicated to you, Ruthie!

To our children and grandchildren, my primary circle of love. Bekah, Nate, Ashley, and Brenna, Aiden, and Carson, you are the apples of my eye, my greatest pride and joy, my everything in life. Each step of the way, our family has been a source of life and health, and unbeknownst to you, the passion behind each paragraph I've crafted. This opus is ultimately for you, with my prayers that you will earnestly pursue the discerning life for yourself and pass it along to everyone who crosses your path.

To the various teams and individuals at Leadership Transformations and the Pierce Center at Gordon-Conwell Theological Seminary, this book is written for you to receive as a gift to our shared ministry now and in the future. Your dedication to our vision and mission, your commitment to one another, your partnership in service, and the scope of our reach to others is a daily inspiration to me. Let's continue to live as discernmentarians in our generation, all for the glory of God.

Because this book was written during the COVID-19 pandemic, I can't help but see this as a silver lining to the world-shaking outbreak that shut down the world. During this season, our ministry pivoted completely online, which meant that my travels elsewhere and even my thirty-mile commute to the office came to an abrupt stop. But during that time frame I secured this contract with Zondervan Reflective and was able to carve out many creative blocks of time to write. I'm saddened by all the loss of life around us but grateful to the Lord for giving me strength, health, creativity, and hope to complete this manuscript on time.

I'm profoundly grateful for four individuals who read my early drafts of the manuscript and offered some incredibly helpful suggestions for editorial revamping. Beginning with Ruth, who read one chapter at a time and offered ongoing feedback. Also, to Rick Anderson, my amazing partner in ministry, who looked the manuscript over from a 30,000-foot vantage point with gracious insight. David Currie, one of the smartest men I've ever met, read the draft from the perspective of a church historian and theologian. Brother David Vryhof, my longtime spiritual director, combed over each paragraph and offered pages and pages of affirmations and suggestions for which I am profoundly grateful.

Finally, the Zondervan Reflective Team. Thank you for

believing in me and this project. I am overwhelmed by your support and look forward with you to the impact this book will have in the future. Thank you, Ryan Pazdur, for your initial interest in this book project. Kyle (and Liz) Rohane and Chris Beetham, I'm indebted to you for your patience, godliness, and editorial excellence. Your friendship and partnership in publishing are gifts I treasure deeply.

All praise, honor, and glory belong to God: loving Father, gracious Savior, empowering Holy Spirit. My heart's desire is that the Lord will be pleased to bless the work of my hands and multiply the prayers of my heart. May a new generation of leaders and learners choose to embody the discerning life, notice God in everything, and daily *practice a preference for God.*

About the Author
and Leadership
Transformations, Inc.

The Rev. Dr. Stephen A. Macchia is founder and president of Leadership Transformations, Inc. (LTI). LTI is a ministry that focuses on the spiritual formation needs of leaders and the spiritual discernment processes of leadership teams in local church and parachurch ministry settings nationwide. In addition to his pioneering work with Leadership Transformations, he is the director of the Pierce Center for Disciple-Building at Gordon-Conwell Theological Seminary, where he also serves as co-mentor of the Spiritual Formation for Ministry Leaders Doctor of Ministry track. Steve is an ordained minister, conference speaker, retreat facilitator, leadership coach, and spiritual director. He is the author of fifteen books, workbooks, and devotionals, and serves as creator and host of *The Discerning Leader* podcast. He and his wife Ruth live in the Greater Boston (Massachusetts) area and are the proud parents of Rebekah and Nathan, daughter in-love Ashley, and the joy of their hearts, granddaughter Brenna Lynn and her twin brothers, Aiden Joseph and Carson Stephen.

Leadership Transformations, Inc.

On July 1, 2003, Steve and Ruth Macchia founded Leadership Transformations, Inc. (LTI). Since then, this ministry has grown to become one of the most fruitful spiritual formation organizations in the nation. Leadership Transformations serves leaders and teams in congregations and ministry settings, with the belief that "as the leader goes, so goes the organization" and more importantly, "as the soul of the leader goes, so goes the leader." Soul care for leaders and teams is top priority and the ministry initiatives of LTI include *Selah*, Certificate Program in Spiritual Direction; *Emmaus*, Certificate Program in Formational Leadership; soul care retreats and soul sabbaths; and online workshops and retreats. LTI also facilitates discernment processes with leaders and teams; created the Church Health Assessment Tool (CHAT), the Team Health Assessment Tool (THAT), the Rule of Life website (ruleoflife.com), and *The Discerning Leader* podcast. LTI also offers their SpiritualFormationStore.com, featuring hundreds of resources created or vetted by the LTI team. The vision of LTI is "for Christian congregations and organizations to be filled with leaders who place spiritual formation, discernment and renewal above all other leadership priorities." Learn more at www.LeadershipTransformations.org.

Notes

Introduction

1. Rueben P. Job, ed., *A Guide to Spiritual Discernment* (Nashville: Upper Room, 1996). This six-week guide to spiritual discernment has been used several times over the years by Leadership Transformations, Inc., whenever we are seeking to help leadership teams embrace the concept of spiritual discernment. With permission from Rueben's widow, Beverly, and the team at Upper Room Books, we have been granted permission to share this out-of-print material as an appendix to *The Discerning Life*. It is the author's hope that this material will be used by many teams seeking to understand spiritual discernment as a lifestyle and not simply during times of decision-making. Rueben's definition of discernment as "practicing a preference for God" is a guidepost for us throughout this text.

Chapter 1: What Is Spiritual Discernment?

1. Leadership Transformations, Inc., is the ministry founded in 2003 by Steve and Ruth Macchia. It started with a dream; God woke Steve up with words and phrases and a clear image for leaders and teams to engage in for personal and collective discernment. Discerning God's presence and calling led to the founding of LTI several months later. Today LTI is a national ministry focused on the spiritual formation, discernment, and renewal needs of leaders and teams. More information can be found on their ministry website, www.LeadershipTransformations.org.

2. Paul Anderson, project director, The George Fox University Congregational Discernment Project (Newberg, OR, 2009), from documents shared with the national team serving as part of the National Discernment Initiative. For more, see "Congregational Discernment Project," George Fox University, https://www .georgefox.edu/discernment/index.html. As of the time of the publication of this book, this project is currently on hiatus.

3. Dan Graves, "John Wesley's Heart Strangely Warmed," Christianity .com, May 3, 2010, www.christianity.com/church/church -history/timeline/1701-1800/john-wesleys-heart-strangely -warmed-11630227.html. At Aldersgate, 8:45pm: "Someone read from Luther's *Preface to the Epistle to Romans....* While he was describing the change which God works in the heart through faith in Christ, I felt my heart strangely warmed."

4. Evan B. Howard, "Christian Discernment," in *Brazos Introduction to Christian Spirituality* (Grand Rapids: Brazos, 2008), 379–80, 397.

Chapter 3: Listening

1. As I write this story of "snowmageddon," I'm aware of those who have lost their homes due to extreme hurricanes, massive wildfires, destructive tornadoes, and other natural disasters. Any form of destruction like this is disquieting and disrupting, and I certainly don't want to equate my story with any of these tragedies. Our hearts can hardly fathom what it would be like to endure such hardship. Prayer becomes all the more important in these situations, for without God we simply cannot face the sufferings and sadness of life.

Chapter 6: Empathy

1. Since 1999 I have been researching and writing about the vitality of the local church, as recorded in my first book, *Becoming a Healthy Church: Ten Traits of a Vital Ministry* (Grand Rapids: Baker, 1999) and subsequently through Leadership Transformations' online Church Health Assessment Tool (CHAT), which helps churches listen to one another as they discern God's direction for their shared

life and ministry. For more information visit www.HealthyChurch .net.

2. Stephen A. Macchia, *Becoming a Healthy Team: Five Traits of Vital Leadership* (Grand Rapids: Baker/LTI, 2005) was written to help ministry teams work toward greater effectiveness together in service to others. In this book, and its accompanying handbook of noncompetitive exercises, teams are invited to consider the five key principles for their health: trust, empowerment, assimilation, management, and service (for which the acronym is TEAMS). In addition to the book, LTI also has an online Team Health Assessment Tool (THAT) available for leaders and teams.

3. Danny E. Morris and Charles M. Olsen, *Discerning God's Will Together: A Spiritual Practice for the Church* (Nashville: Upper Room, 1997), 56–63.

Chapter 7: Focus

1. David L. Fleming, *Draw Me into Your Friendship: A Literal Translation and a Contemporary Reading of the Spiritual Exercises of St. Ignatius of Loyola* (St. Louis: The Institute of Jesuit Sources, 1996), 138–45.

2. Leadership Transformations offers a myriad of services for leaders and teams who are seeking to shift toward the discerning life as individuals, teams, and communities. Become familiar with the resources made available to you and your team at www.LeadershipTransformations.org.

Chapter 8: Process

1. There are excellent resources available for those who want to learn more about how other Christian movements and denominations practice discernment. For more information about Benedictine discernment, consult "Belmont Abbey Discernment Guide," Belmont Abbey.org, https://belmontabbey.org/wp-content /uploads/2019/03/Belmont-Abbey-Discernment-Guide.pdf; for Augustinian discernment, see the article "2236 Spiritual

Discernment," Augnet, www.augnet.org/en/works-of-augustine /his-spiritual-tradition/2236-spiritual-discernment/; for Franciscan discernment, see "Discernment," Franciscan Friars: Province of Saint Barbara, https://sbfranciscans.org/be-a-friar/discernment/; for the Quaker's Clearness Committee, see "Clearness Committees— What They Are and What They Do," Friends General Conference (FGC), www.fgcquaker.org/resources/clearness-committees-what -they-are-and-what-they-do; for the Wesleyan Quadrilateral, see "Glossary: Wesleyan Quadrilateral, the," The People of the United Methodist Church, May 26, 2015, www.umc.org/en/content /glossary-wesleyan-quadrilateral-the.

Chapter 9: Lifestyle

1. Stephen A. Macchia, *Crafting a Rule of Life: An Invitation to the Well-Ordered Way* (Downers Grove, IL: InterVarsity, 2012). Written as an interactive workbook, this resource walks the reader through the process of articulating a personal rule of life.

Appendix B: Practicing a Preference for God

1. All of Rueben P. Job's writings in appendix B are taken from the introduction to *A Guide to Spiritual Discernment* (Nashville: Upper Room, 1996), as well as the introductory article for each week of readings. Used here by permission.
2. John S. Mogabgab, "Editor's Introduction," *Weavings: A Journal of Christian Spiritual Formation* 10.6 (Nov/Dec 1995).
3. Timothy Kelly, "A Spirituality of Watch," *Alive Now*, Nov/Dec 1994.
4. Robert K. Smyth, "Meditation for April 21," in *The Upper Room Disciplines 1993* (Nashville: Upper Room, 1992).
5. Ron James, "Meditation for June 14," in *The Upper Room Disciplines 1994* (Nashville: Upper Room, 1993).
6. Stephen V. Doughty, "Glimpsing Glimpses: A Quest for Communal Discernment," *Weavings: A Journal of Christian Spiritual Formation* 10.6 (Nov/Dec 1995).
7. Wendy M. Wright, "Passing Angels: The Art of Spiritual

Discernment," *Weavings: A Journal of Christian Spiritual Formation* 10.6 (Nov/Dec 1995).

8. Susan Ruach, "Meditation for May 7," in *The Upper Room Disciplines 1993* (Nashville: Upper Room, 1992).

9. John S. Mogabgab, "Editor's Introduction," *Weavings: A Journal of Christian Spiritual Formation* 7.5 (Sept/Oct 1992).

10. Minerva G. Carcano, "Meditation for July 14," in *The Upper Room Disciplines 1993* (Nashville: Upper Room, 1992).

11. Phyllis R. Pleasants, "Meditation for April 5," in *The Upper Room Disciplines 1991* (Nashville: Upper Room, 1990).

12. Flora S. Wuellner, "Were Not Our Hearts Burning within Us?," *Weavings: A Journal of Christian Spiritual Formation* 10.6 (Nov/Dec 1995).

13. Wright, "Passing Angels."